Naked Through the Gate

A Spiritual Autobiography

Joel Morwood

Published by

Center for Sacred Sciences
Eugene, Oregon
www.centerforsacredsciences.org

Second edition

Copyright © 1985 by Joel Morwood
All rights reserved

Printed in the United States of America

From *The Way of Life* by Lao Tzu translated by R. B. Blakney. Copyright © 1958 By R. B. Blakney. Copyright Renewed © 1983 by Charles Philip Blakney. Reprinted by arrangement with NAL Penguin Inc., New York, New York

Cover photo by Nihat Belbez. Used with permission.

ISBN 978-0-9620387-3-0

"An illuminating testimonial of the heart. Highly recommended."
— *L.A. Resources*

"Written for all of us who seek a greater and lasting happiness by a man who learned how to communicate masterfully with words. ...This intoxicating blend of readability and profundity is indeed a rare treat."
— *Meditation Magazine*

"An invaluable document for anyone Wishing to pursue this path."
— Franklin Merrell-Wolff
Author of *Pathways Through To Space*

"I resolved to write it as honestly as I could, with all the warts showing — the kind of book, in fact, that I had always wanted to read during my own journey but never found."
— Joel

Acknowledgements

First among the many people who have contributed to the publication of this book I must give humble thanks to my editor, Maggie Goswami, for her painstaking efforts to render a very sloppy manuscript into acceptable English. I am also grateful for all the comments and suggestions offered by those many friends, too numerous to mention, who consented to read this work in manuscript form.

For permission to use sections of his original translation of the *Bhagavad Gita*, I want to thank my friend, Amit Goswami.

Author's Note

This is a true story. However, the names of those characters not engaged in public work have been fictionalized. This was done out of respect for their privacy.

For Athena, naturally

Contents

Prologue	1
One: The First Noble Truth	5
Two: Finding a Corpse	19
Three: Samantha Jones and the Holy Grail	33
Four: The Hardships of Learning	47
Five: Fear and Trembling in the Court of the Soul	61
Six: What Is Truth?	79
Seven: Trouble in the Soul	97
Eight: Adventures in the Subtle Realm	115
Nine: Images of Light	135
Ten: Enchanted but Unchanged	151
Eleven: Hand on the Plough	173
Twelve: The Discovery of Gnosis	195
Epilogue: World Without End…	213
About the Author	225
References	227
Endnotes	229

Prologue

It was by eating of the fruit of the Tree of the Knowledge of Good and Evil in the primordial Garden that man became Man, and the fruit of this tree is metaphor. By the power of metaphor, man creates images; and by the power to imagine, he makes distinctions; and by the power to distinguish, he compares; and by the power of comparison, he names; and by the power of naming, he names himself. And the name of man is Adam, which means 'I'

I am *homo sapiens*, the one who knows. And everything I know is given to me through metaphor. Metaphor is the basis of all my knowledge and culture, the source and substance of every art and science. All that I create is created by this power. It is my greatest asset and most potent weapon. Without metaphor my species could never have survived. Still, I must eat of its fruit "in sorrow" all the days of my life.

For by naming myself 'I', I also and necessarily name all that which is not-I the 'world', so that in every act of naming myself I am already implicated in the experience of duality, or separation between 'I' and 'That', 'self' and 'world'.

But further, in order to name, I must compare; and by comparing, I must see the world as diverse and know these diversities as harbingers of joy and suffering, pleasure and pain, good and evil.

And by distinguishing joy from suffering, pleasure from pain, good from evil, I am impelled to seek the one and flee the other until everything reveals itself to be ultimately ephemeral and ungraspable, and I am finally confronted with the image of my own ephemerality, which is the metaphor of death.

Thus am I driven from my primordial home in Paradise. Its gates are sealed to me by my own knowledge. And by this knowledge am I also condemned to exile and bewilderment, to wandering and doubt, to seeking and despair in a world of fleeting forms whose final meaning I can never fully comprehend. Such is the life and destiny of every being born human, or so it seems... In fact, this destiny is a lie.

For, lest we forget, there also stands in that original Garden another tree, which is the Tree of Eternal Life; and the fruit of this tree is not knowledge but Gnosis. And whoever eats of the fruit of Gnosis knows that the True Life is not human but divine, that the Real World is not many but One, that I am not separate from or other than That One, but I AM That One, or the Reality, which is God, Brahman, Nirvana, or Allah—call it what you will. It cannot be named because It stands prior to all names; it cannot be imagined because It is the ground of all images; it cannot be distinguished from anything because It is both the origin and content of everything; nor can anything be compared to It because nothing exists outside, or beyond, or above, or below It

It is not something to be found, for It was never lost; not something to be revealed, for It was never hidden; not something to set right, for in It nothing is amiss. It can only be remembered before all remembering; and what is remembered is this very World, radiant and perfect just as it is, without a seam or flaw anywhere to be seen—for we have only dreamed it otherwise in the great sleep of 'I', that fabulous phantom play of metaphors and images that veils men's eyes. But the one who eats of the fruit of Gnosis Awakes from this dream and this sleep and is free of all metaphors and images forever...

Yet to eat of this fruit, we must return to the Garden and to the Tree that bears it. Nor is this an easy journey to make; for, lest we also forget, the gate to this Garden is guarded by an assembly of angels with a flaming sword that "turns every way," so that whoever would enter must first submit to the ordeals imposed by these angels with their sword. And the fiery function of this sword is to purify consciousness of every image and vestige of 'I' and 'that', 'self' and 'world', until we stand utterly naked, as we were in the beginning before all metaphor. Then and only then can we pass through the Gate into the Garden of our primordial Home where grows the Tree of Life and its Eternal Fruit

This journey is the True Destiny of every individual who comes into the world, and this book is a testimony to that Truth, written by one who has made the journey. Nor was this journey made by an extraordinary individual, but rather by an ordinary man born into all the ordinary circumstances of a metaphorical life, who yet found his way Home. For

Prologue

this Way is open to all, and this Truth is available to all, simply because there is no one who can ever depart from this Way, and there is no one who is other than this Truth.

Therefore, listen to my story not as the tale of someone else's journey, but as the story of a journey you have already made, only in another form. And hear my testimony as the testimony of your own heart, remembering this journey and longing to make it again in your present form, for I tell you truly, we are all Only ONE.

Prologue

One:
The First Noble Truth

The first Noble Truth of Buddhism is simply that there is suffering and death and that these are the unalterable conditions of human existence. This may seem commonplace, but I spent most of my life trying to avoid just those conditions. All my undertakings, great and small, were motivated by a desire to escape the inevitable. In the end, of course, every such effort must prove futile, but it took me nearly forty years to learn this lesson, which is the very first lesson of all spiritual journeys.

This is not to say I grew up totally naive. I was born in New York where muggings and murders, suicide and insanity formed a dark undercurrent in the flow of city life. Usually, however, such grim dramas passed me by, much like the echo of subways rumbling impassively beneath the avenues. Once I saw a black kid shot to death in a gang fight, and again, a mafioso gunned down on 4th Street, but still, I was, as they say, just an innocent bystander.

My parents were middle-class professionals, and I was educated in liberal private schools, wrapped in an atmosphere of tolerant humanism. "Decency" and "progress" were the watchwords of the era, and we were taught that the pursuit of happiness lay along the path of conformity and convention. Death was shunned as a morbid subject and suffering regarded largely as the result of ignorance and scarcity, social evils that must inevitably succumb to the slow but steady march of civilization. In the meantime, there was nothing much to do.

The most urgent task my generation faced was getting into college, preferably one with ivy-covered walls. Beyond this lay the prospect of a secure and prosperous career in some reputable profession, a family of 2.4 children (then the national average), and perhaps a summer house in Connecticut or on the Cape. All in all, it was not a future that promised any great challenges, spiritual or otherwise.

It wasn't until I was fifteen that I realized for the first time that I was going to die. I woke up one summer night with the sheets damp and sticky against my skin and thought, "Someday I won't be here." In my mind's eye I could see the whole world continuing just as it was — full of rivers, mountains, roads, people, houses, the moon and stars — but without me. I would simply cease to exist. I would become nothing.

This was no mere passing thought, but a completely experienced image, so detailed in its desolations that, for several hours, all I could do was lie paralyzed in bed, overwhelmed by terror and the knowledge that I was utterly alone in an alien universe.

Afterwards, I began to wonder who or what this entity called 'I' really was? This led to a quasi-spiritual quest that consumed the latter portion of my adolescence. I attended lectures on Zen Buddhism by Alan Watts, pondered D. T. Suzuki's tantalizing essays, and made snowy meditations on my roof, gazing at the North Star, hoping to find some counterpart in my own soul upon which to fix my destiny. One night, wrapped in a blanket, with a million flashing snowflakes falling out of a black sky, I actually did catch a glimpse of the Eternal Void, but it faded quickly.

More often, however, I pursued these vaguely mystical yearnings in a far more hedonistic manner. Inspired by Jack Kerouac's rebellious novel *On the Road*, I started hanging out in sweaty jazz clubs and McDougal Street cafes, sipping espresso laced with gin, hoping to find IT in the apocalyptic poetry of the beats or in weekend benzedrine jags and teenage joy rides, feverishly groping girls in the back seat as though the mystery of all life were hidden beneath panties and brassieres. Still, no matter how fast and far I pushed such excesses, I could never outdistance the morning's bleak dawn and my own mortality.

Somehow, in the midst of these hormonal storms, I managed to graduate from high school. But then, in 1961, I dropped out of college to hitch west, following Kerouac's vagabond call, and eventually ended up in Mexico smoking dope with the local fishermen whose language I couldn't speak. It was there, in an isolated little village by the sea, that I made a sad discovery that would haunt me for the next twenty years. One day a fisherman caught a large sea turtle, dragged it up onto the beach, and slit its flippers so that it couldn't crawl back to its watery home. There was no taint of cruelty in this act, only the sober logic of necessity. Without proper refrigeration, dead flesh spoiled quickly in the tropical sun, and fresh meat was precious to these impoverished people.

All afternoon I watched the turtle die, its dark red blood seeping down and away into the white sands. That night the old señora cooked it up into a tasty stew that I didn't think I would have the heart to eat. But I was hungry. In the end I ate the stew — and, more, I relished it. In that one moment of enjoyment I understood the inexorable link between pleasure and pain — that all joy has its shadow of suffering, every life its night of tears. With that my time on the road came to an end. I had still not solved the riddle of my existence, nor had I found a psychic North Star to guide my soul, but by now I had grown weary of looking.

A year later I was back in New York, prepared to accept the world more or less as it had been given to me. Somewhere during my travels I had discovered the magic of film. The New Wave of directors then rolling in from Europe — Bergmann and Fellini, Goddard and Truffaut — fired my imagination, and eagerly, I set out to imitate them. I enrolled in production classes at N.Y.U., began free-lancing on documentaries and commercials, and forgot all about shining eternities and dying sea turtles. At last I thought I knew who I was — a filmmaker, and this became my passport to society. I got married, landed a full-time job on a network sports show, and for a while it looked as though I might end up with that house in Connecticut after all.

Then came Vietnam.

No one understood why I went, least of all myself. The year was 1965. The news was full of bombing reports and troop buildups, and everyone knew the war was escalating. All my friends scrambled around for various military deferments, and there was no reason why I couldn't have secured one as well. But when my draft notice arrived in the fall, I just let events take their course. I felt strangely hypnotized by history's darkening swell and made no resistance to its momentum as it carried me away; nor in my innocence did I have the faintest idea of what changes it would bring.

In February of 1966 I was inducted into the United States Army and, the following year, received orders for Vietnam. On the eve of my departure, I had an astonishingly numinous dream, crammed with epic images whose full significance I was not to fathom until many years later. It concerned a journey to the East to see the great Man and a period of exile overseas, but it ended with a promise that someday I would return home to my native land. I took this dream as a beneficent omen that I would survive Nam, and I did. But there was no honor in it, nor was it possible to gather back the scattered threads of my old life.

What shall I say about Nam? The sun rose every morning and set in the evening just like anywhere else. Some days were bright and clear; on others, it rained. We ate, slept, sweated, and swore. We worked and partied, made friends and enemies, knew sadness and joy. Occasionally things got crazy, but much of the time it was boring and routine. Like people everywhere, we had jobs to do and problems to solve—only in our case the job was killing, and the problem was staying alive.

Even so, in many ways it all seemed very mundane, and that was perhaps its greatest horror. Here, carrying a weapon felt as natural as toting a lunch pail, and some guys collected human ears the way kids collect stamps or coins. Progress was measured in firepower and body counts, and no one thought it indecent when the boys in GR played practical jokes with pieces of corpses. Indeed, the only thing indecent in Nam was *decency* itself. That was a bad joke, justly jeered by the mad laughter of machine-guns and the rude whistling of mortars. Here, suffering and death were perfectly acceptable, and the only real shock was that no one had ever told us it could be so. Yet, it was true. This was the bloody bedrock of civilization—the flip side of reality, where everything we had been taught to believe was cancelled out in a precisely balanced equation that would finally add up to exactly zero.

But of course, none of us saw this at the time. We were too busy trying to survive to bother with any such long-term, moral calculations. Besides, we were deceived more than anyone by Nam's surface appearance, its smells, its touch, its dazzling light and fierce monsoons. It seemed to us a physical place—a bit of mud and jungle that one could eventually escape, like a tourist fleeing a bad vacation. Thus, we dreamed only of going home and leaving it all behind. How were we to know that the real Nam wasn't outside us, but inside—a secret psychic terrain from which we could never decamp?

It wasn't until three hours after I was discharged that, hunched over a bourbon in the purple glow of the Seattle Airport bar, I knew something was wrong. I had been away a full year, all the time acutely aware of being a foreigner in foreign lands. But now, back on the soil of my birth, listening to a couple of baby-faced executives chatting excitedly at my elbow about the price of beach-front condos and the latest in hot vacation spots, I realized that none of this meant anything to me anymore. I was still a foreigner. In some strange way, I had not come home at all.

At first I thought it was I who had changed, but it was the world that had been changed forever in my eyes. The old metaphors no longer worked, nor did the old conventions I had once shared with family and friends. To them Vietnam was a horrible mistake, best forgotten. But you do not forget the kiss of napalm or the touch of charred flesh so easily. I had seen the Buddha's Truth firsthand, and it was no mistake. The shadow of the little sea turtle's suffering hung over the entire world, and it was a shadow that no amount of cultural imagery or civilized pursuits could ever hide or erase.

Shortly afterward I got divorced and drifted out to San Francisco on the already ebbing tide of flower children. For several months I lived with a hippie family in their attic, collecting unemployment, smoking dope, and abandoning myself to a kind of aimless, sensual anarchy. The year was 1968. The Summer of Love had faded, but there were still girls enough willing to share their beds and bodies, as freely as their flowers, with any stranger who happened into orbit, and I floated between one pair of nameless legs or another until they all seemed like the common appendages of the same impersonal being.

Meanwhile, the Haight was going to hell. Junk had appeared on the streets, and everyone was moving away, or getting ripped off, or busted. But I didn't care. At the center of my universe was an emptiness untouched by any ordinary human concerns.

Then, one day I found a new image on which to reconstruct my life.

I was standing on Haight Street, gazing indolently in the window of a poster shop, when a passing panhandler stopped long enough to exclaim, "Hey, you look just like him!"

I looked to the poster he was pointing at. Che Guevara, the famous Cuban revolutionary, stared back at me with blazing eyes, and it was true. I did look a bit like him. His beard was scraggly like mine, and his hair whipped loose and free beneath a rakish black beret adorned only with a single, red star. Mostly, however, I concentrated on his face. There was an ascetic heroism in that countenance, and you could see immediately that here was a man of purpose. It was this, above all else, that impressed me.

The next day I borrowed a book about Che from a friend and, almost inadvertently, got my first lesson in Marxism.

"The history of all hitherto existing society," states the opening chapter of *The Communist Manifesto*, "is the history of class struggle." It goes on to declare that this struggle has always and inevitably resulted in one class ruling, exploiting, and oppressing the other classes of society by virtue of its ownership and control of the means of production. This, according to Marxism, has been the principle cause of all human misery and suffering throughout the annals of history.

In our present capitalist epoch, it was the bourgeoisie that ruled and the proletariat that was most exploited. Unlike previous, relatively stable systems, however, capitalism was relentlessly dynamic and had to be forever fueled by increasing profits and expanding markets. All modern wars—particularly imperialist wars like Vietnam—stemmed directly from this incessant drive to expand. Thus, as long as capitalism reigned, war, exploitation, and oppression would ever be its bitter fruits.

This Marxist analysis, at once ruthlessly rational and wildly messianic, seemed to fill exactly the void in my life. Here was a viable explanation not only for the horrors of Vietnam but for a host of other inequities as well. Moreover, it offered a bold and sweeping solution that, if it could not obviate the biological fact of death, promised to mitigate it to a great extent by investing individual life with historical meaning. The choice was clear: either join one's destiny to the inexorable tide of proletarian revolution, or be swept away with the rest of the flotsam and jetsam of the past. It was an appeal to both logic and honor I found impossible to resist. Marxism was to be a crusade against the Shadow itself, and in such a cause I was willing to take up arms once again.

That summer I joined a Marxist collective, making propaganda films for the New Left. Cameras in hand, we mounted the barricades, our red arm bands proudly proclaiming us enemies of all capitalist states. Nor were we alone. From Tokyo to Paris, Washington to Berlin, massive anti-war demonstrations and student protests had rocked the governments of the Western world, while at home farm workers went on strike, and Black

Panthers were shooting it out with the police. The tide, indeed, seemed to be turning, much the way Marx had predicted.

There was, however, one flaw in the communist ointment—at least, as it had been applied so far—and that was Russia. Though nominally a socialist country, the Soviet Union appeared to have abandoned its international obligations in favor of a policy of national, even imperialistic, self-interest. What had gone wrong?

A complicated theory of "revisionism" was devised to explain this Soviet aberration, but of far more significance was the example then being set by the People's Republic of China. There the flame of the Great Proletarian Cultural Revolution was still burning bright, and with it, the torch of proletarian internationalism—or so it seemed to us. Since Mao Tse Tung was the leader of this "revolution within a revolution," we became not just Marxists but Maoists. This is a crucial point, because it was a trip to China four years later that finally convinced me that the Marxist model was inherently and hopelessly flawed.

Actually, China was but the straw that broke the camel's back.

Almost from the beginning, I had harbored instinctive doubts about the possibility of a communist utopia ever being realized, and over the next few years these doubts sprouted like weeds in my soul. By 1970 the once fluid American Left had solidified into dozens of dogmatic factions and was splintering under the pressure of tiresome, internecine quarrels, which all too often masked only petty struggles for personal power.

Even more discouraging was the obvious indifference of American workers to our heroic conception of their great historical task. In spite of sporadic alliances over local issues of wages and working conditions, all our efforts failed to rally more than a handful of genuine proletarians to the Marxist standard, and I began to wonder why.

It is axiomatic in Marxist doctrine that man's primary drive is centered on the acquisition of life's basic necessities. All other motives are seen to be dependent upon and subordinate to this singularly materialistic ambition. Thus, greed, envy, pride, and the will to power are considered not as innate in the human psyche but as pathological responses to the fear of material deprivation. When all material wants are satisfied, the argument goes, then these passions will vanish, and with them, the shadow of human suffering.

And yet the world abounded in examples of men who had amassed more wealth than they could possibly dispose of, and still their appetites remained insatiable. Nor did such individuals seem to be exceptions to the race as a whole. Everywhere, everyone — whether they possessed a lot or a little — appeared bent on acquiring more. It was almost as though tangible wealth and even the intangibles of power were mere symbols for some deeper need — a need that the symbols alone could never fully satisfy.

But if this was the case — if such a need existed — then it meant that no purely materialistic solution to the problem of human suffering was possible. The shadow was within us. Our own rapaciousness would always outstrip our wealth, our own unassuageable lust give rise to further exploitation and oppression. In the long run the revolution would be in vain.

The trouble was, I had no idea what this "deeper need" might be. Besides, in the face of manifest global poverty, disease, and war, such speculations smacked of bourgeois intellectualism. What was so obviously and painfully called for was not philosophical hair-splitting but action. At the very least, society should provide the basic human necessities, and socialism promised to shoulder this responsibility. Thus, I swallowed my doubts and tried to keep the noble image of Che polished in my heart.

In the summer of 1971, several months before I knew I would be going to China, there was a curious and very uncharacteristic development in my life that had nothing at all to do with politics. I got interested in horses.

It began on a bright Sunday afternoon. I was lying on a beach with Colette, the first woman I had had a steady relationship with since Nam, when several people on horses came galloping by, racing the surf. It looked like fun, and later we discovered there was a rental stable nearby. For the next few Sundays, Colette and I went riding on our own. Then came cheap group lessons, and soon I was reading everything I could get my hands on about horses — books on breeding, history, training, dressage, etc. What had started out as a passing inspiration of a summer afternoon quickly exploded into a full-blown passion which rivaled even the Revolution itself.

This was not an easy passion to justify to my comrades, who were not a little horrified by what looked suspiciously like a thoroughly bourgeois pastime. At one point criticism became so intense that a sympathetic friend went so far as to translate from the German letters exchanged between Marx and Engels in which Engels specifically cites horseback riding as excellent therapy. These august pronouncements notwithstanding, my new hobby won only scorn from most of my peers.

Indeed, it was hard to explain this sudden passion, even to myself. Although my father had taken me riding as a child, I had hardly seen a horse in fifteen years. There was no denying, of course, that I now felt these equestrian excursions with Colette to be a welcome break from the rigors of revolutionary life, but why *horses*? Why not basketball, or bowling, or some other respectably proletarian sport? Frankly, I was as baffled as anyone.

It was early fall when I learned I was going to China, and it came as a complete surprise. In the past, groups of American leftists had been invited to Cuba and North Vietnam but never, as far as I knew, to the People's Republic, which still lay firmly behind the proverbial "Bamboo Curtain." The trip was planned to last eight weeks, and our party would be composed of a dozen representatives from various collectives around the country. My job was to take color slides to be used in lecture tours on our return. Because we were under constant government surveillance, everything happened very fast and in great secrecy.

Within a few days I was off to Montreal where our whole group was to assemble, hopefully beyond the watchful eyes of the F.B.I. It took five days for everyone to trickle in. In the meantime I befriended some of my fellow travelers and wandered around the city. Mostly, I was interested in horses and would stop to chat with carriage drivers near the park about their animals. Once I even borrowed our only rental car to attend a very chichi horse show on the outskirts of town, for which I was soundly criticized by my new comrades. Even before we got off the ground, as it were, I was acquiring a reputation for being something of a horse freak.

Our next stop was Paris, where we had to switch airlines with a two-day layover, waiting for the once-a-week-only flight from the West to the People's Republic. Although I had never been to Paris before, I couldn't work up any enthusiasm for the city. Strolling the streets by day, it looked to my eyes like any other decadent bourgeois metropolis. At night along the Seine, with all the buildings lit up, I had to admit there was a certain bygone grandeur about the cathedrals, but even so, it all seemed to belong to a doomed age. I was only interested in the future, and as far as I was concerned, the future lay in the East, in Mao's China.

From Paris, we continued via Air France, touching down at Athens, Cairo, Karachi, and finally Shanghai, where we transferred that same night to a Chinese prop plane and flew up to Peking. The full impact of actually having arrived in China, however, didn't hit me until the following morning when I woke up at dawn in an elegant old colonial hotel, with teakwood floors and leaded-glass windows, and looked out past Tiananmen Square to where the ancient red-peaked roofs of the Forbidden City pushed up through a blue mist to catch the first pink rays of sun. Then I knew how Marco Polo must have felt a thousand years before, and I also knew that nothing had really changed. I had come to China to see the future, but instead I had found the eternal past.

We spent the first couple of weeks in Peking visiting factories, schools, hospitals, foundries, museums, historical sites, and department stores. Everywhere we were bombarded with figures concerning production quotas, current output, and future projections coupled with confessions of past mistakes, all designed to prove that the Great Proletarian Cultural Revolution—under the personal direction and leadership of Chairman Mao Tse Tung—had saved China from ossifying into a reactionary, bureaucratic state.

At that time it was still very much Mao's China, and every wall and building was adorned with his portrait. What's more, everyone from high party officials to grade-school children could quote to you from the famous *Little Red Book*, which contained sayings by the Great Man and had become the veritable bible of this prodigious social endeavor. But what had the Cultural Revolution really accomplished?

Stripped of political rhetoric, Mao's goal (and hence, the goal of the revolution) had been nothing less than to create the New Man—an individual purged of all self-interest, whose entire life would be dedicated to building a perfect socialist society, and who would take a full measure of joy simply in serving others. It was not an ignoble idea, but had it worked? By the time we left Peking for three weeks in the countryside, I had begun to suspect not.

We embarked by train but ended up traveling by bus, car, and plane as well. We covered a lot of territory, visiting army camps, communes, rural factories, dams, produce markets, and peasant villages. Here, the official line was the same as in Peking: Mao Tse Tung and the Cultural Revolution had turned the tide and kept the revolutionary vision alive.

But even as the spokesmen spoke and the officials officiated, you could feel the whole nation heaving a collective sigh of relief that the tumult had finally run its course, and everyone could begin to settle back down to business as usual. That great national goals had yet to be achieved, no one questioned; a sound agricultural base had still to be secured and a commensurate heavy industry developed. But that the future China would not be a model of selfless socialist society was also obvious. Its primary aim would be to shield and protect the Chinese people in their own ancient pursuit of what everyone else appeared to want: personal prosperity and private happiness. China, like the rest of the world, had its Shadow, which even the Cultural Revolution could not erase. By the time we reached Yenan I had no doubt that Mao Tse Tung would go down as one of history's greatest leaders. I also sensed that, judged by his own high standards, he was going to prove one of its most colossal failures.

Yenan had been the cradle of the Chinese revolution, roughly equivalent to our own Valley Forge. Indeed, it was maintained and displayed in much the same way. Here you could visit a cave where Mao wrote a famous treatise and see the very bed he slept in, or you might stand on the exact spot from which he delivered a decisive speech. Guides would take you to battlefields and barracks and recite stirring tales of tactics and heroism from the annals of the People's War. Being something of a history buff, this was for me one of the highlights of the trip. But the *pièce de résistance* was yet to come.

During our travels in the countryside I had, of course, been particularly interested in the horses at various farms and communes and had annoyed my comrades no end by nagging our interpreters for information as to their care and breeding. Everyone knew by now of my quirky obsession, and I took a lot of ribbing for it. On our last day in Yenan, however, we were taken to a dusty provincial museum that housed mementos of the Long March.[1] Here, under a tin roof slung over adobe walls, were glass cases displaying arms and ammunition from the period—tattered flags, rusty mess kits, yellowed maps—all accouterments of a peasant army on the move. Our guide on this particular day was not the most inspired of speakers and droned on and on, describing each relic in windy detail. But as we neared the end of our tour of the first chamber, my eyes caught something in the adjoining room that made my heart race. In the middle of the floor, completely enclosed by glass, was a stuffed, white pony, and I could already guess to whom that dwarfed equine had once belonged.

When we finally got around to this exhibit, our guide described in reverent tones how this very animal had been Mao Tse Tung's personal mount during the trials and tribulations of the Long March. Now for the first time during our own little journey, my comrades paid respectful attention to a horse, simply because the Great Man had ridden it. For my part, on closer inspection, I was a little disappointed in our hosts' attempts to preserve the noble carcass. The skin had already yellowed and was peeling at the seams, and I wondered how long it would last before going the way of all flesh.

Five weeks from the day of our arrival, we were back in Peking, and after the privations of rural life it was nice to be ensconced once again in our elegant hotel with hot baths and bellhops who greeted you with steaming hand towels every time you walked in through the massive front doors. But the schedule had been hectic, and there were still two weeks to go, one of which we would spend down in Shanghai. Before leaving Peking, however, I had a startlingly vivid dream.

In the dream I woke up in the same hotel room in which I had actually gone to sleep, only now I was aware of an unusual disturbance in the hall outside my door: an enormous black stallion had gotten into the building and was coming toward my room, scattering waiters and busboys from his path. In a moment he burst through the door, prancing around my bed, nostrils flaring and ebony coat glistening with foam. I was terrified, but the stallion kept nodding his head and whinnying anxiously until I realized that he wanted me to climb onto his back. Swallowing my fear, I obeyed, curling my fingers into his thick mane and clinging to his giant flanks with my legs. He neighed approvingly and, in an instant, leapt through the leaded-glass windows, bounding up into the night sky and out over the peaked roofs of the Forbidden City, carrying me westward and home.

It was, I knew, the symbolic end of my romance with Maoism.

We went to Shanghai as planned, then returned to the States.

Colette and I got an apartment together, and for a while I continued working with the film collective, attending rallies and going to meetings, but the bloom was off the lily. Instead of being reassured that our Chinese comrades were keeping aloft the banner of proletarian internationalism, I had come away convinced that the real dynamic at work in China was the restoration of her own national power and pride, which had been so humiliatingly lost to Western colonialism in the last century. This is not to say that I hadn't admired the Chinese people but simply that, as far as I was concerned, China would go the way of Russia, as would, by implication, all other Marxist revolutions. The communist utopia was undeliverable, and the ideology on which I had based my life collapsed almost overnight.

I cannot say that when I left San Francisco a year later, I had discovered any coherent alternative, nor was I looking for one. All idealism had been exhausted in me. I had, however, read a number of popular books in the new field of sociobiology by such authors as Konrad Lorenz and Robert Ardrey. According to their metaphor, the human being—like any other animal—was governed by inherited instincts, genetically selected as adaptations to a harsh and competitive environment. We were, in effect, biological robots programmed to survive at any cost, and I might as well make the best of it.

Besides, I was tired of tilting at windmills. It was time, I thought, to grow up and face "reality." At least, I still had Colette with whom I had fallen quietly in love. Now all I wanted to do was forget the past and live a normal life, and for a while I succeeded. But the past, as Karl Marx himself wrote, has a way of catching up with us:

> Men make their own history, but they do not make it just as they please; they do not make it under circumstances chosen by themselves, but under circumstances directly encountered, given and transmitted from the past. The tradition of all the dead generations weighs like a nightmare on the brain of the living.[2]

The First Noble Truth

Two:
Finding a Corpse

Whoever has known the world has found a corpse.[3]

So declares Jesus in *The Gospel According to Thomas*, and for the better part of my adult life, this had seemed to be true. But then, what I had known of the world—as both a soldier and a revolutionary—had been mostly war. Now I was ready to sue for peace, and on any terms. If I could not change the world, I would pursue the world—and the things of the world, and I didn't much care how I did it. I lay down my honor, put my soul to sleep, and headed south, hoping to hitch a ride on the American Dream.

It was a rainy February night in 1973 when Colette and I arrived in Los Angeles. We had a thousand dollars cash, a battered VW bug, which carried all our earthly possessions, and a German shepherd puppy named Captain Blood. I had just turned thirty, and my ambition was to break into Hollywood.

Somewhere near Bakersfield, we heard a radio commercial on a country-and-western station advertising a school for broadcasting. The announcer promised that, among the many glamorous benefits of such a career, graduates would "hobnob with the stars."

"That's what we're going to do," I told Colette, "hobnob with the stars."

She made a face, indicating she didn't think much of the idea, which, in retrospect, probably wasn't a very auspicious beginning to our sojourn in Glitterland, but then neither were my circumstances. I had no connections in the movie business and no immediate prospects. I spent the next few months looking for a job as a film editor but without any luck. By summer our money had run out and Colette went to work as a secretary to support us. Though her salary was meager, we were still able to rent a tiny house in Burbank with real plum trees in the backyard, shop in gaudy, air-conditioned supermarkets, and get our very first credit cards. I was beginning to feel like a genuine U.S. citizen once again.

In the fall I won a writing fellowship at the American Film Institute, and by the following year I was picking up odd jobs as a script reader and trying to write screenplays of my own. Colette continued working without complaint, and I vowed that if I ever "made it," she would get her chance to pursue whatever dreams she might have. In the meantime we were married and, although still poor, quite happy.

Two years later, however, I had not made much progress in my career. I had fantasies of myself as a six-figure-a-year writer with a house in Malibu, a Porsche in the garage, and champagne on the table—and I was hungry for it all. Of the three screenplays I had written on spec, however, not one had sold, and my only two salaried jobs had been for non-union producers who paid next to nothing. Colette was still bringing home the bacon, and though we made ends meet, I was starting to feel guilty and frustrated. What's more, I was pushing thirty-three, and in Hollywood, where youth is at a premium, thirty-three already sounded old. Almost every week in the trades, I would read about some kid in his twenties getting promoted to a studio vice-presidency, and a little muscle in my gut would wrench with envy.

I began sending letters and resumes to producers and company executives requesting any kind of position, but still without results. If I could only squeeze my foot in the door, I was confident that I could play this game and come out a winner.

In January 1977 I got the break I had been longing for: I was hired as a story editor by an independent producer named Lewis Simak, who had a contract with Warner Brothers. My starting salary was a meager $250 per week, which Colette insisted was much too low, but I didn't care. The Success Express had finally stopped long enough for me to hop aboard, and I was off at last.

In the beginning we were just a three-person operation:

Lewis, myself, and his secretary, Jean. But by the end of the year we had our first movie-for-television in production, and its producer, Lee Mario, joined the company on a permanent basis. The following year Jean took over my job as story editor, and I became the executive in charge of production at triple my original salary. By now we had a full-time production manager, several more secretaries, a gofer, and a receptionist — all in all about ten people.

With our fortunes rising, Colette and I purchased a spacious, two-bedroom house with a huge studio wing, and I bought the first brand new, right-off-the-showroom-floor car I had ever owned. It was a cream-colored Audi 5000 and cost me over $13,000.

By the end of 1980 Simak Productions had produced two more movies-for-TV and a major Hollywood feature on which I had served as Associate Producer with my name on a single card in the opening credits. I was the envy of my friends and the pride of my parents, who had suffered through the tumults of my youth wondering gloomily if I would ever amount to anything. For the first time in my life, I felt completely in control. I had willed all this into being. I was, at last, master of my destiny.

Colette, too, seemed to be enjoying our new affluence. By now I was making $60,000 a year plus bonuses and an unlimited expense account, so she could well afford to quit her job. She dabbled in the stock market, bought a Triumph convertible, and still we had, as they say, money to burn. We dined in restaurants where they don't list their prices on the menu, because if you have to ask, you shouldn't be there. We made business trips to New York, flying first class and staying at the Plaza, where we drank champagne and ate clams on the half-shell every night before going to bed. We took a vacation in Tahiti, attended studio premieres and cocktail parties in Beverly Hills. In short, it was all coming true; we were hobnobbing with the stars...but the wine of success had already started to sour.

It was little things at first, subtle things you hardly notice. My Audi, for example — it was a truly beautiful automobile, equipped with sun roof, Blaupunkt stereo, push-button windows, cruise control, and front-wheel drive. It was more luxurious than my living room, yet handled like a race car. In the beginning every time I slid behind the wheel, I would get a palpable thrill and think, this is what it's all about. Poverty sucks. I'll never be poor again.

Then one morning, fighting traffic over Coldwater Canyon, with my mind working out a strategy for the meeting I was late to, I suddenly realized I was no longer aware I was driving an Audi. It was just another car, a hunk of metal, a means to an end. Afterwards I tried to recapture the old sensation, but it was never the same. If I wanted that feeling again, I knew, I would have to buy something newer and more expensive, a Mercedes maybe, or that Porsche I had dreamed of.

Restaurants, too: the first time I went to La Serre was with Lewis and a writer to talk story, but I wasn't paying much attention to the intricacies of plot and character. Instead, I was musing, here I am with real French waiters emptying my ashtray even before I finish a cigarette and calling me "Sir." A few years later I could wolf down a plate of asparagus and caviar and polish off a glass of twenty-dollar Chardonnay without missing a single line of dialogue. It had all become just part of the day's routine, nothing more.

Even our house: the night we moved in, with boxes still stacked in the halls, eating take-out from a Chinese restaurant because our cooking gear had yet to be unpacked, I remember going out into the backyard and sitting under the stars, thinking, this little sliver of land is mine. I own it. I am a landlord. It felt good, and it was a good house, roomy and well-designed, in a nice neighborhood with nice neighbors. Colette fell in love with it and devoted most of her time and energy to fixing it up. She and my father planned a garden, and she supervised the Mexican worker who put it in. After a while, however, for me the spell of ownership wore off. It began to feel like just another place to live, four walls — something to keep out the rain.

Nor did I fail to recognize these signs. It was that shadow of insatiability, which I had pondered so philosophically as a Marxist, only now it was no longer philosophical. The shadow had fallen over my own life, seeping into all its pleasures and joys. I was like the proverbial kid at Christmas opening his presents, playing with them for a week, then consigning them to the shelf to collect dust until finally someone gives them away to Goodwill. If you have money, which I did, of course, you can keep on buying yourself new presents. But I began to ask where it was all leading, and such questions often prove fatal.

Far more important than any possessions, however, was my relationship with Colette. In spite of her cool reaction to my joke about hobnobbing with the stars, I had always assumed she wanted this success as much as I did, and it was true she enjoyed its fruits. But at the same time, she was becoming indifferent, if not actively hostile, to the life-style that bore them.

In a town that made little distinction between friendships and business associations, it was almost as crucial to socialize with the right people as to make deals with them. Indeed, the two often went hand in hand, and if it took a bit of flattery or deception to win someone's favor, I was not beyond employing such means. Colette, however, despised all sham and pretense, and this led, with increasing frequency, to sharp, irresolvable arguments or, worse, periods of sullen silence that could last for days. In retrospect I think that at a certain point, she would have been perfectly happy to stop the clock and stay where we were with food in the cupboard, a roof overhead, some spending money in our pockets, and a little cushion against the future. The trouble was, in show business you couldn't stop. You were either on your way up or down, and there was nothing in between.

In the meantime I had come to the conclusion that what was wrong with my life wasn't the industry per se, but only the somewhat sordid role I had come to play in it. Years ago I had dreamed of being a director like Fellini—architect of a new art form, but had succumbed instead to the allure of a cheap prosperity and ended up a mere administrator in the Hollywood machine. I might never be a Fellini, but directing could at least provide something of the creative satisfaction I still felt I lacked. To this end, then, I began developing in my spare time a short, dramatic film that could showcase whatever directorial talents I possessed.

After reading and discarding a number of stories by other writers, I decided to try to write one of my own. I toyed with a few horror plots but quickly gave them up. The whole point was to do something *meaningful*, but the truth was, I no longer had anything meaningful to say. Still, I persisted, playing at my typewriter on weekends and dreaming of Oscars at night, totally unaware that the whole nightmare of the past was looming up behind me, about to come crashing back with devastating consequences.

Even now it astonishes me that I went to see *Tracers* without the slightest idea that it might have any import for my life beyond the possibility of finding a couple of quality actors for my film. The play had opened in a little theater in Santa Monica to rave reviews, with special accolades for the thespians, and it was for this reason—and this reason only—that I dragged Colette across town to see it. The fact that it was about Vietnam and had been written, directed, and was being acted by Vietnam veterans made no special impression on me whatsoever. It was almost as if I had forgotten that I myself had once been there.

The theater was tiny, with cramped bench seating that could accommodate perhaps fifty people. There was no curtain. The set was bare, the costumes and props largely improvised. The script, however, was fluid and powerful. The actors shifted roles and scenes with lightning speed, recreating vignettes of horror, humor, and despair—like snapshots from the war—with consummate skill. Judged by even the most critical standards, the production had to be rated excellent. Yet, by the end of the evening none of that mattered to me in the least.

I was back in Nam.

Time had been obliterated, the thirteen years since my return utterly wiped out. I could smell the shitpots burning, taste the acrid gun powder on the air, hear the rush of Phantoms in the smoke-filled skies—and it was all happening *right now* in some psychic fourth dimension eternally suspended between past and present where not one fragment or detail was ever lost nor their impact diminished by a single degree. Tears welled in my eyes, and by the time we left the theater, I was shaking so badly that Colette had to drive us home.

That was in the spring of 1981, but the emotional fallout continued for more than a year. A police helicopter buzzing overhead would make my blood surge, or the crack of a car's backfire shoot a stream of adrenalin through my brain. Sometimes, waking from a restless sleep, I would slip out into the backyard's black stillness and listen once more to cries of "incoming?" and the thunder of a thousand feet dashing for the bunkers in the sultry jungle night. And if I closed my eyes, I could see again red rain on the perimeter and the pop of yellow flares.

The most troubling thing about these images was not that they arose but that I actually enjoyed and even cultivated them. For somewhere interwoven in the shuddering memories of war, I sensed, as well, an elation and vitality that I had long since lost or relinquished but that now suddenly made all my current pursuits seem not only vaguely unsatisfying but starkly empty and vain.

The nightmare of the past had, indeed, caught up with me, and riding like a specter on its back was the Buddha's first Noble Truth. Out there in the world, beyond the self-created confines of my fatuous life, suffering and death continued as the dark underbelly of existence—the ultimate end of everything.

For many months I found it almost impossible to give voice to this inner maelstrom of remembered scenes and clashing feelings, even to myself. Mostly, they just boiled in the threshold of consciousness, but sometimes they would burst upon the foreground, coalescing into a single, overwhelming urge to return to Nam—an urge that, even to my distraught sensibilities, seemed totally perverse. How could anyone else understand?

Colette, of course, was not unaware that something convulsive was going on, but when I tried to talk to her about it, I could see the fear and confusion gathering in her eyes. She had no idea what was happening to me, nor could I offer her any coherent explanations. I felt isolated and alone, and the gap between us widened.

The one avenue of expression I did have was writing, and I availed myself of it in the form of a script for my showcase film. At last, I felt I had something to say and soon worked out a story about two contemporary vets trying to cope in a society that had been stripped of all relevance. I called it *Winter Warriors*.

I also started attending weekly sessions of a veterans' rap group that met in a Venice storefront every Thursday night. The vets in this group came from a mixed bag of economic and racial backgrounds, and many had problems far more severe than mine, but the essence of our reactions was, in almost every case, identical. In spite of all its horrors, Vietnam had been the "most exciting thing that ever happened to us." Moreover, everyone expressed feeling at times that they "didn't belong in this world," but in the one "back there." It was almost as if we all sensed that something had been left undone in Nam, but what?

I began reading books and articles on the psychology of veterans and learned about post-traumatic stress disorder, survivor guilt, etc., yet found none of these answers completely satisfying. They all sounded too pat. Something was missing, but I couldn't put my finger on it. Besides, there wasn't much time for heavy thinking. I was still floundering around in my old life, trying to keep it anchored to some fixed ground, and that ground was Colette. Our relationship, however, was quickly unraveling and would soon snap in an agonizing manner.

One night just before Thanksgiving we got into an argument over something trivial. I hardly remember what it was about, except that I had been drinking too much and was probably more belligerent than usual. At any rate, she left the house in tears, saying only that she would be staying at her uncle's. She had done so before on occasion, so I wasn't particularly worried.

In the morning she was still gone, but this, too, was no cause for alarm. I was certain that she would be home for dinner and took Captain Blood for his daily walk in the park. Upon returning, I noticed that someone had left a message on the answering machine. Thinking it must have been my secretary calling about a rescheduled meeting, I punched the replay button, but it wasn't my secretary. It was Colette.

Her voice was slow and a little dull-sounding but quite deliberate. She had called, she said, simply to inform me that I shouldn't feel responsible for what she was about to do. That was all. But it was enough. And it made my spine freeze. There was not the slightest question in my mind that she had meant suicide.

I called the office with some lame excuse about being ill, but asked Lee to come over right away. We had become good friends in the last few years, and I didn't want to be alone. Next I telephoned everyone Colette and I knew, saying only that she had left the night before and asking if anyone had seen her. No one had.

Lee arrived and spent a few hours with me being as sympathetic as he could, but eventually he had to get back to work.

By evening I was physically sick. I lay down on the floor in the living room by the phone, put my arms around Captain Blood, and cried until dawn. It was absolutely the blackest night of my life, Vietnam not excluded.

The following morning, when there was still no word from Colette, I called the police to report a possible suicide. Two officers were dispatched to the house to take down the facts — age, weight, color of hair, color of eyes, etc., but there was obviously nothing they could really do. There was nothing anybody could do.

After they left I just sat down in a chair and tried not to go crazy.

Colette returned late in the afternoon. I saw her through the window, opening the side gate to the yard, and I could hardly believe my eyes. It was like seeing a corpse risen from the grave. Later, I learned that she had, indeed, gone to a motel and there swallowed half a bottle of Valium. In the morning, however, she had awakened with no more harm done than a bad night's sleep and the worst hangover of her life.

My first reaction was unutterable relief. But during the next few weeks, I spun round and round through a revolving door of every conceivable emotion, from doubt—She must have known half a bottle of Valium wouldn't be lethal—to rage—How could she have done that to me!—but always whirled back to my own crushing sense of guilt. Whatever the seriousness of her intentions, Colette had been driven to a desperate act, and I had been the merciless driver, spurring her on at every turn with a cold and callous indifference. Perhaps, as was commonly believed about Vietnam vets, the war really had irreparably damaged something in my soul.

In any case, we both started seeing shrinks. Mine was a classic Freudian named Dr. Mark. He explained that my war-induced symptoms actually had their origins in childhood traumas, which it was the task of therapy to unearth. Suddenly, however, it struck me that this couldn't be true. My "symptoms" were essentially no different from all the other vets I knew whose backgrounds were so varied. Hence, childhood experiences could have little or nothing to do with it. In fact, whatever had happened in Vietnam had actually superseded such experiences, as though some mysterious Force had invaded all our lives with a dark will of its own, so that, in a very real sense, we were no longer separate individuals but had become part of some larger communal Psyche.

At the time I failed to realize the full implications of this thought, which ultimately raises the question, "Who, then, am I?"—the question that begins all spiritual journeys. Nevertheless, I had intuited that the problem of Vietnam wasn't exclusively "my" problem, and thus, in the end, no amount of personal therapy was going to solve it.

This intuition was born out by a dream I had shortly thereafter in which I went to see Dr. Mark with a cut finger. Being busy with another patient, he offered me a band-aid and directed me to the bathroom. As I tried to bandage the wound, huge quantities of blood spurted out all over the place. I called Dr. Mark in to see, and he was stunned. "You can't be bleeding so much!" he exclaimed. But I was...

After that I stopped seeing him.

Meanwhile, the situation at home with Colette wasn't improving. All arguments between us had ceased, but so had any real communication. She now appeared incredibly fragile to me, and I was terrified that I might do or say something that would prompt her to try suicide again, this time with fatal consequences. As a result I guarded every word that came out of my mouth and tiptoed around her like the fabled bull in a china closet, holding my breath, but the strain was becoming unbearable.

The impasse was finally broken in late December when Lewis got a studio go-ahead to finance another feature. This one would be shot on the island of Malta in the middle of the Mediterranean. I was to depart immediately to prepare the way for principal photography, which would begin right after the first of the year.

Colette came to the airport to see me off and, when the loudspeaker announced boarding time, threw her arms around my neck and wept. I knew she still loved me, and I loved her, too. But at the same time I felt like I was being strangled. Later, on the plane, I recalled the old adage that we kill what we love the most and was shocked to find that it had come true. Our marriage was dead.

The two months on Malta were exhausting. As soon as shooting started, a dispute arose between the star (whom I'll call Jo) and the director, with Lewis caught in the middle. Jo felt that the director was mishandling the script. Although not a great work of art, it was more than decent by Hollywood standards, and I sided with her in trying to protect it. But the energy required to maneuver through the Byzantine set politics was enormous.

In my free time I wandered the island's barren coasts and rocky ruins. Malta was drenched in history, its roots extending back to a natal age when unknown voyagers had washed up on these forbidding shores long enough to leave behind huge megaliths of ringed stone that now stood watch over the centuries. Most of these monuments were bare of decorations, blank boulders set on edge, leaning upon one another like silent, ancient ancestors, the wind alone whispering in their bones to tease you with mysteries—where had they come from? And where had they gone across the blue, restless sea? I longed to know.

One of the few representational figures left by these archaic peoples was an enormous Goddess carved in tawny rock—a primal, moon-faced mother with full-moon breasts, a giant moon belly, and wide, moon-round eyes. I used to go and sit in front of her for hours, trying to fathom her frozen secrets, but the veil of Time hung between us as heavy as the rock itself. Still, she seemed to want to speak to me—of what, I could not tell.

In the port city of Valetta I strolled along the massive ramparts erected by the Hospitaller Knights of St. John, who flourished here in the Middle Ages, and visited the ornate cathedrals where these warrior monks had said confession and received the sacraments before plunging off in their swift, well-armed galleys for the Moslem coasts of Africa and Turkey to rape and pillage and return home with holds chocked full of gold, jewels, and women. How had they managed it—to serve the supreme God of Love with the bloody spoils of war?

But at least, they *had* a God, and such anomalies didn't seem to trouble them. Though sworn to chastity, they had turned Malta into an immense brothel. They had vowed poverty, but wallowed in all the luxuries the East could yield. Obedience was their law, but they had become a law unto themselves. Their history was Man's history in microcosm, riddled with all its frustrating contradictions, and pondering it, I couldn't decide where I fit in: was I a cynic or a romantic? a sensualist or an ascetic?

On Sundays I took the ferry, escorted by blue dolphins, to Godzo, visited Calypso's Cave, and brooded on my fate. The cave overlooked a jagged, inhospitable beach and was said to be the spot where Odysseus had tarried for seven years with seductive demigoddess Calypso on his way home from Troy, and I felt a sudden affinity with the Greek hero. We had both fought in a war far from our native land, and now, years later, like Odysseus, I too felt lost and still at sea. I remembered my first night back from Nam, sitting in the airport bar, a foreigner, and realized that, all the intervening years notwithstanding, I had yet to find my way home.

But if home was not to be located on any geographical map-which apparently it wasn't—then where was it, this Ithaca of my heart?

Despite these gloomy questions, however, in the air of Malta I sniffed some Mythic Realm that transcended all the wasted trivia of our ordinary lives. I began to feel, very faintly, that I must be something more than a mere biological organism, a simple collection of odd molecules aimlessly thrown together for an imperceptible blink of eternity, only to be dissolved and scattered again in death.

What was *death*, anyway? I thought of Nam and how I had been torn, after moments of combat, between exaltation and despair. Exaltation, because I had met death and, surprisingly, conquered it; despair, because I knew the victory to be only partial. Could death ever be conquered once and for all? Was that the task left undone?

It sounded absurd, and yet, there was something in Malta that bore witness to this possibility, something that seemed to outlive all its own forms: the Goddess's primordial mariners; Christ's vanished knights—even the old men who today drank their beer with knotty, blackened hands in sad fisherman cafes; and the very rocks themselves. Still, I couldn't quite put my finger on it...

In the meantime it became all too obvious that Jo and I were fighting a losing battle on the film. Near the end, Lewis had to leave Malta, and the studio, afraid of cost over-runs, put the production manager in charge of the set. The picture came in under budget, all right, but it was also a creative and commercial disaster.

When we got back to L.A., I told Colette I wanted to separate.

She assented stoically and moved into her uncle's temporarily vacant apartment, leaving me with the house and Captain Blood. I continued working for Lewis's company, but Malta had killed my taste for Hollywood. The fun had simply gone out of it. Nevertheless, I clung to the hope that I might yet derive some satisfaction from directing films of my own and plowed all my spare time and money into making *Winter Warriors*.

With the help of two actors from the *Tracers* cast and a crew of friends, we began shooting it on weekends and in the evenings, but the urgency and enthusiasm I had once felt for the project were gone. Although

Finding a Corpse

Vietnam would continue to haunt me from time to time, I no longer regarded it as the central issue of my life. Since Malta, I had come to think of it as only part of some larger mystery that extended beyond anything I had comprehended so far; nor, I was beginning to suspect, would I find the answer in any earthly pursuits. I had known the world and the things of the world—great and small, and they had all turned to dust in my hands. If the world, for me, was not quite yet a corpse, it was definitely terminal.

On April 14, 1982, we finished shooting *Winter Warriors*. I was pleased with myself for having brought the project to completion, but I was also now certain that I would never be a director. This left a huge hole in my life. That same night, however, I had the following dream, which I recorded in a journal I began keeping at that time.

> I am walking through a gentle meadow with no particular destination in mind when the meadow turns into foothills. It's still easy-going and pleasant, but then, gradually, I realize I am climbing the steep slope of a mountain. This is harder work, and soon I find myself scaling a sheer granite cliff, fingers and feet clutching at cracks and toe-holes, a fierce wind whipping around my body. I look down and am terrified to see the earth thousands of feet below. For a moment, I freeze. But an inner voice urges me to keep going: "After all," it reasons, "a fall from here or higher up will kill you just the same."
>
> With great difficulty I struggle on toward the top and, at last, I make it. I look out over a breath-taking landscape spread at my feet. The seven continents and seven seas extend before my eyes to a 360-degree horizon. Both the sun and moon are simultaneously visible in the sky, one half of which is night, the other, day, and a sacred hush envelops the world. Suddenly, I become aware of a woman standing at my side, wearing a helmet. She hands me a sword and says, "This sword is as bright as the moon and as sharp as the stars, and with it you can cut through the heart of truth."
>
> I take the sword and hold it in the palm of my hand, and it feels powerful and good. Then I turn to the woman and ask, "Who are you?"
>
> "Don't you know?" she laughs, gently, "I am Athena and I've been with you always."

Ever since I was a child I had always had colorful and dramatic dreams, but—except for the one before Nam—none like this. I awoke in a state of awe, feeling humbled and strangely blessed. Although I knew that

Athena had been the goddess who guarded and guided Odysseus on his voyage home, and that the gift of a sword had symbolic antecedents in legend and myth, I made no attempt to analyze these things, for the dream did not seem to point to anything beyond itself. It had its own reality, a reality so numinous and self-evident that, by comparison, the wake-a-day world appeared but a pale counterfeit. What's more, the message was perfectly and profoundly clear and needed no additional interpretation. I also knew it was a message I could ignore only at the peril of my soul.

Three: Samantha Jones and the Holy Grail

I mark this dream, in which Athena first appeared, as the beginning of my quest. I say *first* appeared, because, although I never actually saw her again, Athena was to stay with me as a distinct presence, an inner voice — I am tempted to say, a personality — for the next sixteen months, guiding my thoughts, sending me dreams, prompting me to action when appropriate, and restraining me when necessary. At times — as fantastic as it may sound — she even seemed able to manipulate the external world in order to teach me some lesson or other. If she didn't actually control events, she certainly had foreknowledge of what was destined to occur and took advantage of it for my benefit. In all this, however, she never once explained herself — either who she was or what she was about. Everything was in the form of terse injunctions: *Go there. Do this. Don't do that.* Which is not to say that I was totally devoid of choice in my dealings with her. There were occasions when I rebelled against Athena's dictates, but always to my regret. Eventually, I came to accept and trust her so thoroughly that when she would absent herself for certain periods, I would yearn for her tutelage once more.

Immediately following the dream, however, I had no way of knowing all this was going to happen; our relationship would take weeks and months to unfold fully. What I *did* know was that something radical had occurred at the very core of my life. I had been handed an instrument of inestimable worth, and I had better learn how to use it.

The problem was, I had, as yet, no idea where to turn for such instruction. But I needn't have worried. Athena, my disincarnate guide, had already begun her work. Even then, I was being led in ways, and to ends, that I could never have imagined. And one of those ways was a very incarnate, flesh-and-blood woman named Samantha Jones.

Actually, I had first met Samantha three years earlier, and from the beginning there was something bizarre about our relationship—the way we met, for instance…

It was in the fall of 1979, and I was busy with pre-production of Lewis's first feature. Jean had been doubling as both my story editor and secretary, but with the increased work load, we needed a full-time secretary. I interviewed a dozen candidates over a week's period. They shuffled in and out of my office, parading a variety of skills and personalities, but the last seemed by far the best. She was sensible and energetic, could type and take dictation. The only drawback was that she had never worked in the film business before, but this was relatively unimportant. I would have hired her on the spot except that a glance at my calendar revealed that she was not the last candidate, after all. Jean had penciled in another appointment for me the following day. Nevertheless, I was sure this girl would have the job and told her so. We shook hands, and she left, but I never saw her again, because the next day's applicant turned out to be Samantha.

The minute she walked in the door, I knew I was going to hire her. What's more, Samantha seemed to know it, too. The interview was a mere formality. She was perfectly relaxed and answered all my questions with the air of someone getting inconsequentials out of the way. Yes, she could type, take dictation, and even had prior industry experience. But somehow, I knew all this already, and although I was certain I had never laid eyes on her before, the more Samantha talked, the more I sensed something overwhelmingly familiar in the sound of her sonorous voice, the way she brushed back bangs of blond hair from her forehead, and the flashing, almost conspiratorial expression in her large brown eyes. After a while, I began to feel she was, indeed, someone I knew, but in disguise, that at any moment she might pull off wig, hat, and false nose, and I would recognize an old, old friend, playing a very clever practical joke.

But, of course, she didn't. She just sat there waiting patiently for my next question with a slightly ironic smile, as though she had actually come on some other, secret mission that had nothing to do with anything as mundane as a job. It was disconcerting, to say the least, but in the end, she had all the qualifications of the previous girl, plus experience, and so there was nothing else to do but hire her.

Samantha began work the following Monday. Within a few weeks, however, something even more disconcerting happened. Lee was preparing a TV movie to be shot in Europe later that year but, in the meantime, maintained an office down the hall from us.

He and Samantha hit it off immediately, and a couple of times, he took her out to lunch. One day he came into my office and closed the door, signaling that he had something private to say. It was that he and Samantha had started dating. To avoid company gossip, they were keeping their relationship discreet, but because we were friends, he wanted me to know. Although I assured him that, as a matter of office policy, I had nothing against such romances and that whatever they did after hours was fine with me, the truth was anything but that and had nothing to do with formal policies. It was wholly personal. My stomach tightened, my breath caught in my throat, and a sick chill passed through my flesh. I was rapidly succumbing to all the symptoms of an intense, physical jealousy.

The absurd part about it, however, was that, to the best of my knowledge, I wasn't in love with Samantha or anyone else except my wife. In those days Colette and I were still very happy together, and I had no interest in other women.

Within a day or two the symptoms passed, but they left me genuinely puzzled. Working at a film studio, I was exposed daily to ladies far more alluring and attractive than Samantha, but they had produced no such reactions. Besides, psychologically, she wasn't even my type. While I was a hard-headed pragmatist, Samantha seemed almost to have a screw loose somewhere. Often, during lulls in office activity, I would catch her staring off into some private space of her own and would have to call her name more than once to bring her back to *terra firma*. On such occasions she always looked sheepish and apologetic, but as long as these little astral flights didn't interfere with her work, I had no complaints. And I had to admit that her work was superb...sometimes uncannily so.

It was not unusual for me to be sitting behind my desk midmorning, about to ask Samantha for a cup of coffee, when in she'd sally, coffee in hand. Even stranger was to yell out the name of someone I wanted on the phone only to find that she was in the midst of dialing that very number. Or to request a script and discover that she had already put it on my desk an hour before. These weird incidents notwithstanding, however, we quickly settled into a smooth and comfortable working routine, and as the start date for our picture drew near, I had other things to worry about.

Actually, in the beginning I probably learned more about Samantha from Lee than from anything she herself said. Most of it concerned her financial struggles. According to him, she was deeply committed to spiritual growth and spent all her money on various conferences and workshops. As a result, she could barely keep food on the table. Lee, of course, was telling me all this in the hopes of wangling her a raise, which I think she finally got. In any case, what Samantha did on her own time was really no concern of mine.

Shortly after Lee left for Europe, Samantha showed me an unpublished treatise she had written on *Science and Higher Consciousness* and asked for my opinion. Frankly, at the time I thought the content a lot of pseudo-scientific bullshit, but the writing was something else again. I had read enough best-selling authors to recognize marketable talent when I saw it, and Samantha was better than most. I had also plowed through enough junk to know just how rare such talent was.

From then on I began to take a new, almost fatherly interest in her. At the end of the day we would often share a glass of wine, and listening to her talk eagerly about the great questions of religion and philosophy and how they might be resolved in the light of recent theories in the fields of physics and biology, I would recall my own adolescent zeal for mysticism and Zen and smile inside. Like me, someday she would have to grow up and face the "real world," and if I could help steer her in that direction, so much the better—especially in view of her prodigious literary potential for which she herself seemed to have no appreciation. The first thing, however, was to get her to tackle something a bit more commercial than "higher consciousness."

When I learned that Samantha had once been married to a rock-and-roll singer, I suggested she write a book based on this experience. I even had a hot title for her—*Rock Wife*. In my mind's eye I could already see rows of paperbacks filling the supermarket racks. All she would have to do was write up a few chapters and an outline, and I was sure I could make a sale. Samantha politely promised to think it over, but never mentioned it again.

Finding a Corpse

One afternoon in December I returned from lunch to find a single red rose sitting on my desk. It was Samantha's way of giving notice. We said our goodbyes two weeks later at the office Christmas party. I kissed her and quipped that it was a good thing she was leaving, because if she didn't we'd probably end up having an affair. It was a joke, of course, but I had grown truly fond of her. I knew I would never have another secretary as sensitive and skilled as Samantha, and I was right. I also thought I would never see her again.

About that, I was wrong.

Shortly after I came back from Malta, Lee mentioned that he had run into Samantha recently and that she had asked about me. It sounded like a bit of social courtesy, and I didn't give it a second thought. A week later, however, she called to invite me to lunch.

We met at a little restaurant in Hollywood that served continental cuisine on an outdoor patio with a slatted roof. I don't recall much of the conversation except that, in spite of the fact that we hadn't seen each other in three years, it was easy and animated, and we laughed a lot. Samantha had a wonderful way of laughing. It would just sort of erupt, spontaneous and full, from some deep well of delight, and it warmed me to hear it again, especially after all the anguish of the past year, haunted by memories of Nam and breaking up with Colette.

Towards the end of the meal, I noticed how the sun and shadows from the roof fell in bars across her face, like the lighting in old black-and-white movies from the forties, and realized for the first time that she was positively beautiful. How had I missed it before?

Without anything specific in mind, I picked up my wine glass, peered at her radiant face through its amber contents, and suddenly asked, "So, are we going to have that affair or not?"

Samantha said, "Yes."

What can I say about the next few feverish weeks? I had been in love before, of course — and deeply so with Colette, but this was bewilderingly different. Where Colette's love had been human and earthy, textured by a myriad of domestic rhythms and subtle joys, Samantha's was all liquid fire, rolling through my life in great transporting waves of tender torment and holy lust. We stole lunch hours, snatched evenings, consumed whole weekends, bodies snapped together like fleshy magnets perfectly aligned. Nor did it seem to matter whether we were physically close or not. I could be lying in her bed, locked to her sweating bones, or on the other side of town in the middle of a business meeting, when the tide would come pounding up from some molten nether-sea with a thundering will of its own to engulf all my senses and leave me gasping. Even at its ebb, this current never really left me. I could always feel it coiled somewhere in my bowels, hissing softly like a fuse that simmers between charges but is never fully extinguished. Where had it come from? Who had lit this serpent flame, and how? Was it carnal or divine? Sacred or profane? I knew nothing of Athena then and didn't stop to ask; there wasn't time.

The truth is, I had never intended to fall in love with Samantha.

She was only meant to be a little diversion, a toy to cheer me up. I didn't even realize it was happening until she wrote me a poem. In marvelous, myth-rich imagery, she had captured the essence of our incendiary affair; but one verse, in particular, drove straight to my soul:

> but I sent for you, I charged the ether
> with a plaintive north star song of old
> my wolf call melody to the moon

Long ago I had wished for some north star to guide my life and inform me of my destiny. I had stalked it in the wanderings of my youth, hunted it in the jungles of war, tracked it through the quicksands of revolution. But in the end I had lost the scent and given up. Now, here it was again, unbidden and almost forgotten — that ancient siren song born in some lost province of the heart, singing to me from eternity through Samantha's guileless mouth, and I was hooked.

Actually, although I failed to realize it at the time, the poem was also, like her rose, Samantha's delicate way of giving notice that, as far as she was concerned, our romance had temporarily run its course. Shortly afterwards, she suggested we "take a breather." I wasn't exactly thrilled by the idea, but there was nothing else to do, so I agreed. Besides, I was about to start shooting *Winter Warriors*, and for a while all my free time would be occupied.

I didn't see Samantha for about a month, but I telephoned her once or twice and wrote her a letter, which she answered. It wasn't easy maintaining a distance, yet I realized that our relationship had to switch gears, or we would both burn out. When the shooting was over, however, I called to make a date for lunch.

Ever since that first day she walked into my office, I had always been able to read the substance, if not the details, of Samantha's thoughts, no matter how impenetrable a mask she tried to put on. Thus, the instant I saw her face, I knew in my gut something was wrong. I also knew what it was; she was seeing someone else.

Samantha admitted it was so. His name was Ralph. She had met him at some consciousness-raising workshop, and they shared, she said, a lot in common. It was true that Samantha had never made me any explicit promises, but I was angry and hurt nonetheless. After all, she might have had the courtesy to mention Ralph in one of our phone calls or her letter and save me the embarrassment of this meeting. But it also occurred to me that—sex and poetry aside—Samantha and I shared almost nothing "in common." What was there to build a relationship on? All that was really at stake was my punctured masculine pride, but so what? It was time to do the gentlemanly thing—wish her luck and bid her farewell. I opened my mouth to say just that, but that's not what came out. Instead, I insisted that I was going to fight for her with everything I had.

Samantha looked as surprised as I was by this spontaneous declaration and even a little pleased. When I asked for another date, she agreed, and I went away, pride restored, confident that I would win her in the end.

The first thing I did was change my tactics. I started taking her on "real" dates. We went out to dinner, movies, and even on a whale-watching expedition. I also began paying more attention to her moods and thoughts, likes and dislikes, and found them both fascinating and exasperating.

Although she had been raised in a middle-class, suburban home, Samantha was by no means unsophisticated in the ways of the world; yet she still maintained some amazingly child-like predilections. She loved to watch Sunday morning cartoons on TV but shunned the news because its violence upset her. She could become tearful for days over some slight delivered by a thoughtless colleague at work, but also go into paroxysms of joy at the simplest kindness. She was trusting to a fault and would believe almost anyone or anything—including shoddy magazine and TV advertisements, whose mail-order claims often left her sorely disappointed. Samantha herself, however, was never scheming or vindictive. Indeed, she had a genuine and innocent faith in the ultimate Goodness and Truth of Life, and it was this, more than anything, that captivated my heart and bound me to her.

Most of Samantha's faith, intellectually at least, was based on the ideas of New Age thinkers, and it was she who first introduced me to them. We discussed theories she had culled from the works of John Lilly and Teilhard de Chardin, Lyall Watson and Fritjof Capra. Though I remained outwardly skeptical, by now I had had my Athena dream and was becoming inwardly intrigued. Was there really some greater reality standing behind this ephemeral and apparently pointless existence? And if so, how could it be reached? Samantha used words like *transformation*, *realization*, and *enlightenment*, but I had little idea what they meant—nor did she seem to have a very clear conception either—and sometimes we argued. Nevertheless, such thoughts began to take root in my soul.

The real source of my frustration, however, lay neither in Samantha's naivete nor in her beliefs—both of which I actually found refreshing, but stemmed from the fact that I could never quite pin her down or figure her out. There was always something elusive and enigmatic in her nature that kept me forever unsettled. The only thing I knew for certain was that I wanted to spend the rest of my life with her, and I began to fantasize what that life might be like.

I would stay in the film business, but only as a means to finance our private adventures. We would travel the world, cultivating a stylish circle of friends composed mostly of writers, artists, philosophers, and the like. Samantha, of course, would be free to pursue her own literary muse full time, but I was no longer interested in pushing her in a commercial direction. She was a true artist in her own right and deserved all the patronage I could offer.

In this fanciful scenario, I would be her Knight-Protector, she, my Lover-Protege. It appealed to a kind of decadent, anti-hero image I had of myself as a tough-minded man of the world, but one who secretly wielded his power in the service of Art and Innocence. It was a lovely dream. The only problem was that Samantha didn't share it.

Everything fell apart during a weekend we spent in Santa Barbara. I thought two days alone would cement our relationship and give me a final victory in our lovers' war. But Samantha must have sensed the hour of surrender approaching and balked. From the outset she was aloof and unresponsive, which, in turn, made me feel clumsy and tense. Nothing specific happened. We never quarreled nor even exchanged a harsh word. Indeed, the whole weekend passed much *too* politely, and by the time I dropped her off at her Westwood apartment that Sunday evening, I knew my little daydream would never come true.

The trouble was, I was both unable and unwilling to give her up completely. What's more, Samantha herself was being mysteriously coy. Several times I phoned for a date, and each time she sweetly put me off without, however, asking for a definitive break. Finally, one night in a fit of drunken frustration I showed up at her house, banging loudly on the door and frightening her so badly that she refused to open it. Later, of course, I called with an apology—which she coolly accepted, but I realized I had better lay off for a while, if not for good. I had lost control of the situation and, more disturbingly, of myself.

A few days later I got out an old pack of Tarot cards I had and, purely as a lark, asked them whether I should just forget about Samantha entirely. I used the Celtic cross method, described in the instruction booklet, and chose the Knight of Swords to represent myself. I had already decided that the Queen of Cups would represent Samantha, should it turn up. On the first layout the Queen of Cups *covered* my Knight. I reshuffled and dealt again. Again, the Queen of Cups appeared, this time *crossing* the Knight. Thinking that I must not have shuffled very well, I spread the cards all over the floor and reassembled them at random. I dealt a third layout, and once again, the Queen of Cups popped up, this time *above* my Knight in the position that, the book said, symbolized what I had yet to achieve.

According to the Tarot, then, I couldn't get rid of Samantha even if I wanted to. As I pondered the mathematical probability—or should I say, improbability—of these readings, I suddenly felt Athena hovering at my shoulder with what sounded suspiciously like a chuckle. Spooked, I carefully packed away the cards and never again tried to use them for divination.

It was sometime in June that I attended what I later came to regard as my first Public Teaching, and this too was indirectly prompted by Samantha. She had mentioned once taking a series of classes on alchemy given by a

Dr. Stephan Hoeller at a place called the Philosophical Research Society. One day while browsing through the Times Calendar Section, I spotted a notice for another lecture to be given by Hoeller, this one titled "Parzival and the Grail in our Souls."

As a child I had been raised on tales of King Arthur and his Knights of the Round Table (where Parzival had held a legendary seat), so the subject immediately piqued my interest. Besides, I was still wondering about the meaning of Athena's sword and thought there might be a symbolic connection between it and Arthur's famous Excalibur which Hoeller could elucidate. It was for these reasons, plus a secret hope that Samantha might be there as well, that I drove down to Los Felix Boulevard on a warm Wednesday night to see what he had to say.

I paid my $2.00 donation at the door and walked into the rather large auditorium feeling somewhat out of place. There were perhaps a dozen people already seated, mostly older, mostly female, and to my eyes, mostly odd-looking—the kind of women you see in occult bookshops with long flowing skirts and heavy jewelry. I took a seat near the rear and waited. A few more people of like ilk straggled in, but that was it—not exactly an overflowing crowd.

A few minutes later Dr. Hoeller arrived, striding purposefully up the aisle, clutching a heavy briefcase. He was a short, rotund man in his late forties with a ruddy face and black goatee. He wore a full-length, black raincoat and, incongruously, an Australian bush hat with the brim pinned up. After withdrawing some notes from his briefcase and arranging them on the podium, he launched into the evening's topic with flare and humor.

Dr. Hoeller was, I later learned, a self-described Jungian Gnostic and Bishop of the local Gnostic Church. He was also an extremely erudite scholar of the esoteric traditions—both East and West—and a challenging speaker, given to corny jokes and sometimes long digressions in which he would take to task rigid orthodoxy for knowing neither the *ortho* (right) nor the *dox* (teaching). Originally, he had hailed from Hungary and still spoke with a hefty accent, which made me think of an impassioned Faustian professor of the last century. In any case, he was a far cry from most modern gurus with their jumbled jargon and unsupported insights. In short, he was an ideal first teacher for someone in my skeptical stage of development.

Hoeller began by placing the Grail legend in historical perspective. Although its plot and characters were derived largely from Celtic sources, its romantic spirituality had come, by way of the troubadours, from the south of France where the mysterious Cathar heresy flourished during the twelfth century. Hoeller's own interpretation was based on Wolfram Von Eschenbach's *Parzival*, which Hoeller presented as an example of the archetypal Questing Myth as delineated by Jung.

To begin with, Parzival (whose name means to *pierce right through the middle*), like the classic Questing Hero, grows up unaware of his true identity — in this case, that he is, in fact, the Grail King's nephew and heir. The first person to inform him of this is his cousin, Sigune — a woman, and this information is what sets the plot in motion. What's more, as Hoeller pointed out, it is always a woman who appears at critical moments to keep it going.

In the meantime, however, Parzival still has no idea of how to claim his birthright and, after leaving home, falls under the tutelage of a magician named Gurnemanz. But the magic Gurnemanz teaches is *goetic*, or earthly magic (as opposed to *theurgic*, or spiritual magic), and suited only for worldly pursuits. Finally, Parzival realizes that this is not his destiny and departs.

Next, Parzival meets and marries Condwiramurs (*conduit of love*) to whom he will be faithful for the rest of the tale. After their honeymoon, however, he ventures out into the world again. Inadvertently, he stumbles on Munsalvaesche, the mystical Grail Kingdom, only to find that it has been turned into a wasteland by some mysterious enchantment. Nevertheless, Parzival gets a chance to meet the Grail King (who suffers from a wound that won't heal), but because the young hero has been taught proper "worldly" manners by Gurnemanz, he is too polite to ask the essential question, "What's wrong here?" This failure on Parzival's part causes the Grail Kingdom to vanish, and he is returned to mundane reality, hardly realizing that he has lost a golden opportunity to win the Grail and fulfill his destiny.

Parzival then travels to King Arthur's court where he performs numerous deeds of chivalry that earn him praise from the whole noble company. Hoeller's interpretation of this episode was that Arthur's court represented a spiritual training ground in which the "lords and ladies of the soul" are reconciled and integrated in preparation for the great transformative tasks ahead. The danger, however, is that the seeker can be lulled into a fatal complacency by his accomplishments here and so lose the motivation to carry his quest to completion. Indeed, this is what almost happens to Parzival But at the zenith of his courtly glory, a hag-witch, Kundry, appears to publicly chastise him for failing to achieve the Grail when he had the chance. Like the ancient furies, she pursues him mercilessly until, finally, he vows on his knightly honor to undertake the quest once again.

Though somewhat bitter about the harsh fate God has decreed for him, Parzival sets out a second time to find Munsalvaesche, sustained now only by his love for Condwiramurs. "If I am to strive for the Grail," he declares, "the thought of her pure embrace must drive me on." But Parzival can make no real progress until he meets a mendicant hermit, Trevrizent, who counsels him to purify his heart towards God. Only then is he allowed to find his way back to the Grail Kingdom where he is again ushered into the wounded King's presence, this time to ask the magic question, "Uncle, what is it that troubles you?" Instantly, the wasteland is transformed into a realm of overflowing abundance. The King is healed, and eventually, Parzival himself inherits the Grail throne, thus becoming *that which he sought*. According to Hoeller, then, the whole epic symbolizes the eternal journey towards Gnosis, the spiritual transformation that is potentially the birthright of us all.

Although I knew little about Jungian psychology at the time, I was completely enthralled. Here was a metaphor that, if it offered no "explanations," seemed to express many aspects of my own experience. I could easily identify with Parzival's perennial sense of unfulfilled destiny. I didn't know who I was anymore or what I was supposed to be doing in this world, but I felt there must be *something*. That I had spent the last decade learning "Gurnemanz's magic" was evident, but it was equally evident that it had not been sufficient to prevent my own life from turning into a wasteland. Like the Grail King, too, I seemed to be suffering from a wound that wouldn't heal (as represented in my dream of Dr. Mark and the cut finger). Also, as with Parzival, it had been a woman—in the form of Athena—who had handed me the sword (emblem of knighthood) and started me on this quest, and another woman, Samantha (conduit of love), who had encouraged it, even, coincidentally, steering me to this very lecture. Finally, like Parzival, I seemed already to have missed some crucial opportunity in Nam—the task left undone—for which I was now paying. But if these mythic parallels promised some clarity, there was much more that remained hidden and problematic.

What, for instance, exactly was the Grail? Or, more practically speaking, what was it that I should be looking for? Historically, the Grail had been an object shrouded in mystery. In Wolfram's saga, it was conceived of as a kind of philosopher's stone, and in later versions influenced by the Church, it had evolved into the cup used by Jesus at the last supper. Earlier accounts, however, were much more vague. All that could be gleaned from these was that it seemed to be a vessel of sorts, imbued with magical powers to transform the individual and his reality—but in what way? I realized, of course, that the Grail was not to be taken literally as a physical object, but even clues to its possible psychological significance thoroughly escaped me.

Next, I was completely baffled by the meaning of the question, "What's wrong here?" It was a question I myself had been asking a lot lately. So far, however, it had failed to transform my world into a land of abundance on any level.

I was also puzzled by Parzival's interlude at King Arthur's court and the spiritual instructions he received from the hermit Trevrizent. Did this mean I should seek out a guru and undertake some form of spiritual discipline? If so, which of the almost countless varieties would be right for me, and how would I know? But this was a step, I decided, that I wasn't ready for.

Nevertheless, that night proved to be a pivotal point in my journey. I had all but exhausted the things of the world; now I would begin to pursue the things of the spirit, to reorganize the priorities of my life—slowly, at first, but with ever-increasing speed—until this pursuit superseded all else. I had, in fact, almost without realizing it, taken my first, tentative step on the path, a path that—through Athena's grace and Samantha's love—would eventually pierce all worlds *right through the middle.*

But the discovery of Gnosis cannot be made, nor even the real quest begun, until the things of the spirit themselves have been exhausted. Thus, it would take me a full year of further explorations, of trials and errors, obstacles and tests, of wanderings up and down blind alleys and dead ends, before I returned to the naked simplicity of this very moment and, like Parzival, divested of all other purposes and with only a woman's love to sustain me, actually and literally set out to find the Grail.

Four:
The Hardships of Learning

I continued attending Hoeller's lectures on Wednesday nights and also began reading voraciously on psychology and mysticism, but still, this whole business of "transformation" made little sense. One of the first books I read was Carlos Castaneda's *Teachings of Don Juan*; the following passage expresses my predicament very concisely:

> When a man starts to learn, he is never clear about his objectives. His purpose is faulty; his intent is vague. He hopes for rewards that will never materialize, for he knows nothing of the hardships of learning.[4]

One of the first "hardships of learning" was trying to understand Don Juan himself. His teachings seemed to consist mainly of certain shamanic practices designed to help the seeker penetrate a visionary world that sounded closely akin to states of consciousness induced by hallucinogens. (Indeed, the use of peyote played a large part in his methods.) Aside from the outlandish nature of some of these techniques—like sewing up the eyes of lizards and following them across the desert—I was confused about the ontological status of this psychedelic world itself. Did Don Juan mean to suggest that it was somehow more real than ordinary reality? Apparently, he did. Still, I failed to see its relevance to the problem of transformation. I had taken acid and mescaline in my younger days, and although I found the experiences illuminating, I certainly hadn't been transformed by them in any fundamental way. What, then, was the point?

Moreover, I was by no means ready to so totally surrender a materialistic worldview or my critical faculties. What I sought in practice was a rational way to explain such phenomena as Athena's presence and my uncanny relationship with Samantha, and for a while I thought I had found such an explanation in the works of Carl G. Jung.

If Athena seemed to me something more substantial than a mere fantasy, concocted by my own unconscious, I could at least recognize in her a possible archetype of Jung's collective unconscious. Also, the idea of a collective unconscious threw some light on my growing perception of some mythic aspect to reality that I had first sensed so strongly in Malta. Exactly how all this fit with a scientifically rational cosmos, however, was still somewhat of a puzzle. Was Jung trying to imply that the collective unconscious stood metaphysically apart from or above the material world? Or was it merely the conscious manifestation of biochemical processes in the brain, which were genetically transmitted and then replicated in each individual? Jung himself seemed to flirt with the former position, but when pressed, fell back on the latter.

I could also see how Jung's concept of anima projection might explain the intensity of my feelings for Samantha and my peculiar helplessness in their sway. What's more, if Samantha was only the passive recipient of a purely subjective projection—and not linked to me by any objective circumstances—then the possibility existed that this projection could be dissolved by my own independent efforts. In the end this turned out not to be the case, and eventually, I had to abandon Jung's model. But in the meantime, it was to provide an important framework for the next phase of my development.

It should also be said that Jung did me the great service of pointing out that the contents of the psyche are not "merely psychological" (as our culture so likes to dismiss them) but *just as real* (as psychical entities) as anything tangible to the five senses. Thus, whether or not God exists, the psychic *image* of God certainly exists and has had a profound influence in shaping human destinies.

The immediate consequence of this last recognition was that I began to pay much closer attention to my own psychic images and dreams. This opened a rich inner line of communication with the same ground from which Athena had sprung and proved a valuable source of guidance and reinforcement during the entire rest of the journey.

An example of one such communication came in the form of a dream I had in mid-July. Colette's uncle had returned to claim his apartment, and she wanted the house back. I found a small, two-bedroom cabin in Topanga Canyon, whose remoteness from Hollywood promised the seclusion and privacy I was lately beginning to yearn for. The night before I actually moved, however, I spent an hour or two idly thumbing through the *Whole Person Catalogue*, a kind of shopper's guide to the New Age. The next morning I awoke convinced that I had seen an ad in this catalogue for an institute called The Center for Consciousness Transformation, located on the same street as my new house. I even started looking through the catalogue again for its address. Then suddenly, I realized I had dreamed the whole thing. This imagined Center for Consciousness Transformation was none other than my own future abode!

In Topanga, too, I started a rather strict schedule of daily meditation, which became a permanent feature of my quest. At first, these meditations were based on a book authored by Dr. Hoeller and titled, *The Royal Road: A Manual of Kabalistic Meditations on the Tarot*. Although I knew next to nothing about either the Kabala or the Tarot, meditation appeared to be a requisite of all spiritual paths, and since I had come to trust and admire Hoeller, his manual seemed as good a place to begin as any.

In the first part of the book Hoeller correlated the twenty-two cards of the Tarot's major arcana with the intricate pathways and stations on the Kabalistic Tree of Life. The second part was the manual proper. Here, the cards were not used for divination but rather as icons to be contemplated and absorbed, marking out the spiritual terrain on the road to Gnosis. Each card was pictured along with a brief explanation of its symbolism, a motto drawn from one of the mystical traditions, and the meditation itself. By way of example, the meditation on *The Hermit* read,

> In the lonely hour of my soul, thou comest to my chamber, O beauty and love sublime. I lean upon the rod and staff of my insight, and though I walk through the valley of solitude, and scale the summits of loneliness, I know that my lover awaits on the mountaintop, from whence ever cometh my help. In the midst of the turmoil of living, I am but a lonely wanderer seeking my love. A pilgrim of eternity am I homeward bound among the stars.[5]

Although the prose was a bit flowery for my taste, the images of being a "wanderer," scaling a "mountain-top," devotion to a "lover," and "homeward bound" — plus an overall sense of loneliness — all seemed hauntingly appropriate to my own psychic condition. But the cards were more than just reflections of images already in my consciousness. They also served to keep at least part of my attention constantly focused on the quest, vague as it yet was. One effect of this new focus was actually to intensify my loneliness by further distancing me from friends and associates. Yet this very distance facilitated a subtle shift in day-to-day perceptions that soon began to generate small flashes of insight. One such flash came in the midst of an important business meeting, which otherwise would have totally absorbed me.

After the Maltese debacle Lewis switched the company's strategy. Instead of concentrating on feature-film development, he decided to break into the television-series game. For the past several months we had been hammering out a dozen or more plot formulas for TV sit-coms. Now we began a round of meetings with our agency representatives, who would try to package and sell these ideas to the networks. Aside from the fact that television was even less appealing to me than movies, I began to see all our activity with a new, more disinterested eye.

The meeting I remember in particular took place in a modern, brown-and-beige agency office. The six or seven young agents facing us across the table were also all dressed in color-coordinated, brown-and-beige suits and ties. Even Lewis, I noticed, as though obeying some primal instinct, had donned this uniform, while I still wore last year's blue blazer and grey slacks. Somehow I had missed the change in fashions. Who dictated such things? I wondered a bit uncomfortably.

As the meeting progressed, however, my discomfort evolved into an odd, though not unpleasant, sense of detachment. I became aware not so much of what was being said but of *how* it was being said. All the words and phrases were drawn from the same reservoir of stock Hollywood lingo I had been hearing for years—a lingo, however, that I now realized had very little substance behind it. It was as though we ourselves had become actors, reading lines in a bad TV show. Even our gestures and expressions seemed stale and mechanical, and I found that I could actually predict what everyone was going to say next.

At one point, to emphasize the salability of a particular idea about adolescent romances, Lewis banged the table excitedly and exclaimed, "Don't you realize what we've got here, fellas? We've got teenagers humping at eight o'clock!"

For some reason the seriousness with which he said this struck me as hilariously funny, and I started to laugh out loud. Surely everyone understood that this whole scene had turned into a parody of itself. When I looked around the room, however, no one else had so much as cracked a smile. Apparently, these actors had forgotten we were in a play!

Later I thought of something I had read in Idries Shah's book about Sufis: "Humanity is asleep," a famous Murshid had said, "concerned only with what is useless, living in a wrong world." I was beginning to suspect that this might be quite literally true, but if humanity was living in a wrong world, where was the *right* one, and how to get there? Woefully, I seemed to be drifting in a limbo somewhere between the two.

After days like this, it was always a relief to get back to my little cabin in Topanga. The trip took forty-five minutes, the first half hour of which was bumper to bumper on grueling, smog-choked freeways. But during the last fifteen minutes, climbing the narrow, switch-backed road that curled up into the canyon, with the sea's clean taste on the wind and the orange sun slashing through pines and scrub oak, all the hustle and bustle of the work-a-day world fell away like soiled clothing.

I spent the evenings reading quietly or taking Captain Blood for long, solitary walks in the raggedy hills where we rarely met another soul. It was an isolated life, but not without its consolations, as this July 29th entry in my journal indicates:

> This morning, I awake to the softest purple light creeping into the valley. Something tugs at the antenna wire running down past my window—a jet-blue bird, scrounging for his breakfast. This place is alive with peace.

But, as I said, it was also a lonely peace and sometimes hard to bear. Another entry on August 5th reads,

> I listen to the moon-full bark of a misty, midnight dog and imagine that I understand all the deeper mysteries. But the dog knows different and I know the dog knows. Sometimes I hear the wind sniffing in the trees, nudging branch and leaf to life, and my heart leaps to the rippling dance that spreads up and down the valley like some infectious tribal rite, but I cannot sing the tune, nor mark the measure of the beat. What riffs solitude will produce; a wild careening between the most ludicrous sorrows and inflammatory joys!

Many of these "ludicrous sorrows" and "inflammatory joys" were evoked by fantasies of Samantha. In spite of all efforts to "dissolve" her as an anima projection, Samantha continued to stalk my thoughts like some shadowy angel driven underground. I spun long, imaginary dialogues with her in my head and frequently felt a compulsion to call her up and try them out.

Athena, however, now began to intervene on a regular basis. As soon as I reached for the phone, I could feel her invisible hand restraining mine. Whenever I disregarded these checks, conversations with Samantha proved strained and difficult.

But there were times, too, when Athena would actually urge me to call her, even though I had nothing in particular to say. On such occasions, Samantha always responded warmly, often making some remark like, "I knew it was you!" or "I had a feeling you would call today." — all of which left me with the distinct impression that something or someone was trying to keep us connected, if only intermittently. Increasingly, I began to feel we really were bound together in some larger mythos whose true ends and purposes had yet to be revealed.

But I also came to realize that Samantha was not—as I had always assumed—any more conscious of these ends and purposes than I was. In fact, if anything, she was less so. Her coy remarks and enigmatic looks, which I had taken as signs of a private wisdom, in reality expressed little more than a natural, girlish coquetry. And whereas the mystery of our nexus had become a focal point in my life, it was only peripheral to hers. Thus, there was no point in trying to force a deeper level of intimacy between us. I could either accept our relationship as given and attempt to work with it or let Samantha slip forever into the passing stream of time. Faced with this choice, I resolved to try simply to be her friend and see what would happen next.

What happened was a test of this new resolve, and by surviving it, I received my first clear lesson on wielding Athena's sword.

In July Samantha attended a ten-day conference at a place called Sky Hi Ranch, run by a New Age teacher named Dr. Richard Moss. I had read Moss's book, *The I That Is We*, subtitled *Awakening to Higher Energies Through Unconditional Love*, but had been less than enthusiastic. His panacea of unconditional love sounded rather idealistic, and I was skeptical about the existence of any "higher energies." Nevertheless, when Samantha returned, it was obvious that she had undergone some very potent experiences, the consequences of which were not altogether blissful. On the phone she said that she hadn't slept in days and was having a hard time functioning back in her job—all of which made me even more skeptical.

One evening a week or so later, Samantha invited me to her apartment for dinner. I showed up early and, finding no one home, waited on the balcony smoking a cigarette. In a few minutes Samantha arrived loaded down with groceries and wearing a haggard expression. I could tell she was still suffering the effects of Sky Hi and made some mildly sarcastic remark.

"Look!" she snapped, eyes flashing with uncharacteristic anger, "I'm in no mood for your combativeness tonight. If you're going to be that way, you might as well leave right now!"

Her words stung me sharply, not because no one had ever accused me of being combative before—indeed, I had heard it often in my life—but because I realized the truth of it with a sudden and astonishing clarity. I was a combative person and had always been so. I was even secretly proud of this trait. It was part of who I was!

Or was it? Now, in Samantha's ruffled presence, I was no longer sure. Certainly, I hadn't *intended* to be combative with her. On the contrary, what I had really wanted to do was snatch the packages from her arms, kiss her on the forehead, and tell her that, no matter what she was going through, I cared for her deeply. Then why hadn't I done it? Did I not have a will of my own? Was I, like my colleagues at work, unconsciously playing some role in a master script that I had no hand in writing? Was I also asleep?

More important than these questions, however, was the shift in perception that had allowed them to occur at all. It was not unlike the agency meeting in which I had become detached enough from my surroundings to see them in a new perspective; only in this case, I had somehow become detached from *myself*. Indeed, for a moment there seemed to be two selves—the old, familiar one who had thoughts, feelings, and performed various activities; and now suddenly, a new one who simply watched. Moreover, in the very act of this observation, the old self's combativeness just seemed to dissipate on its own.

Students of almost all spiritual traditions will recognize this phenomenon as *mindfulness* or *witnessing*, which is not to be confused with ordinary self-awareness. Self-awareness, as we commonly experience it, is always predicated on an image of who we think we ought to be and usually produces an effort to correct or maintain behavior in conformity with this image. True mindfulness, on the other hand, is not predicated on anything, nor does it motivate any activity. It is a purely neutral mode of observation or, at most, a kind of self-questioning, but one which carries no necessity for an answer.

Having no knowledge of such things at the time, however, I simply formulated it as Athena's first Commandment—PAY ATTENTION—and began trying to observe myself in other situations as well.

In the meantime Samantha and I managed to get through the evening as friends, and I even discovered in my soul a new empathy for her in this current ordeal, which she described as "a hurricane of emotions, blasting through my life, turning everything upside down." Was this the transformational process in action? I began to think it might be and vicariously found the prospect both fearful and exciting.

Samantha also told me in more detail about the techniques used at Sky Hi for achieving expanded states of consciousness. One of these was called *energy balancing*, and a week later she gave me a surprising demonstration of its efficacy. This took place at my house the following Sunday. Samantha arrived bright and early in good spirits. She had brought a record by Steve Halpern, which she put on the stereo while I lay on my back in a comfortable position. Then, after a brief, silent meditation, she began to move her hands slowly over the surface of my skin without, however, actually touching it. At first, I remained dubious about the whole procedure, but soon I did start to feel something like waves of energy surging up and down my body. These were very physical, concrete sensations; yet the energy did not seem to be confined to any ordinary biological channels such as the blood or nervous systems. Instead, it had a generalized quality, rather like waves of heat or electricity.

Finally, these waves acquired considerable force and even seemed to overflow the boundaries of my skin to form a kind of magnetic field that enveloped the organism. So intense did this field become that, after the session, I felt painfully cramped inside the walls of my small cabin and had to go out onto the sun deck until the sensations subsided.

Energy balancing is, in fact, closely akin to a whole class of meditative disciplines that might be termed the Yogas of Subtle Energies (i.e., Hatha, Kundalini, etc.), and later I was to become very much intrigued with this approach. In the meantime, however, I did not miss the fact that it was Samantha who had, once again, unlocked a new gate on my path and thus continued to play, consciously or not, the role of incarnate guide. As I noted in my journal on August 9th,

> This morning I had a funny thought which made me chuckle out loud. I set out to conquer Samantha, in the way of my warrior soul, and failed; but by some subtle psychic alchemy, she seems to be conquering me.

It was true, and in the aftermath of our energy session, I grew quite complacent. Friendship with Samantha was proving easier than I had anticipated, and though I still had no clear idea of what my ultimate objective was, I appeared to be making some sort of progress. It's like being back in school, I thought, taking a new subject. At first, you don't understand anything, and it all seems impossibly difficult. But soon, you begin to pick up fragments of knowledge and fit them together until, finally, they assume a definite shape. All I had to do now, I supposed, was continue collecting insights and experiences, and they would eventually coalesce into a comprehensible whole.

But spiritual paths do not work this way—quite the opposite. What they require is not an accumulation but a divestment, the stripping away of all experience and surrender of every form of knowledge. Consequently, my light-hearted optimism was far from warranted. In fact, I was about to be rudely disabused of it by a sequence of painful shocks that culminated in a temporary but serious setback.

The first of these came in the middle of August. One of the key organizers for the veterans' rap group was killed in a car accident. His name was Tom Ambrose, and I went to the memorial service held at the Vet Center in his honor.

In his eulogy, the minister said, "Tom had no hidden personal agenda," and it was true. Veterans organizations, like any others, have their share of politics and egos, but Tom was utterly devoid of both. He was so quiet and unassuming that sometimes you hardly knew he was in the room. But if called upon in any emergency—day or night, he was always there to do what he could, asking no reward and demanding no special recognition. In short, he was the closest I had ever come to meeting an authentic saint, and yet, he had been recompensed with a senseless and premature death. In this tragedy I saw again the Shadow of the World, rising to mock all our feeble human efforts towards righteousness, and it made me suddenly bitter. What could be the point of any spiritual transformation in the face of such Cosmic caprice? Perhaps it was better just to look out for one's self, after all.

In the days that followed, I tried to talk to Samantha about Tom's death. She had become my only confidant in such matters, but Samantha was entering another period of withdrawal, and all I got from her were sweetly aloof platitudes about "acceptance" and "surrender." Apparently, our friendship wasn't working out, either.

One windless evening, with the hot, soggy air hanging heavily in the trees around my cabin, I began to brood about our relationship. To hell with friendship, I thought. It didn't make sense, anyway. We had more in common now than ever before. Why weren't we together?

I drank half a bottle of wine, sweated, and brooded some more. Old, imagined dialogues with her began to play again in my head, over and over. And the more they played, the more I became convinced that the logic of our love was unassailable. It was only Samantha's cowardice that stood in the way. Finally, in a state of absolute frustration, I grabbed the phone and called her, insisting that I had to come over right then and talk. She agreed, but I could hear the reluctance in her voice. I could also feel Athena shaking her head vigorously over my shoulder, but I didn't care. I was pissed off and determined to have it out with Samantha once and for all.

When I arrived, Samantha listened politely to all my arguments. We had the same interests, we understood each other, there was already a lot of water under the bridge, and we shouldn't let it go to waste, etc., etc. And what was her answer to this impassioned but well-reasoned plea?

Krishnamurti once said, "When someone says, 'I love you,' you don't say, 'Let me think it over.'" That, however, was precisely what Samantha did say and bid me a prompt goodnight.

Outside her apartment I was once again stunned. This had nothing to do with the evening's outcome, which had really been a foregone conclusion, but stemmed from the fact that I had again been *witnessing* the whole scene, knowing every moment that it was a gigantic blunder yet, this time, unable to stop it from happening. It was exactly like being in a car, roaring down a mountain with no brakes.

Back home I made a one-line entry in my journal that read simply, "Why can't you keep your big mouth shut?" — an excellent question, indeed, but perhaps better phrased, "*Who* can't keep his big mouth shut?" It certainly hadn't felt like "me."

During the next ten days or so that it took Samantha to make a formal reply (she had her own rhythms in these things), two other events of significance occurred. The first I learned about when I arrived at my office the next morning. Norman Garey, a renowned Hollywood lawyer, had committed suicide.

Although I had only met Garey once, I knew him well by reputation. Among his clients were some of the most prestigious names in the business. A year before, when a friend and I had almost partnered in a company of our own, she suggested we use Garey to draw up the papers. I was hesitant, because I knew he was expensive, but my friend insisted. He was worth it, she argued. Merely to say that we were handled by Norman Garey would give us clout, and I had to agree. You could hardly find a more successful or respected man in the entire industry. Yet, at noon the previous day, Norman Garey had left his luxurious office, returned to his home in Beverly Hills, and put a bullet through his head.

At first, I read the various accounts of his death in the trades carefully, looking for an explanation. There were rumors of financial troubles, a deal gone sour, even the venomous whisper of scandal, but nothing concrete. It was all conjecture. Then suddenly, I realized that it didn't matter. Whatever the specific circumstances, I knew the real reason Norman Garey had chosen oblivion. He had faced what Camus once called the only truly serious philosophical question — whether life is or is not worth living. For both Garey and myself, this had meant a preeminently worldly life. But Garey had pursued and won a far greater proportion of the things of the world than anything I had yet achieved. He had reaped a prodigious harvest, tasted all its fruits, and given his answer. It was an answer, moreover, with which I found myself in sympathy, and almost immediately, I began looking around for something else to do with my life.

The second incident took place several days later. For the last few months Colette and I had been getting together occasionally to talk over practical matters. Although these meetings were often painful, I was not averse to them. I was still frightened of her desperation and didn't want her to feel that I was completely incommunicado. In a funny way I loved Colette as much as ever. It was just that her love was a country with rigorously defined and jealously guarded borders beyond which I had already trespassed and to which I could no longer return.

On this particular occasion, we met for dinner at a Japanese restaurant in the valley. Colette had always been too proud to broach the subject of reconciliation before, but now, halfway through a plate of sushi, she launched into a lengthy and well rehearsed appeal for just that. "We shared," she said, "the same interests, we knew each other well, there was a lot of water under the bridge which it would be a shame to waste, etc."

I don't recall exactly what I said when she finished, except to mumble something about a reconciliation not being possible. The truth was, I really didn't know what to say, because I no longer knew who was talking. Colette had delivered, almost word for word, the very same speech that I had given Samantha. It was like watching two different actors playing the same character, and again, I was left with the spooky sensation that everything had been pre-scripted.

I remembered also my experiences with the vets in the rap group and the realization I had had in Dr. Mark's office that, as vets, we all seemed to have become part of some larger Psyche. At the time I had thought this a peculiar consequence of the war, but now I began to wonder if it didn't apply to everyone? Perhaps what appeared to each of us as a distinctly personal mental life was, in reality, only a kind of local computer readout of the same Master Program being accessed through a myriad of different brains. And just as we don't attribute the software content of a program to the specific piece of hardware through which it is retrieved, perhaps it was a mistake to presume that mental life "belongs" to any single organism. But if this were so, if the thoughts and feelings that I had experienced were not really "mine," then in what sense could I be said to be a unique or discrete individual? Suddenly, I had no subjective point of reference for the world, nor could I perceive the origin of my own activity in it. For several hours I simply didn't know who I was.

Eventually, my old, discrete sense of self returned, but the question remained: "Who was I?" Until it was answered, I knew, there could be little ground for security in anything I undertook. Thus, that night I got my first glimmer of an objective to this quest and also of (what would prove to be) the primary instrument of its accomplishment—the question itself: *Who am I?*

Meanwhile, in the beginning of September a "Dear John" letter arrived from Samantha. Actually, it was a kind of prose poem, so delicately and poignantly wrought that I almost felt it was worth losing her to receive it. In any case, I wanted to make some sort of response, just to let her know that I harbored no ill feelings. I composed several drafts of a letter of my own, but, compared to her masterpiece, they all sounded second rate, so I decided to call instead.

Our conversation turned out to be surprisingly pleasant and free of all the usual strains associated with a farewell. Samantha thanked me for my "understanding" and said things were improving for her. She was having less difficulty at work, sleeping better, and looking forward to spending a relaxing two weeks at her parents' house when they went away on vacation the following month. She also told me she was considering getting a kitten for a pet, and I was glad to hear her sound so buoyant over the prospect. Finally, there was nothing left to say except goodbye. An entry in my journal, noting this conversation, concludes with the remark, "And so Samantha Jones passes out of my life forever."

What had it all meant? From the beginning there had been that uncanny sense of familiarity, the flavor of some deeper, mythic purpose to our dance that had remained a mystery through all its phases. She had been my secretary, my lover, and my friend; yet all these shifting roles still seemed only an outward masquerade, disguising some connection of far greater significance—but what? It was a puzzle that I had never solved, and now I had to resign myself to the fact that I probably never would. It was the end of an era—or so I thought.

Finding a Corpse

Five:
Fear and Trembling in the Court of the Soul

> He [the seeker] slowly begins to learn—bit by bit at first, then in big chunks. And his thoughts soon clash. What he learns is never what he pictured or imagined, and so he begins to be afraid. Learning is never what one expects. Every step of learning is a new task, and the fear the man is experiencing begins to mount mercilessly, unyielding. His purpose becomes a battlefield.[6]

So warns Don Juan. I had, by now, run across other warnings as well. Hoeller had cautioned against the risk of insanity for those who take the Royal Road, and there are references to this risk scattered through most of the mystical literature. So far, however, I had encountered nothing of the sort. I had been baffled; I had been confused; I had felt pain and guilt and longing, but not fear and certainly nothing akin to madness. I was, however, about to enter a stage in which I would experience both in spades. And when the time came, I would be grateful for this advice, also from Don Juan:

> And what can he do to overcome fear? The answer is very simple. He must not run away.[7]

But in the days immediately following my breakup with Samantha, though sad, I was also curiously relieved. For the first time in months, my mind was free of anxious yearnings and an endless stream of fruitless fantasies. Now I could turn my attention to more practical matters.

After Garey's suicide I knew that I would eventually have to get out of the film business, but what would I do for a living? It occurred to me that my experiences as a revolutionary might make an exciting and salable book. I had known many of the leading figures of the era and participated in most of the local struggles, including the violent San Francisco State strike and the battle for People's Park. I decided to stay on with Lewis long enough to write my memoirs, which I could do in the evenings and on weekends. Then, if I got a publisher, I could cut all ties with Hollywood and become completely independent. With considerable confidence, I cranked the first page into my typewriter and went to work.

I also made a decision to start dating other women. If I couldn't fathom what had happened with Samantha, I wasn't going to sit home and mope about it. There was a talented and attractive actress at a little theater group I belonged to. Her name was Elanore, and I began taking her out to dinner, plays, even dancing. In fact, Elanore had been a dancer before turning to acting. She told me funny backstage stories of chorus-line intrigues and also of her current adventures and misadventures trying to break into the movies, all of which I enjoyed immensely. She was young, vivacious, and great company, and being with her made me feel like my life was finally coming together again.

This is not to say that I had lost all interest in things spiritual, only that such interests no longer held the same sharp urgency. I still went to lectures by Hoeller, who warned that the mystical journey was not something to be undertaken half-heartedly. "You can't negotiate with God!" he would thunder and insist, "God is not an uncle. God is an earthquake!" But once again, I was leaning more towards a purely rational explanation of all this esoterica.

With Samantha's departure from my life, Athena, too, had started to fade, and I began to wonder if I hadn't attached too much significance to both of them. I knew that this kind of wild romanticism was often symptomatic of male middle-age crises, and I was pushing forty. I was also reading more of Jung's traditional works and had become particularly impressed with his analysis of psychological types and its solidly therapeutic implications.

All people, according to Jung, can be divided into two basic categories, introverts and extroverts, depending on whether their primary orientation is toward self or objects. Within these broad categories, individuals can be further classified based on one of four psychic functions: thinking, feeling, intuition, and sensation. Although all four functions operate in every individual, in practice, one of these functions usually dominates. Thus, a person's "type" is a combination of his general orientation and predominant function. For example, someone might be an extroverted thinking type or an introverted feeling type, etc.

One of the goals of Jungian therapy, then, is to achieve a more harmonious interaction between these functions within a given individual and perhaps mitigate an overly pronounced extroverted or introverted tendency. The idea is a better balanced and integrated human being who has free access to the full range of psychic possibilities.

Perhaps, in the light of this schemata, the Grail Quest, or spiritual journey, did not require such a radical and mysterious self-transformation as the mystics seemed to indicate. Instead, might not the extravagant and ambiguous symbolism of mystical literature actually stand for perfectly intelligible psychic processes that were only now being mapped and elucidated by modern psychology?

I began to think so and, on a conscious level at least, adjusted my sights accordingly. If I could master Jung's formulae and apply them to my life, I thought, I would at last be able to manipulate my destiny at will. In retrospect, it was almost as if my old, purely rational mind was taking advantage of Samantha's sudden absence in order to mount a counter-attack and regain its former position of supremacy. And for a while it seemed to succeed.

What I was completely unaware of, however, was that a revolution was brewing in my subconscious, along parallel lines but towards drastically different ends—ends that, in Don Juan's words, I could never have "pictured or imagined." Truly, my psyche was about to be turned into a "battlefield."

The first hint that such a tempest was in the offing appeared as a subtle element of fear creeping into my meditations. In addition to following Hoeller's manual, I had also begun spending a half hour before breakfast each morning sitting Zen-style as I had done as a teenager. These sessions usually produced a mild euphoria, but a September journal entry reads,

> This morning I meditate outside on my sun-deck and get a whiff of cosmic waves flowing everywhere—waves in the wood grain, waves undulating in the branches of trees, waves locked into rolling hills, waves in the currents of the clouds, waves passing through my tissues. At one point, my body begins to rock of its own volition and, suddenly, I feel my center start to slip away. Frightened, I pull back.

On the whole, however, meditation—like my studies in Jung—seemed to be serving a healthy readjustment to the world, and, in fact, the "world" was about to make a final and dramatic bid to reclaim my allegiance.

During the last few weeks, Lewis had been engaged in a series of hush-hush meetings with some mysterious bigwigs, but I had been absorbed in other things and paid scant attention. One afternoon he summoned me into his office to make an important announcement. He had accepted the presidency of a well-established and much larger company and offered to take me along as his vice president.

If, in my heart of hearts, I knew that this offer had come too late to change the course of my life, all I could think of at the moment was that less than ten years ago I had been a penniless hippie on the streets of San Francisco, and now I was about to become a vice president of a major corporation. It was, as they say, an offer I couldn't refuse. We would make the move in November.

Ironically, it was on that very same day that my subconscious fired the opening salvo of its own offensive that would ultimately carry my life off in a totally different direction. Having a clear calendar for lunch, I had asked my secretary to order a sandwich from the local deli and settled down behind my desk to read. Suddenly, and without the slightest warning, a series of images exploded on the screen of my consciousness with such graphic force that every other perception was momentarily obliterated. My desk, the office, even the book in my hands, all vanished in the brilliance of this mental slide show in which an unknown Knight and an ancient Emperor were depicted in some archetypal struggle. I saw this not as a full-blown, coherent scene but only in flashes, like a few random frames chopped from an archaic film; yet I knew the story's essence instantly, and as soon as I had recovered from the initial impact of this "white heat" (as I later came to call such episodes), I dashed off the following brief notes in my journal:

> The Knight must seize the throne and become the Emperor. This will be achieved only through courage and sacrifice. "Only he who is not afraid of death by a thousand cuts can unhorse the emperor!"
>
> The High Priestess presides, but where does she fit in, and when will she unfold her scroll?

Though not, properly speaking, hallucinations (as they didn't appear anywhere outside myself), these images were no less vivid or intense. In fact, they had the same numinous quality as Athena's Dream, and I suspected her signature in this work. At any rate, they obviously heralded some important metamorphosis underway in my psyche, and, still radiant with their glow, I added a few thoughts:

> If there are archetypes, can there be archedramas as well? Both personal and historical? If so, how does one transcend them—break the grip of maya, shatter Karma, attain Grace, find salvation, regain the garden?... All questions and no answers.

All questions and no answers, indeed! The Knight and the Emperor were both figures from the Tarot and evidently represented two sides of a conflict. The quote about "unhorsing the emperor" had been a Maoist slogan in the sixties and confirmed the theme of revolutionary struggle, but by whom and against what?

The High Priestess was also a figure borrowed from the Tarot. The reference to a "scroll" came from the way she is depicted in the Rider Deck, withdrawing from her robes a scroll marked *Tora*, or The Book of Sacred Law. Significantly, however, the scroll is still rolled up and, thus, as yet unreadable—as was the meaning of these images. At home that evening I looked up Hoeller's meditation on the High Priestess, searching for more clues:

> On the ship of the desert, I ride across the vast wasteland of the soul. O thou silvery moon, my guide and light, shine on my path! All ye stars and luminaries of the heavens, guide me through the perils of the great journey, so that I may arrive at the supreme crown of my being, and enter the ineffable splendor of the last chamber of the palace! The road to the great crown of final victory leads through the peril of the abyss, where the quicksand of temptation may destroy me. Only balance can save me from plunging into the pit. Therefore, I will invoke into my personality the power of balance; and poised between the light and dark pillars of my being, serenely and firmly I shall hasten to the mysterious place where the voiceless voice of the beloved calls to me day and night.
> 8

In the past I had always associated this passage with Samantha, and reading it again only served to reinforce this impression. The symbolism of the guiding power of "moon," "stars," and the "voiceless voice of the beloved" immediately brought to mind her "plaintive north star song of old" and "wolf call melody to the moon." Yet, Samantha was already out of my life, so the symbols no longer seemed to have a referent. Could they stand for Athena herself? But I had never thought of Athena as "my beloved," and it was strange trying to think of her that way now.

In the midst of these perplexities, I hardly noticed that, on the Kabalistic Tree of Life, the High Priestess corresponds to the Thirteenth Path. As diagrammed on the Tree, this path follows the main trunk, running from Tiphareth (Beauty) to Kether (The Crown), or in other words, *right up the middle*. Thus, still unbeknownst to me, the first White Heat contained the image and prophecy of Parzival's path, which was to become my own. But perhaps, if I had known, I never would have taken it, for Hoeller described it as "possibly the most perilous of all paths" — but then again, "also the most beautiful and mysterious."

In the days ahead I focused my attention on the image of the Knight overthrowing the Emperor, still under the delusion that I could arrive at a purely analytic solution. It seemed that the Knight and the Emperor must represent two aspects of my personality, perhaps symbolizing two of Jung's psychic functions. If so, then there must be two more figures, as well, to complete the quartet, and I began to hunt for them in my past. This was a coldly rational process. I set out to examine all the different roles I had played during various stages of my life. I wanted to trace them back to their origins in concrete experience, plot their curves, map them on a conceptual graph. If I could construct such a map, I thought, I would finally know who I was.

I spent several days dredging through random memories. At first, it was frustrating. There seemed to be no more order to these recollections than one might find among old relics dragged up from the bottom of the ocean. After a while, however, a pattern began to emerge. Everything was pointing back to the year I had turned seven as being axial. This was the first real memory I had of myself as a coherent person operating in a continuous stream of time. It was also, significantly, the year I entered first grade at an Episcopal-run school.

I had been enrolled in this school not because my parents were religious (quite the contrary) but simply because it had a good academic reputation. In fact, the curriculum was strictly secular. But we did assemble every morning in an ornately decorated church, and once a week a priest celebrated mass with appropriate pomp and ceremony—all of which had a marked effect on me. For the first time I encountered a structured cosmology in which everything had its appointed place under a supremely reigning God. Nor did I have any trouble finding my own place, for—as the nuns were fond of telling us—we were all God's children. Much to their dismay, however, I took this dictum literally. As God's son, I improvised my own masses with pilfered wine and bits of Wonder bread, heard confessions from my classmates, and dispensed my own divinely inspired wisdom. All this came quite naturally to me, and it was only the negative reactions of my parents and teachers that forced me to consider my relationship to God as somewhat unusual. Thus, I learned to differentiate a specific *spiritual* aspect of myself and guard it from the eyes of those around me.

On the other hand—and to my seven-year-old mind, not incompatibly—I was also very much aware of being a physical entity, capable of responding with pleasure to appropriate stimuli in the environment, like the naked bodies of little girls, for instance, as experienced in games of "house" and "doctor." But as I was often scolded for initiating such impious pastimes, I learned that this, too, must be a special facet of existence to be differentiated and protected.

Another momentous discovery I made that year was the tender power of romance. I had been given the lead in a toddler's adaptation of *Orpheus and Eurydice* and soon fell head-over-heels for my leading lady, a nymphet named Heather. Although in our first-grade version of the Greek tragedy, Orpheus finally did rescue Eurydice from dark Hades, there was to be no such happy outcome to my own off-stage love. Heather showed not the slightest interest in the stormy yearnings of my childish heart, and after the curtain fell on closing night, she ignored me completely. Thus, I learned early something of love's bittersweet mysteries, and this also became a clearly identifiable aspect of myself that needed careful handling.

Finally, it was in first grade, too, that I began to discern the ways of the world and how to manipulate them. As the oldest member of my class, I became its *de facto* leader, endowed with all the temporal power such a position entails—mostly for disruption. But I also discovered that this power could be used to make subtle bargains with my teachers. Good behavior—especially on a mass scale—had its price, and I grew bold and crafty in exacting it.

To curb such precociousness, the following year I was skipped a grade and effectively stripped of my power. But I learned another lesson in the process. Like my spiritual relationship to God, my strategic relationship to the world constituted a distinguishable and, to others, suspect side of my nature and, in the future, would have to be exercised with more caution.

Having completed the above analysis, I congratulated myself. I had, indeed, been able to trace four aspects of my personality to four sets of concrete experiences, and these closely approximated Jung's four psychic functions—(spirituality) Intuition, (sexuality) Sensation, (love) Feeling, and (strategy) Thinking. Moreover, I could see that, at any given period in my subsequent life, one of these functions usually dominated at the expense of, or at least in conflict with, the others. It now seemed that I was making real progress in "solving" the riddle of my identity. My subconscious, however, was not about to let the matter rest on such superficial ground.

At home alone one evening about a month later, I was seized by a second White Heat. In another burst of images, even stronger than the first, I actually saw how the court of my soul was organized, and it had nothing to do with any abstract "functions." It was a living, flesh-and-blood drama in which four distinct characters perpetually vied with each other for control of my psyche.

Again, as soon as I was able, I grabbed my journal and jotted down the following names and descriptions:

> *Orpheus*, watching helplessly as Eurydice slips away. Orpheus, who goes mad with sorrow and rejoices at his own dismemberment. Orpheus, the megalomaniacal melancholic, frozen in a starry constellation of perpetual grief. Orpheus, who looks to the end of time, to death, and for whom all the world is but an antechamber to eternity. Orpheus, who is a fool in the eyes of men, an object of pity for women, a fragile puff of petals to be blown away in the slightest breeze, a miserable fake—Why fake? Because Orpheus is also...
>
> *Odysseus*, the crafty one, schemer par excellence, deviser of stratagems, liar, conniver, a player of roles, actor to please any audience, posturing as beggar or king, seeker of revenge, prideful of lonely devices, mistrustful of all—even Penelope, incapable of giving away his heart,

wanderer on desolate seas, homeless, rootless, forever disillusioned by the beacon that beckons him home to Ithaca; but forever coming home, coming home from Nam, coming home from China, coming home from Malta—always coming home to find home infested, corrupted and cut off, because Odysseus is also...

Parzival, the innocent; seeker of Holy Things, receiver of visions, dreams, magic, the voice of angels and poets; of sad voyages and sweet love for all beings; who cries over dead animals on the road, and butchered elephants, and the children of the dust, and would accept all the burdens of the world without complaint, but is afraid of being taken advantage of, of being cheated and deceived and thought a—God forbid!—sentimentalist, because Parzival is also...

Pan, reveler in flesh and wine, heartless breaker of hearts, enemy of reason, of manners, of morals—the Outrageous One, who loves to shake his cock at the world; who rejoices in blood and battle; who laughs at Fate; who tempts illness and madness, but only up to a point—who is finally afraid of the Great Leap; who harbors secret defenses; who is a coward in the face of his own demons, and who ends his debauches in cynicism and despair.

These words came in a spontaneous flood, without any time to pause or think them out as I wrote. But when I read them over, I was astonished by their accuracy. I had been—and still was—all these personae; yet at the same time I was also none of them. Though manifested in my psyche, they seemed—like the gods and goddesses of Malta—to have sprung from some other, mythological realm beyond my own felt existence. It was as if I had merely "identified" with them, the way one does with characters in a movie, at times rooting for or against this one or that as they played out their various archedramatic roles through the vehicle of my organism. But who was the "I" who performed these acts of identification?

I decided there had to be a fifth entity—a *me*—who cognized and, to some extent, controlled these personae. At first, I thought of this entity as Arthur, the legendary court ruler, and described him thus:

Arthur, aloof, unswayed by emotion, proud of his lofty loneliness, benevolent autocrat of the soul, dispenser of cool wisdom, master of his feelings, skeptical of all joy, disdainer of all sorrow, unreachable on his throne, but always ready to retreat.

Arthur conquers by division. His chief weapon is ridicule. He pits Odysseus against Orpheus and Pan against Parzival. If Odysseus can silence Orpheus, Arthur promises him a safe return home. And if Pan can seduce Parzival, he will inherit all the pleasures of the flesh. But under such conditions, home proves loveless and Pan's pleasures, empty.

Arthur is the "Emperor," but who is the "Knight" who will overthrow him? Orpheus is too distracted, Odysseus too cynical, Pan too cowardly, Parzival too weak. Who then will wield Athena's sword? And what of Athena herself? She is not one of the court but stands behind these lords, ready to lend her strength to whomever comes forward.

Although this description was not a product of the actual White Heat but a kind of afterthought, it reflected well the "I" that I imagined myself to be. Mythologically, however, I had made an error in casting Arthur in the role of villain, and thus the imagery's full significance remained hidden until the next White Heat when this error was corrected, and the whole conflict reached a climax.

In the meantime, the drama continued to unfold, but now I began to *witness* it consciously in day-to-day life. That is, I would become acutely aware in a business meeting, say, that it was Odysseus who was in command. Or at dinner with Elanore, I might suddenly feel Pan gazing lasciviously at her through my eyes. Such moments contained more curiosity than fear, but at other times this destabilization of my psyche could and did produce episodes of real terror.

With increasing frequency during meditation I experienced that sensation of "losing my center," as though the very coordinates of my being were dissolving away. Once, while sitting cross-legged on my bed, staring at my reflection in the night-darkened window, I was alarmed to see it change into the face of a werewolf staring back at me.

One of the most frightening incidents—but also one that ended on a hopeful note—I described in my journal as follows:

> A disturbing day. Driving home, I am preoccupied with thoughts of work, scripts, business conversations, etc. After dinner, I have to read another script; only then do I have time for meditation. But it is difficult to get into, and I can't make my muscles relax. Finally, I give up, get into bed, and read Jung's Answer to Job.
>
> Halfway through, I am struck by the profundity of what Jung is saying: God is an evolving psychic entity, struggling to become conscious of

himself. We, as part of the world of God making himself manifest, are part of this process. He works through us and is us.

Suddenly, I feel out of control, swamped, as though God were actually taking over inside of me, usurping all my functions. I turn off the light and try to sleep, but everything has a numinous, charged energy that gives rise to an awesome and nameless fear. I wrestle with it and remember Don Juan's warning—once fear wins, a man is lost! The only thing to do is stand your ground.

I call on Athena and hold still, trying to maintain my balance in this psychic storm. Finally, the fear abates somewhat, and I am left with the question: "What am I supposed to do in this life?" There is no answer.

After a while, tired and frustrated, I try again to sleep. But just as I am about to drift off, a voice calls my name from the other side of the room. It is a real, distinct voice, and I sit bolt up in bed, heart pounding. The voice is followed by a thought—a promise: I am to be given a *gift certificate*. Shaken, I get up and go sit by the fire wondering what this gift is to be and where I am to cash the certificate?

As things turned out, I would have to wait three weeks to find out. I was, however, about to receive another gift of no less importance, delivered by Athena's infallible hand.

On Saturday morning in the beginning of October, as I drove down from Topanga to do my weekly shopping, I saw great rivers of gray and brown smoke pouring into the autumnal sky. It looked as if the whole West Valley was ablaze. Suddenly, I thought of Samantha. She would be staying at her parents' house now, and although I had never been there, I knew it was located in the vicinity of the fire. "Perhaps she's in danger," a distinctly feminine voice whispered in my mind. It was a voice I knew well. Athena was back.

I called Samantha from a pay phone in the supermarket parking lot. She sounded a little surprised to hear from me but said she wasn't in any jeopardy. The fire was quite far off on the other side of the freeway, and I could tell she was puzzled at my concern. I said goodbye and hung up, feeling like the world's worst idiot and not a little annoyed at Athena for having so misled me.

It took less than an hour to do my shopping, but when I came out of the supermarket, the fire looked even bigger than before. Half the sky was now glowing orange and black with smoke.

Driving home, I turned on the radio and heard a news report that the flames had jumped the freeway. In Los Angeles, that meant a serious conflagration, and once more, I heard Athena whisper Samantha's name, full of apprehension. This time, however, I was determined to ignore her. Even if Samantha were in danger, she had plenty of friends and relatives to call on. I wasn't going to make a fool of myself twice in one day. But Athena persisted, and by the time I got home, she had won.

Again I called Samantha—though still very much against my better judgment, but this time she said that she could see smoke and flames close by and was getting worried. Without hesitation, I told her to pack her valuables and come right over. She arrived half an hour later. In a journal entry, I described the afternoon:

> On the surface, nothing has changed with Samantha, but how different it is being with her this time. I feel charged with energy, but not the same maelstrom of passions as before. I make her tea. We take a walk. Talk. Read on the sun deck like an old married couple. I can tell her things I would never mention to anyone else. How I've missed her company.
>
> She says she was thinking of me last night. She always says this when I call out of the blue, and I've always tried to dismiss such remarks as mere coquetry, but perhaps it's true. Suddenly, I don't care. It's enough just to have her here. I am no longer Orpheus, dragging around his heavy baggage of sorrows. Or Odysseus, weaving stratagems of conquest. Or even Pan, swollen with red desires. I am Parzival in simple and sweet communion with a sister soul...

There was a complication to our afternoon idyll, however; Elanore and I had made a date for that night. But as evening approached with the fire still raging visibly beyond the low hills, I didn't want to leave the area. And I certainly didn't want to leave Samantha. I decided to break the date with Elanore and take Samantha out to a local restaurant in the Canyon instead. But when I called Elanore to explain the situation, she insisted on driving all the way across town to join us. My journal continues,

> Dinner is at The Inn of the Seventh Ray. Samantha and I get there first, and I fear the worst. Oddly, when Elanore arrives, all goes reasonably well. Officially, Elanore is still my "date," Samantha only a "good friend" I am helping out of a jam. It's true enough to be innocent, and innocent enough to be true. We all play our roles. Samantha is on her best social toes, finds things to chat with Elanore about. I mediate with a bit of humor. Never realized how astute

Samantha could be in such situations. Like me, she can lie with perfect grace. It's a conspiracy of pretense. But the social fiction doesn't match the psychic reality. Samantha's eyes are full of cryptic looks, and every time we brush glances I hear again that north star song of old and fall deeper under its spell. All other realities pale...

Back at my cabin, Samantha accepts an invitation to join us for another glass of wine and a little smoke. She's pushing it, I think, but am delighted and a little intrigued. She has her own version of fun and games.

Samantha goes to the kitchen to pour the wine. Elanore takes a seat on the couch. Trying to remain neutral, I flop on the floor in front of the fireplace. Samantha enters with the wine glasses, sits delicately on the couch next to Elanore, and smiles. And suddenly, I know that Elanore is history. What's more, I know that it will always be this way. It won't matter who I am with—be she the most ravishing, stunning woman in the world—someday, somewhere, she will sit on a couch and, in my mind's eye, Samantha will come and sit down beside her with that same devilish smile, and that woman, too, will be history. It is finally all beyond my will. I am being delivered up to unknown gods and no longer try to resist.

Several glasses of wine and a couple of joints later, Samantha leaves. Elanore coaxes me to bed, claiming her rights. We make love, but my heart isn't in it. Samantha has taken that with her.

I took Elanore out a few more times after that night, but she could sense something was wrong. Finally, I had to tell her it was time to go our separate ways. We parted friends, but it was the end of all my hopes for a "healthy readjustment" to any kind of normal life. The two White Heats and now Samantha's reappearance had shattered that possibility forever.

With my social life once more reduced to zero and only the details of shutting down Lewis's old company to attend to at work, I turned my full attention back to the drama still being played out in my soul. So far, I had been merely a somewhat astonished observer of these personae in their mysterious struggles. Now I was anxious to speed up the process, but how?

I began to ponder this problem in every spare moment. Once or twice my secretary even caught me gazing off into space, mulling it over, and had to call my name several times to bring me back to reality. I remembered doing the same to Samantha and laughed. What ironies life dishes up! Still, I was at a loss as to how to proceed.

In the meantime, I had been attending a series of lectures on Shamanism being given by Hoeller. At one of them he announced he would demonstrate some of the actual techniques at a special Saturday seminar. I made a point to be there.

The seminar was held at the Gnostic Society, located in a seedy, Hollywood Boulevard storefront decorated with occult paintings and portraits of Jung. Recently, I had been toying with the idea of asking Hoeller to take me on as his personal student, and I thought this would be a good opportunity to check out his practice, but it was to prove disappointing.

For one thing, the seminar really wasn't about Shamanism, but Ceremonial Magic. After an introductory talk, Hoeller and his assistant donned ritual robes and displayed their instruments—magical swords, amulets, mirrors, lamps, etc.—none of which appealed to me. Next, they performed some sample rites taken from medieval grimoires and alchemical texts, designed to invoke various psychic powers. Somehow, I just couldn't see myself parading around in elaborate costumes calling on weird entities with Arabic-sounding names. In the end I decided against taking Hoeller as my teacher, but the seminar did give me a clue for accessing the lords of my own psyche. I would invent a shamanism of my own.

I already knew something about such practices, because several years earlier I had done considerable research for a story based on Wicca.[9] I had even gotten to know a few practicing witches and been invited to one of their rites, held in the back room of an occult bookstore. This, too, had been a rather stylized affair, but according to some witches, at least, Wicca didn't depend so much on the proper garb or implements as on the practitioner's intentions. In any case, I was familiar with some of the fundamentals. Most important was the Circle of Protection, a real or imaginary circle inscribed on the ground with a sword or knife, in which the practitioner remains while summoning potentially dangerous spirits. I also knew the principle of the Four Directions, their attributes and elements, and could easily correlate these with my four personae. As a note in my journal indicates, I began that very night:

> Tonight I take Captain Blood out to a hillside clearing, draw a circle in the earth with my staff, and wait. For what? I don't know. I try to mumble a few incoherent words of invocation, but they die in my throat. I feel awkward and embarrassed. Nothing happens. Then, just as I am about to give up, a huge Doberman appears on the ledge above me, snarling and barking furiously. Instantly, I'm up, staff in hand, adrenalin pumping, ready for a fight. The Doberman takes off into the darkness, but the incident is so strange and startling that I cannot help but read into it a sign that I should continue.

The staff referred to was a wooden walking stick that I used to carry for just such encounters with stray dogs (this was the only time I ever met one), and now I converted it into a sword substitute. Every night I would go out to the same clearing, draw a circle in the earth with this staff, and experiment with various improvised invocations. Mostly, I called upon my lords to appear, and often I could sense their presence projected at the appropriate compass points on the circle: Odysseus in the East, Pan in the South, Orpheus in the West, and Parzival in the North. Still, I found it hard to take myself too seriously and was constantly afraid some neighbor would stumble into the clearing and think me mad or ridiculous or both. Fortunately, no one ever did.

After a week or so, I decided, partly out of embarrassment and partly out of impatience, to drop all the mumbo jumbo. I continued to visit my spot and to summon my lords, or "guardians" (as I now called them), but without the ritualistic rigmarole. Of course, I was aware that to do so was considered extremely dangerous by all practitioners of the occult, but as I said, I didn't take myself too seriously. Perhaps I should have. My journal entry for October 22nd reads,

> Tonight I draw no circle of protection, make no entreaties to my guardians. I sit on the bare earth, let come what may. At first, nothing. My mind races with trivia, back muscles cramp, neck tightens, head constricts. I try to focus on my breath—one (breathe), two (breathe), three (breathe)—but my thoughts wander off along a thousand byways of daily concerns. It's no good. I've lost my guardians...
>
> A half hour goes by. Back aches, legs grow weary. I feel foolish and betrayed. Everything seems empty and senseless. I almost give up.
>
> Then, I feel the earth shift slightly under my feet. I look up. The sky glows, throbs. Across the canyon the mountains are undulating. The universe seems to be coming apart at the seams. I'm terrified and feel

like I'm losing all control. I grip my staff tightly, close my eyes. It's true, I'm definitely going insane. Panic! Instinctively, I want to run back down the hill to the safety of my cabin. But a voice says:

"No. Endure this. There's no place to run to anyway." Very well. If I am to go crazy, let it be here and now.

I relax my grip on the staff, sit up, feel muscles uncoil, head expand. I am floating. The lights on the hillsides become jewels; distant cars pass like meteors on ribbons of silver energy. Matter dissolves into colored waves, and I can no longer feel where my skin ends and the warm breeze begins. Then suddenly, I am flooded to the point of tears with a great torrent of Love.

Now I actually see them—Odysseus in the east, Pan in the south, Orpheus in the west, Parzival in the north—each standing at his appointed place on the compass. Then others appear as well! Wide-eyed Aphrodite next to Pan, calm Penelope beside Odysseus, lovely Eurydice with Orpheus, and the High Priestess herself next to Parzival. So they each have their feminine counterparts, and Love is not the exclusive province of Orpheus, as I had thought, but flows through them all, and now I can feel it like a river encircling me. And, as I watch, they begin to dance, these Lords and Ladies, joining hands, moving around me in this river of emotion, swirling faster and faster until they become a single, pulsing blur of ecstasy.

Then they slow to a more stately step, but with hands still joined, and I realize I am sitting on a table—the Round Table. This is my court, and these Lords and Ladies are pledged to my service. And I see, too, that it is not Arthur who is Emperor, but Mordred, the imposter, who has seized the throne; and it is Mordred who must be overthrown so that Arthur, sleeping in Avalon, can rise again and assume his rightful place, which he is, in fact, already doing, stirring somewhere in my depths; and Mordred grows weaker by the moment, dissolving into the dark from which he grew, dying, dying...

With this, the vision faded, as did these characters begin to fade out of my life from that night on. I had sailed safely between Scylla, the monster of insanity, and Charybdis, the whirlpool of fear. My old center had, indeed, slipped away but was being replaced by a new and stronger one in which the various and heretofore warring personae of my psychic court would make their peace.

By correcting my initial but false assumption that Arthur was the "Emperor," and hence the villain, of the drama, the vision had placed the whole episode back in proper mythological perspective. According to legend, Arthur had been slain by his treacherous nemesis Mordred in a civil war that had ruined Camelot. But Arthur's death was not to be permanent. He had been spirited away by the sorceress, Morgan Le Fay, to the Isle of Avalon from which someday he was to return in triumph and glory; and this, psychologically, was the nature of the revolution now taking place in my own consciousness.

Mordred, I recognized, was the cynical and ignoble identity I had adopted on coming to L.A. In order to maintain this image of myself, however, I (as Mordred) had had to suppress the indigenous lords and ladies of my soul in what had amounted to a subconscious civil war. Now, aided and abetted by Athena (a sorceress in her own right), a new self was emerging to reunite my soul, and this, the third and last White Heat, had marked a turning point in the revolution. Mordred had been unhorsed by the power of Love—a love that (coincidentally?) had just reentered my external life via Samantha's fortuitous return.

In the days that immediately followed, I tried willfully to summon Arthur into my being, but quickly realized that he could not emerge full-blown. Instead, I came to regard him as a kind of seed that had been planted in the soil of my consciousness and would take time to mature. A journal entry at the end of October sums up this revolution:

> There are ups and downs, ebbs and flows, but rhythms, which I used to despise as weakness, I now take more in stride. Every moment can't be a White Heat, and *decisiveness* is not necessarily admirable in all circumstances. Most rewarding, I sense a growing fraternity among my guardians. They seem to be acting more in concert, deferring to one another when appropriate. But at the same time, in this fusion they also grow less objectified and distinct. I know that eventually I will lose them as separate "personalities," and this makes me a little sad. Athena, too, is strangely quiet, but I know I haven't heard the last from her—not by a long shot. I feel as though, having orchestrated these events, she's laying low, letting me deal with things on my own for a while.

In spite of the fact that all this had begun as a purely rational and somewhat amateurish attempt at self-analysis, a Jungian therapist might well have been pleased with the way my subconscious had "turned the tables," as it were, and might also have predicted that a satisfactory outcome was near at hand. I, however, had my doubts, as the next paragraph in my journal indicates:

Also, I can't help but feel, as I read over my journal to date, that everything that's happened so far is but a prelude to the true beginning of my education—a kind of introductory course in which the novice student is exposed to new ideas and experiences in an almost random fashion in order to get him acquainted with the real work ahead.

Actually, though manifested in highly dramatic form, this psychic revolution was still only therapeutic in nature and not, properly speaking, spiritual. Nor, despite the vivid and flamboyant expression in my own case, are such psychological changes as' extraordinary as might be supposed. Most people experience similar if gender transitions during critical phases of their lives, as in the shift from adolescence to adulthood, or from maturity to old age, all of which occur within the context of conventional self-perception. As such, they involve no more than a reorganization and transposition of various psychological forces from one self-image to another. The true spiritual task, however, is precisely the exposure and penetration of *all* images whatsoever—not only of the self, but of the entire metaphorical world.

Still, a period of psychological *purification* is often necessary before the "real work" can begin, because such work requires a courage and dedication not possible to a soul divided against itself. Indeed, although I would rarely again experience the same kind of sharp, sheer panic that my own purification entailed, there would be other even "darker nights" to get through.

In the meantime, however, this whole process had prepared me for a momentous revelation that was to alter the entire character of my quest. My gift certificate was about to come due.

Six:
What Is Truth?

> Pilate therefore said unto him, Art thou a king then? Jesus answered, Thou sayest that I am a king. To this end was I born, and for this cause came I into the world, that I should bear witness unto the truth. Every one that is of the truth heareth my voice.
> Pilate saith unto him, What is Truth?[10]

Most of us have pondered this question at least sometime in our lives — whether as students in a classroom, over the dinner table among friends, or even during moments of serious solitary contemplation; but almost always it remains an abstraction, standing over and above the palpable current of existence to which we are ineluctably drawn back by all the demands of everyday life: the dog has to be walked, a meal prepared, homework done, an appointment kept, or a prisoner judged.

Pilate himself seems to have asked it out of something more than idle curiosity, for he spent a good deal of time interrogating Jesus as if genuinely puzzled by his charge. But Pilate was also, by all accounts, a busy and pragmatic man-of-affairs — the governor of a volatile province, responsible to imperial Rome for its peace and security. And as long as he was locked into such real-life concerns, there was little chance that Jesus' Truth could have anything more than a passing, philosophic interest for him.

Yet all such "real life" concerns are themselves predicated on assumed truths that we hold, often unconsciously, about the fundamental nature of reality and how it works. Pilate, for instance, probably consulted augurs and astrologers before making any important decisions — a practice largely abandoned in our own scientific age, because our basic cosmological assumptions have changed. Thus, ultimately, the question — What is Truth? — is not an abstraction but determines the way we conduct our everyday lives. And that is precisely why we are so reluctant to face it.

As long as our concrete circumstances seem tolerable and comprehensible, we much prefer to cling to the familiar "truths" of the past than risk surrendering them on a mere point of philosophic inquiry, for to do so will inevitably transform our lives in ways we cannot foresee. And because, for most of us, the terrors of the unknown far outweigh the antinomies and petty sufferings of the present, it usually requires some incontrovertible and inexplicable shift in our concrete, "real life" circumstances before we are willing to confront Pilate's question in any personally meaningful way.

I must admit I was no exception to this conservative rule. In spite of all that was happening — Athena, Samantha, the White Heats, I still managed to fit everything into a basically materialistic model of the universe. The "lords and ladies of my soul" need not be taken as actual, self-existent entities but merely as psychic projections, and my "vision" could be viewed as no more than a kind of waking dream state superimposed on a solidly objective reality. What's more, even though I described such experiences in mythological terms, I was careful not to assign to them any fixed ontological status. Nevertheless, these experiences were beginning to put a strain on the ontological assumptions about reality that I did hold.

For one thing, I found it odd that Athena had never appeared as part of my psychic pantheon. It was almost as though she belonged to a different order of phenomena entirely. By now she had become a fully developed presence in my life, but no matter how much I tried to rationalize her as a product of my own imagination, I couldn't shake the sensation that she existed outside of anything I might possibly conceive of as *self*. Could she really be explained away as a mere "projection"? Though it was true that she had never manifested in a form verifiable by others, at the same time she seemed to have access to knowledge — especially in regard to Samantha — that was totally beyond my personal ken. How, for example, had she known that the fire would threaten Samantha's parents' house an hour before it happened? But then again, perhaps it was only a lucky guesstimate on the part of my own subconscious.

Secondly, there was no doubt that Samantha, who was now back in my life, was quite real. But there was also something definitely unreal about our relationship. The timing was just too perfect, as though it had been purposefully designed to "keep the plot moving," as in some well-wrought story. Likewise, every scene seemed fraught with subtle, yet-to-be-revealed meanings, just as an accomplished dramatist might have written them. Was this, too, merely a kind of on-going projection? If so, it was being fashioned with remarkable skill, far beyond any conscious powers of authorship I possessed.

Finally, in reviewing my journal, I noticed that it was peppered with a host of seemingly inconsequential coincidences that, when taken together, gave mounting evidence of a phenomenon Jung called *synchronicity*. For example, an entry made on October 30th reads as follows:

> Spent the afternoon finishing Jung's *Answer to Job* which culminates in a discussion of John's *Apocalypse*, specifically focusing on the vision of the sun-mother, pregnant with child, who, according to Jung, does not appear to belong to this "stream of apocalyptic vision." Jung goes on to analyze the meaning of this motif and concludes that it pre-figures the birth of a second, future Christ as a new form of consciousness in the individuated individual. Heavy stuff!
>
> I close the book, glad for a chance to give my brain a rest. Five minutes later, Samantha calls to say she is on her way over. Thinking to kill a little time with some meditation before she arrives, I pick up Hoeller's *The Royal Road* and, closing my eyes, open it at random to "The Empress" whose motto reads:
>
>> And there appeared a great wonder in Heaven; a woman clothed with the sun, and the moon under her feet, and upon her head a crown of twelve stars. And she being with child cried, travailing in birth...
>
> —which is the exact passage Jung was talking about in *Answer to Job*. This kind of thing has been happening to me with incredible frequency the last few months.

Still, I might have dismissed these quirky occurrences as also just another form of projection if the master interpreter of projections, Carl G. Jung himself, had not attached such importance to them. In his essay *On Synchronicity*, Jung wrote of a "meaningful coincidence of two or more events, when something other than probability of chance is involved." He then went on to examine various kinds of synchronistic phenomena, such as ESP, precognition, parallelism, etc., but could find no causal explanations. He did, however, from his own research and experience, affirm their existence and concluded with the following:

> Synchronistic phenomena prove the simultaneous occurrence of meaningful equivalences in heterogeneous, causally unrelated processes; in other words, they prove that a content perceived by an observer can, at the same time, be represented by an outside event, without any causal connection. From this it follows either that the psyche cannot be localized in space, or that space is relative to the psyche. The same applies to the temporal determination of the psyche and the psychic relativity of time. I do not need to emphasize that the verification of these findings must have far-reaching consequences.[11]

One of these "consequences" would be to all but demolish a strictly biological view of human beings, for if the psyche cannot be localized in time and space, it is hard to imagine how it could be the exclusive product of biochemical processes occurring in the brain. In effect, consciousness would be placed beyond the reach of the laws of cause and effect. But this, in turn, would have even more devastating consequences, because the law of cause and effect is the very glue that holds the entire materialist concept of the cosmos together. If even one exception to this law is admitted, the whole edifice crumbles, for it amounts to the confession that there is a force in the universe that is *non*-material.

Nevertheless, I found Jung's discussion of synchronicity sketchy and confusing, as though he himself didn't quite know what to make of the phenomenon. At the same time, however, I was reading Fritjof Capra's book *The Tao of Physics*, which raised similar doubts about the inviolability of the law of cause and effect, but from a different, more cogent perspective. In describing subatomic phenomena Capra, himself a physicist, insisted that certain of their properties were acausal. Indeed, according to him, this placed the whole structure of classical materialism in absolute jeopardy:

> Quantum theory has thus demolished the classical concepts of solid objects and of strictly deterministic laws of nature. At the subatomic level, the solid material objects of classical physics dissolve into wavelike patterns of probabilities, and these patterns, ultimately, do not represent probabilities of things, but rather probabilities of interconnections.[12]

Even more startling, I gathered from Capra's assessment of the current state of physics that there was no unified theory that could explain in an integrated manner all the phenomena of the microcosm and macrocosm combined. Instead, there existed only a kind of theoretical patchwork quilt, sections of which could elucidate events in their own fields and at

What is Truth?

their own levels but could not be organized into a comprehensive whole. In other words, no one today could actually say what the universe was, simply because no one knew. It was one big Mystery. And yet, I had been clinging to a stringent materialism as though it had some prima facie claim to validity, when even professional scientists were slipping around in its quagmire.

Finally, according to Capra, even in physics, the hardest of the hard sciences, the question of consciousness was cropping up in a way that suggested the same far-reaching (and devastating) consequences that Jung had predicted; for, as Capra wrote,

> At the atomic level, "objects" can be understood only in terms of the interaction between the processes of preparation and measurement. The end of this chain of processes lies always in the consciousness of the human observer.[13]

—or, more succinctly,

> The observer decides how he is going to set up the measurement and this arrangement will determine, to some extent, the properties of the observed object. If the experimental arrangement is modified, the properties of the observed object will change in turn.[14]

Note the revolutionary nature of this assertion, for it says not that a modification of the observer's experiment will *reveal* new properties of the object being observed but that it will actually *change* those properties. Thus, in the field of subatomic physics, at least, the observer is seen as something more than a mere passive viewer of the objective world; in some sense, he or she actively creates it.

At the end of his book, Capra concluded that modern science was pointing to a new worldview of the "oneness of the universe which includes not only our natural environment but also our fellow human beings," but for me personally, it had far more radical implications. I was reminded of a discovery I had made back in high school while taking a course in mathematical set theory that, at the time, caused me quite a shock.

The basic premise of set theory is that mathematics, in its purest form, has nothing to do with anything found in the objective world—not apples or oranges, triangles or planes, or even time or space. It is simply the free play of logic, manipulating abstract symbols according to its own spontaneous assumptions and self-definitions. Thus, it is not necessarily true that 2 + 2 = 4; 2 + 2 can just as well = 5, if so defined.

For me, it was but a short leap from this insight into the nature of mathematics to a comparable insight into the nature of thought itself. Whatever order our intellects perceived in the universe was not something inherently *real*, but rather a process that arose in the mind and was *superimposed* on reality. The world was like a page of random dots that could be connected in various ways to form varying patterns, but there was no one, true pattern existing in the dots themselves. Likewise, there were no ultimate "truths" to be discovered "out there" somewhere in the cosmos. Consequently, to rely on any ideological construction to answer the question, What is Truth? was folly. Today's truth would always be tomorrow's lie, because all such truths were intrinsically ephemeral, as the shifting history of ideas in every field bore ample witness.

Yet ever since I had been handed Athena's sword (and even before, as a Marxist), this was just the kind of truth I had been searching for — a new worldview that would *explain* my existence once and for all. Now, however, I began to suspect that no worldview, whether religious, philosophical, or scientific, could ever carry the value of absolute certainty that I was seeking, because worldviews were, in essence, only *metaphors*. They described reality *as if* it were patterned this way or that but could never reveal reality itself. What difference, then, did it make if I was a materialist, or believed in higher energies, or in nature spirits and wood nymphs? All were ultimately illusionary. Dimly, I was starting to sense that Athena's sword was double-edged; the more I tried to search for Truth, the more it undercut the very basis of that search, and first to fall would be my reliance on any rational constructs.

Such notions, however, were only vaguely taking shape in the back of my mind and remained more or less abstract. As a matter of practical consequences, it was still hard for me to consider seriously any but our culture's own conventional cosmology, governed by all the classical laws of cause and effect. This was the reality everyone around me shared, and any radical departure from it, I knew, would eventually bring censure and social isolation in one form or another. Even Samantha, who was the only one I dared confide such thoughts to, had looked a little askance when I told her about my White Heats. Perhaps I really was a bit crazy, after all. In any case, as I said, none of my experiences so far had positively contradicted any of my more fundamental cosmological assumptions, and, as often as not, I had doubts about departing from them even theoretically. In the end, it would take something exceedingly dramatic and in obvious defiance of these assumptions finally to clear the way for a true inquiry into Pilate's question. And that *something* was to be my "gift certificate."

Meanwhile, life tumbled on, and even had I been more inclined, there wasn't much time for serious philosophizing. Like Pilate, I was still a man-of-affairs and had things to attend to.

In November, as planned, Lewis and I took over the new company. I was put in charge of feature-film production and also given the responsibility for expanding our operations into the burgeoning field of cable TV, an area I knew little about. Out of loyalty to Lewis I tried to give the job my full attention. There was a lot to learn, and even if I no longer felt the same commitment to my career as I had a year ago, it was once more stimulating and exciting — at least, for a while.

At first I had hoped there might still be room in the young cable business for some really innovative programming, but this turned out not to be the case. Instead, it was almost worse than dealing with the networks. The cable executives wanted essentially the same kind of shows, only racier and for less money. This meant either making a cheaper product or arranging complicated financing deals from pre-sales in other markets, which I took no personal pleasure in doing.

At one point Lewis got enthusiastic about developing game shows for syndication, and this too fell into my bailiwick. A producer came to us with an idea for a show called *Hot and Not*, a spurious piece of fluff built around the latest fads and fashions. I groaned and wondered if *Hot and Not* would be my legacy to the world. Fortunately, the idea never got off the ground, but I began to feel that perhaps I should be spending my life in some sort of real service to humanity rather than grinding out a diet of video junk food. This thought was born only as an obscure impulse, but it persisted and eventually grew into a full-blown obsession.

In the meantime my memoirs of life in the sixties had run aground on the same shoals that had almost shipwrecked my brief venture in directing. After writing nearly a hundred pages, I found that I had no focus or point of view. They contained all the necessary commercial ingredients. There were lurid descriptions of hippie drug parties, juicy vignettes from the Smash Monogamy movement, violent scenes of riots, arrests, and jail—but what did it all amount to? Which was another way of asking the same question I had started this whole quest with, What was my life all about? I decided to shelve the manuscript until I had a clearer answer.

Around this time, too, Samantha made a curious and unexpected move. She gave up her Westwood apartment and took a small, one-bedroom studio in Topanga not ten miles from where I lived. Whether she switched abodes to be closer to me or simply because she was drawn to the area, she didn't say, but it certainly teased my interest. At any rate, although you still couldn't call ours a traditional lovers' relationship, we began to spend more time together, and I was glad of her company once again. Besides, I was coming to see Samantha in an altogether different light.

In Japan, as most people know, students of Zen are given koans to contemplate. These enigmatic word puzzles—such as the famous "What is the sound of one hand clapping?"—refuse to yield a logical solution, and that is precisely their point. Eventually, after long hours of strenuous meditation, the rational mind is exhausted, suddenly making room for another kind of understanding to take place.

But koans rarely work in the same way for Westerners, because we usually encounter them out of their traditional context. Imagine for a moment the enormous psychological difference between reading a koan in a diverting book, or hearing one dropped at a cocktail party, and the situation of the Zen student who has committed his entire life to discovering its solution. Consider, too, that the student does not receive his koan in any casual manner but from the lips of a living master, endowed with all the veneration and authority a culture can bestow. Here, the koan carries with it the whole weight of an ancient, esoteric tradition and is thus transformed into the very key to the meaning of life itself.

But in my own soul Samantha had come to embody just this kind of overwhelming enigma, an enigma that also rested at the heart of an ancient (though today debased) tradition, namely, the medieval idea of *Amor*, as expounded by the troubadours. Coincidentally, I was then reading Joseph Campbell's monumental study of mythology *The Masks of*

God in which this mytho-methodology is perhaps nowhere better summed up than in the following:

> Love is born of the eyes and heart: the light world of the godly gift of sight and the dark of the grotto that opens within to infinity. Hence, if the goddess Amor is to be served, neither light alone nor darkness can represent her way, which is mixed: neither Galahad's couch to Sarras nor the crystalline bed of Tristan's cave, but as long as life lasts—and life, after all, is her field—Gawain's Marvel Bed of bolts and darts ("Anyone seeking rest," states the author,[15] "had better not come to this bed"), or the hard war-saddle of Parzival's turtle-dove-branded charger. At the moment of the wakening to love, an object, apparently without, "passes [in the words of Joyce] into the soul forever....And the soul leaps at the call. To live, to err, to fall, to triumph, to recreate life out of life!" Condwiramurs, conduire amour: the guide, the summoner, will have opened a prospect to the castle, the passage to which, however, will have to be earned. And, according to this mythology, the one way is of absolute loyalty to that outward innermost object. By this alone can the two worlds be united and the kingship won of one's proper Castle of Life.[16]

Just so was Samantha for me this "outward innermost object." In a word, she had become my koan.

In one way, she posed an even worse dilemma. The Zen student, at least, chooses his discipline, but I had not chosen Samantha. She had been chosen for me by some ruthless fate from which I could not resign. So far, I had tried actively to love her, court her, befriend her, and forget her, but none of these strategies had worked. What else was there to do? My will was stymied. But I was also now convinced that this enigma could not be solved through any purely psychological or therapeutic processes. Somehow, Samantha Jones's own, very real destiny had become entangled with mine, and I could no more cut her out of my life than be surgically separated from a Siamese twin with whom I shared the same heartbeat. And although I continued to rebel against such a Fate, one by one I felt my options being exhausted. In the end, I sensed, too, that this "koan" would require nothing less than complete surrender, and oddly, I began to welcome it even in the midst of rebellion. Confronted by Samantha, I came to see the whole, mysterious zigzag course of my life as a search for just such a destiny.

In Campbell's fourth volume of *The Masks of God*, I also read the following words of James Joyce's hero Stephen Dedalus:

> I do not fear to be alone. And I am not afraid to make a mistake, even a great mistake, a lifelong mistake, and perhaps as long as eternity, too.[17]

And I wondered if that hadn't been my own problem all along. Was I afraid to make an eternal mistake? Despite the outward appearance of a somewhat adventurous life, I had always been inwardly cautious, willing to commit my body to the field of action, but not fully my soul. Always, I had held something back, watching and waiting, always asking, "Is this my true destiny?"—and always sensing that it was not. Still, I did not believe I would be afraid of daring an eternal mistake if ever I found a destiny worthy of the risk.

On Friday, November 12th, Joseph Campbell was coming to L.A. to give an all-day lecture at the Center for Healing Arts. This was perhaps a once-in-a-lifetime opportunity to hear the great mythologist in person, so I decided to play hooky from work and attend. I don't recall the lecture's exact title, but it was a comprehensive survey of the world's spiritual mythology. The next day I made a journal entry describing it as follows:

> What a mind! What a mine of treasures: stories, symbols, pictures (slides), anecdotes, in all languages and from every culture, spanning more than six thousand years. He [Campbell] ranges up and down the centuries like some shaman of the intellect in pure astral flight, and yet he never gets lost; always he comes back to thread and rethread the eye of the same golden needle buried in the haystack of a million myths. The thematic essence is everywhere and always the same; the death and rebirth of the self, transmuted into Divinity.

Needless to say, I was impressed. For the first time I glimpsed, through Campbell's penetrating eyes, the vast, transhuman meaning of the whole notion of a spiritual quest. What's more, he had made me aware of its universal underlying pattern—its stages, stories, and motifs—which rose again and again in the collective mind of Man as myths and dreams to guide the way. I was not crazy! I was not alone! I was plugged into the deepest circuits of the psyche, standing on the threshold of the Mystery of Mysteries, and I knew that to cross would be the greatest adventure any human being could undertake. This, indeed, would be a destiny worth daring an eternal mistake for; but did I dare it? Frankly, I wavered at the prospect. In committing to such a course, I knew there could be no compromise with the world and the things of the world—career, money, prestige, personal relationships, and security. If need be, all would have to be placed on the sacrificial altar. In some still mysterious but very real way, it would mean, too, my own death and that was awesome to contemplate.

Such were the electrifying though inconclusive thoughts that I took home with me that night, and the excitement persisted into the next day. I couldn't eat, I couldn't read, I couldn't even sit down for long. All I could do was pace the floor, brain bubbling with as yet unintelligible possibilities.

Then, out of nowhere and a little off the subject, an idea flashed through my mind about how to give focus to my abandoned memoirs. I remembered a book I had read several years before called *Black Elk Speaks*. It was the autobiography of a Sioux Indian who had told his story as the unfoldment of a numinous childhood dream. Suddenly, it occurred to me that I, too, had had just such a dream before going to Nam: the journey to the East to see the Great Man. And although I had never written it down before, every detail was as sharp and clear in my mind as it had been that very night. Like Black Elk, I would start my memoirs with this dream and let it guide me through the narrative. Perhaps the dream itself would show me the shape of the events that had followed. In a fever of blind creativity I rushed to the typewriter, spun in a blank sheet of paper, and boldly began to transcribe it for the first time. This is what I wrote:

> I am somewhere in the decaying heart of Europe, amidst cathedrals overgrown with the weeds of relentless time, but I can't stay. I have to travel east—to Asia—to see the Great Man. When I reach the border, however, it is closed, sealed off by armed guards and barbed wire. Just as I am about to turn back, one of the guards points to a building on the other side of the fence—a kind of antechamber cum museum where certain objects from the interior are on display—and I am permitted to enter this far.
>
> In the main room I wander among glass cases and pedestals featuring statues of the Buddha and other religious relics, all collecting dust. Then I notice a door at the far end of the room with a sign which reads: *Magoo, The Great Man*. Thrilled that I might yet fulfill my mission, I steal through the door and find myself in a smaller, ill lit room. Here sits Magoo, but far from being the promised "Great Man," he is a stuffed and lifeless

dwarf with yellow, peeling skin and blind eyes that nevertheless seem to mock me.

Realizing that the sage is a fake, I leave with a heavy heart and head back west, riding a black horse across the dark lands of Europe until I come to Lisbon, the most westerly seaport on the continent. At first glance, the city seems to possess a certain antique charm, but then evidence of modernization quickly becomes apparent. Clanging trolleys run up and down the crowded streets and electric light bulbs are strung incongruously along the ancient balconies—a fusion of old and new that refuses to mix.

I ride on down to the harbor, where a rock jetty extends beyond the fishing boats a mile or so into the open sea. It's land's end and as far as one can hope to go on foot, but I start out anyway, scrambling over the boulders. Soon, I spot a girl standing at the very tip of the jetty, facing the expansive sea. She wears a white, gossamer gown which dances gently on the wind and her golden hair, too, blows softly about her cheeks. Her angelic gaze is fixed serenely on the horizon and I follow it out to the misty juncture of water and sky, where a green and virgin continent rises in the distance, singing with life, and I recognize it immediately: It is America, the pristine New World, as it was before the white man came; emerald of the oceans—my native land.

Now, the girl turns to me and smiles, beckoning me onward and, heart pounding, I continue over the boulders with redoubled effort. But just as I am about to reach her, another woman appears suddenly from behind a rock. She has dark, earth-bound hair and eager, clinging arms which she wraps around my neck, holding me fast to the spot. I struggle against her grip but can't summon the strength to break it. Slowly, she begins to drag me backwards toward the shore. But even as I am being pulled away, I know that someday I will return here and find again the golden-headed angel, who will guide me home across the waves. This is a certainty.

As already mentioned, upon waking from this dream originally I had taken it to mean simply that I would return from Vietnam. Now however, as soon as I typed out the words *Magoo, the Great Man*, it began to dawn on me with shuddering clarity what the dream had actually been about. A simple transposition of the letters *Magoo* rendered *Mao Go*, or *Go Mao*, obviously referring to the real journey I had made to Mao's China in 1971. In fact, the whole first part of the dream reflected this journey in startling detail.

What is Truth?

To begin with, the dream began in the "decaying heart of Europe," which described exactly how I had felt during our actual layover in Paris. Next, the museum in the dream was not only a nearly precise replica of the real museum I had visited in Yenan, but the fact that it was represented as an "antechamber" to Asia, located on the other side of a fenced and forbidding border, neatly summed up the whole showcase character of our trip "behind the Bamboo Curtain."

Moreover, the Great Man, who in the dream had turned out to be a stuffed, dwarfed sage, was an obvious and uncanny symbol for the stuffed, dwarfed horse (with peeling, yellow skin, no less!) that I had actually seen in Yenan and which had been preserved precisely because it had once belonged to Mao—the "Great Man" himself. And just as in the dream I had been disappointed to discover that the Great Man was a stuffed dwarf, so in reality, seeing the stuffed horse coincided with my disillusionment with Maoism. In fact, it now seemed to me that my whole, inexplicable interest in horses, which appeared just prior to my trip to China, had arisen for the sole purpose of directing my attention to this external symbol and marking it for future reference.

Finally, in keeping with the equine motif, the black horse that in this dream had carried me back "across the dark lands of Europe" was no doubt the same black stallion that had burst into my hotel room to carry me home in the dream I had had in Peking.

The symbolism in the second part of the dream was more obscure. On the surface, there was some resemblance between the "clanging trolleys" of Lisbon and real cable cars of San Francisco. Moreover, the "fusion of old and new that refused to mix" could well portray my state of mind after leaving China, but these parallels seemed rather insignificant compared to the rest of the dream. The only association I had with the name Lisbon came from the movie *Casablanca*, where it represented the jumping-off place for refugees fleeing a war-torn Europe. This thought, however, instantly brought to mind another story of refugees by Ray Bradbury called *The Fox in the Forest*, which I had read in high school.

It was set in Mexico City during the 1930s—a time and place whose decadent ambience closely matched that of my "Lisbon." What's more, its protagonists, a man and wife, were also trying to escape a war-torn world —this one, however, placed in the future. Traveling via a time machine, Bradbury's couple hope to lose themselves in the Mexico of the '30s but soon realize that they are being pursued by agents from their own world. Thinking there's safety in numbers, they join a Hollywood movie company shooting on location. Ironically, however, the Hollywood personnel themselves turn out to be agents, and the couple are whisked back to the nightmarish future to face their doom.

Immediately, I recognized in this tragic little tale my own story with Colette in Los Angeles (symbolized by Lisbon in the dream). I too had been a refugee from war, hoping to escape its horrors in the world of movie-making. And like Bradbury's couple, our doom had also been triggered by a company of Hollywood "agents," i.e., the Nam vets in the *Tracers* cast who, in the guise of actors, had sucked me back into the nightmare of another time—though in my case it was the past instead of the future.

The only part of the dream that still puzzled me was the setting of the last scene, the fishing harbor with its rock jetty. As a child, I had played on a somewhat similar pile of rocks in Long Island Sound (which might connect it with my "native land"), but here the resemblance ended. This actual rock pile had been far removed from any fishing harbor or views of a virgin continent.

Nor could I think of any place I had been since that fit the location in the dream. There was one thing, however, that this last scene did make abundantly clear. I now knew why Samantha Jones had always seemed so familiar to me, even on our first meeting. I had, indeed, seen her "somewhere before." She was the angel-headed girl on the jetty, beckoning me home.

Still, as stunningly close to reality as the dream had been, it might have remained nothing more than a rather graphic and curiously clear-cut recapitulation of my life over the past decade except, of course, for the singular fact that I had had it five years *before* any of the events portrayed had taken place. In short, this dream had not been a *recapitulation* at all, but an incredibly accurate and all-encompassing *prophecy*.

As the import of this revelation deepened, I closed my eyes and knew myself to be standing at the most decisive crossroads of my life. I could simply choose to forget I ever had this dream; forget Athena and her sword; forget Samantha Jones; forget my quest and never again ask a single question about who I was, or what was Truth, or Reality, or

Destiny. Or, by inquiring into the dream further and accepting all the consequences of its implications, have the whole current of my existence wrenched from its old, habitual stream-bed and sent spilling out into a vast, inconceivable Unknown.

There was no hurry in this decision. The moment was richly spacious, and I felt I could prolong it indefinitely. All my powers of judgment and every value I had ever held arose in consciousness, as though to give each its own particular counsel, but there was no sense of conflict. The whole process unfolded with a courtly solemnity and almost ritual decorum. When it was over, I took a deep breath and chose the course of inquiry.

First, according to all my previous assumptions about the nature of Reality, The Dream was impossible. Yet it had occurred. Could its prophetic character have been merely an amazing chance coincidence? Was it possible that my subconscious had somehow made an "educated guess" as to what would happen in the future, based on my past experiences and predispositions?

I thought carefully about my life up until the time of The Dream but could find nothing that would suggest to anyone the radical course it would afterwards take. Before Vietnam, I had had virtually no interest in politics and would have considered the suggestion that I might someday become a "commie" positively insulting. Likewise, I had regarded Communist China in the same ideological terms; it was the "Red Menace," completely antithetical to all my inherited values, and the prospect of my ever going there would have seemed remote and absurd. An "educated guess," then, was out of the question.

Somehow, The Dream—or whoever had dreamed The Dream—had known what "I" could not possibly have known. But this implied some form of cognition operating in the cosmos that defied all notions of a purely material universe.

The only halfway adequate metaphor I knew by which to comprehend this phenomenon was one I had read of in Campbell's *Creative Mythology*. It was a rather lengthy quote taken from Schopenhauer. After analyzing the dynamics at work in dreams, in which we appear amid events and characters seemingly willed into existence by someone else, Schopenhauer compares this to waking life where, according to him, the Will to Life functions in a similar manner. He concludes,

> Every event in every individual life must then be implicated in two fundamentally different orders of relationship: first, in the objective, causal order of the course of nature, and second, in a subjective order relevant only to the experiencing individual himself and as subjective, consequently, as his dreams-where the sequence and content of the occurrences are as predetermined as the scenes of a drama, and, indeed, in the same way, namely, by plan of the author. However, that these two sorts of relationship should exist together, and in such a way that every event must be a link simultaneously in two completely different chains with the two conjoining perfectly, the fate of each thus harmonizing with the fate of every other, each the hero of his own drama and yet an actor in all the rest: this is certainly something that surpasses our comprehension, and can be imagined as possible only in terms of the most miraculous harmonia praestabilita.
>
> ...Our timidity before this colossal prospect may be allayed if we remind ourselves that the Subject of this great dream of life is, in a certain sense, only one, namely the Will to Life itself; and furthermore, that all this multiplicity of the phenomena is conditioned by time and space. It is a vast dream, dreamed by a single being; but in such a way that all the dream characters dream too. Hence, everything interlocks and harmonizes with everything else.[18]

Originally, I had read these words of the great German philosopher only as an abstract speculation, but suddenly they came back to roost in the very center of my soul; for now I had actually seen this "Will to Life" (or whatever it was) at work through the window of my own Dream, its Hand shaping my destiny like a machinist's at his lathe.

Far from answering any questions, however, Schopenhauer's hypothesis merely pointed to a second, even more disturbing implication concerning free will. I had always prided myself on making the major decisions of my life freely—that is, often in opposition to societal or peer pressure, but apparently these decisions had not been "free" at all. In reality, they had been the manipulations of some supernal power, firmly guiding my footsteps along a path that had been already predetermined by The Dream. The idea that I had always held of myself as an autonomous being—and which I had only recently begun to question in the most tentative way—now collapsed in complete disillusionment. And what about the present "decisions" I was making (including the one to accept the Dream)? Were they equally illusory? If so, then truly "I" was nothing more than a blind marionette, dangled on the fingers of an unknown Fate.

As I continued to contemplate this state of affairs, I was slowly overtaken by a profound conviction. It was not so much a thought as an utterly bizarre sensation that swept through my whole body. The values we normally attach to dream and reality were becoming totally reversed. *It wasn't my life that seemed real anymore, but The Dream, of which my life was only an insubstantial reflection.*

As this sensation intensified, I could feel myself grow transparent and almost vanish, like a character on a movie screen who, when the houselights come up, is suddenly seen to be no more than a play of projected colors. This condition lasted for several hours but, in spite of its strangeness, was not especially frightening; rather, it inspired a sense of overwhelming wonder.

Toward evening a third implication occurred to me. Although I had carried this Dream in my memory through all the years and events it had predicted and, in fact, had thought about it periodically (it was not a dream one forgot), never before had I perceived any connection between it and my unfolding life. This blind spot now appeared to me almost as incredible as The Dream itself. How, or perhaps *why*, had I missed it?

On reflection, however, I also realized that if I *had* made any connection between The Dream and my life, there would have been the possibility of my "choosing" not to continue living it out. Thus, it seemed that The Dream's significance had been *purposefully* hidden from me until now, but then why *now* had it been suddenly revealed? Could it have been by chance? But this thought made me laugh, for if The Dream proved anything, it was precisely that there was no such thing as "chance." Everything happened according to, in Schopenhauer's words, a *harmonia praestabilita.*

Pondering further, I realized that, except for the prophecy at the end about returning to my native land, all the other events forecast by The Dream had already come to pass — the visit to Paris, the trip to China, the stuffed dwarf, my return and attempt to escape in Hollywood. But now, something else had happened as well, something not actually included in The Dream but only predicted by it. I had found again the angel-eyed girl, Samantha Jones. My life, then, had moved beyond The Dream itself; and the final prophecy was, in fact, about to come true.

Instantly, it all fused together. The Dream had been planted in my consciousness as a kind of psychic time bomb that, when my life had ripened sufficiently, would be triggered to deliver both an immediate message — *that it was time to undertake the spiritual journey in earnest* — and simultaneously, to *certify*, by its very power of prophecy, that such a journey was not only possible but imminent.

The revelation of The Dream's meaning, then, was my promised "gift certificate" — and a wondrous gift it was, for it certified not only the general direction that my life had taken lately but the veracity of all the unsettling mysteries and phenomena that I had been exposed to so far. Suddenly, Hoeller's lectures, the story of Parzival, the Tarot journey, and Campbell's tales of mythology — all ceased to be merely symbolic stories that had happened to others or esoteric speculations of long-dead sages but coalesced into a single, transcendent yet, at the same time, personal goal: *I was going home*.

Everything until now had, indeed, been, as I suspected, only a spiritual kindergarten. Now, the real venture was about to begin. Nor would it be anything as mundane as a simple change of worldview or the adoption of a new cosmology — all such metaphors belonged to the land; but I was back at the point I had left in The Dream, standing at land's end, ready to follow Samantha's "north star song of old" out over the open sea on the great voyage of return. This is what I had always hungered for, yearned for, intuited but never fully cognized through all my wanderings and sojourns. Long had I been in exile, estranged from this world, but now all that was coming to an end. And how sweet the prospect seemed! At last, I would claim my Gnostic birthright; I would learn the answers to Pilate's question; I would find the Grail; I would discover who I really was — all these aspirations became, for me, wrapped in that one poignant and passionate phrase: *I was going home. At last, I was going home.*

Seven:
Trouble in the Soul

In *The Gospel According to Thomas*, Jesus warns,

> Let him who seeks, not cease seeking until he finds, and when he finds, he will be troubled...[19]

In The Dream I had found the key I had been seeking—the key that would unlock my destiny if I had but the courage to use it, and this I vowed to do no matter what the cost. Thus, I learned Athena's Second Commandment—COMMITMENT—but without yet realizing its full weight or all the demands it would entail. In the days ahead I would be troubled, indeed, for once such a commitment is made, there can be no turning back; its fulfillment becomes, literally, a question of life and death.

In the meantime, I was confronted with the immediate problem of how to begin the voyage home. What vessel would carry me across this spiritual sea? Having exhausted and discarded any reliance on intellectual constructs, it seemed that the only avenue left open was *experience*. If Truth was not to be arrived at conceptually, then perhaps it was something to be learned empirically, like riding a bicycle. I remembered the energy session with Samantha and the undeniable state of expansiveness it had produced. Could such states be mastered, and was this the way to Gnosis? By now I had become aware that many traditions, particularly those developed in India, seemed to affirm that this was so. I decided to experiment.

The following week, I stopped by L.A.'s largest New Age bookstore, The Bodhi Tree (of which I had become a regular patron), and picked out a book called *The Fundamentals of Yoga*, written by an Indian doctor, R. S. Mishra. Step by step, it outlined a series of exercises for raising kundalini, the mystical energy that, according to Hindu tradition, lay coiled at the base of the spine but could be enticed, by arduous yogic effort, to rise up through the seven chakras, or subtle energy centers, to the crown of the head, where it was alleged to produce a union between the self and the Divine. There were, however, some preliminaries.

One was to become sensitive to *prana*, described by Dr. Mishra as the "life force" (as distinct from actual kundalini) that circulated throughout the body and the cosmos. This was accomplished by some simple attention exercises, and, sure enough, they aroused sensations very similar to the "energies" I had experienced with Samantha. Encouraged, I continued.

The next step was to practice withdrawal of prana from various parts of the body through a concentrated meditative effort. When successfully performed, that part of the body focused on was supposed to go into a state of *yoga nidra* in which no feeling or sensation would remain. This proved to be more difficult, but I kept at it.

I also, of course, told Samantha about my Dream and described all its prophetic correlations with my life. Initially, I think she took my enthusiastic conclusions with a grain of salt, but the following weekend she came over to my house quite excited about a dream she had just had of her own. Here it is, as I recorded it in my journal:

> Samantha comes to visit me on a Sunday morning. I am with a dark-haired woman with whom I have spent the weekend. Samantha wants to take me to a meeting of Taoist alchemists, but the dark-haired woman is jealous and refuses to let me go. They argue, and apparently, Samantha wins because we do end up at this Taoist meeting where alchemists brew up all sorts of bubbly concoctions in their laboratory vials.

The obvious parallel between the motif of Samantha struggling with a dark-haired woman over whether I am to come with her, which appeared in both our dreams, seemed to confirm for Samantha as much as for me that our lives were, indeed, linked in some deeper order of reality. At any rate, it served to open for us a new period of intimacy that was to last for several weeks.

After this incident Samantha started calling me regularly on the phone, sometimes even at odd hours, just to confide some bit of news or unburden the frustrations of her life and work. Finally, during the Thanksgiving holiday, she took what for her was an enormous step. She was extremely devoted to her parents and had always been guarded about letting me meet them. Now, however, she threw caution to the winds and boldly invited me to their house for dinner. It was, I knew, a token of the greatest trust. I was to be admitted into one of her innermost sanctuaries and was overjoyed at the prospect.

The dinner turned out to be a great success. Samantha's parents treated me with unabashed warmth and hospitality. Her father's interest in photography provided common ground for conversation, and her mother seemed to feel a special liking for me, fussing over my comfort and urging me to eat extra helpings of dessert. Samantha herself was radiant and relaxed and, afterwards, sitting around the fireplace drinking wine, I felt right at home.

Amidst this new-found outer happiness, however, I began to detect a strange and unexpected inner constraint. For the first time in our relationship, Samantha was holding nothing back, but I was. Every time she threw her arms around me in a spontaneous hug, I could feel it—a slight stiffening of the muscles, a tiny tension in my spine, all signs of an unwanted and unwarranted reserve. But why?

I thought of a line from Anouilh's play, *Becket*. When his mistress confesses her love for him, Becket replies, "Somehow, I could never support the idea of being loved." In the play, Becket's inability to love stems from his loss of honor. Was this true of me as well? Had I still not found my own honor? Was I, finally, after all my mad longings, incapable of loving Samantha, or anyone else?

I felt a sick sensation growing in my gut and tried to pretend it wasn't there. But it was. Moreover, by now Samantha and I were much too attuned to each other for her not to notice it as well. How cruel, I thought, to be given this fleeting taste of contentment only to have it all spoiled in the end.

The Sunday following dinner at her parents, house, Samantha and I had a date to pick up a kitten her new landlord had given her permission to keep. When I arrived at her house, however, Samantha was in tears. She was feeling guilty, she said, for neglecting her spiritual practices, partly out of fear. Several times, she too had felt close to insanity. I told her of my own experiences and tried to comfort her, but there was more. Lately, she had been consulting the Tarot cards and gotten consistent indications that deception and betrayal were in the offing. Hearing this, a chill passed through my heart. Was it possible that the cards had been warning her against me? Samantha, on the other hand, felt that it was she who would be the betrayer. Whatever, the readings fostered an abysmal mood between us.

We drove to get her kitten in silence. It was the last of a litter, a black and white runt with an infection in one eye, which nobody wanted. Except, of course, Samantha. It was love at first sight. I told her the kitten had her name inscribed on its heart, and it was true. The trouble was, her name was also inscribed on mine, and I knew I couldn't erase it. Driving home, with the living bundle of fur nestled in her jacket, Samantha was in seventh heaven, but I continued to brood. Things were taking an uncontrollable turn for the worse, and although I didn't know it then, I was slowly sliding into a classic dark night of the soul.

Coincidentally, the following Wednesday I attended a lecture by Hoeller on the Tarot cards and their symbolism. He showed slides from the Knapp-Hall deck, and I was struck, in particular, by The Wheel of Fortune. It depicted an endlessly turning, spoked wheel ridden by two half-human, half-animal creatures. Above them sat an impassive and enigmatic sphinx; I thought I recognized in this card my relationship with Samantha, about to enter another downward cycle. Very well, I thought to myself, let the Wheel turn, but I won't help it along. I'll keep my love steady, like the sphinx, and let Fortune take its course. At first, it seemed to work.

Several nights later, Samantha came over for a wine-and-candlelight dinner, and afterwards, we watched an old Fred Astaire musical on TV, singing along with the actors. Later I wrote of this evening in my journal:

> We lie in each other's arms by the firelight. We talk, laugh, make faces, cuddle, and kiss. She dozes and I stare out the window at the moon shining full in the trees. I can't describe the incredible peace I feel. This is it, I think, a pure moment of perfect bliss. Whatever else happens to you, you'll never forget it.

...and so I haven't.

A week later, however, we met for dinner at a pizza place in the Canyon, and throughout the meal I could feel her retreating once again into her shell. Her voice said all the right, polite things, but she wasn't in it. I looked into her eyes and saw her disappear behind them. For some reason she seemed suddenly afraid of me, and I didn't know what to do. I tried to explain about *Becket* and *honor*, hoping she would have the patience to wait until I found mine, but I only succeeded in frightening her further away.

We ended up in the parking lot late at night with the sea wind blowing up the Canyon and swirling dead leaves and bits of paper about our feet. We kissed, but she was anxious to get away. She climbed into her car, and I watched her drive off, thankful to be leaving behind a man who was half-mad. It was a miserable moment. I was still chained to the Wheel, and I knew that will power alone would never get me off.

As if on cue, too, the ghost of Vietnam returned to remind me that any hope of retreat back to the world was now cut off. A writer friend named Kay had sent me a manuscript by a friend of hers named Alex. It was an ambiguous tale about a series of bizarre murders that may or may not have been committed by a berserk vet. Although the prose was interesting and original, I was puzzled about what the author was trying to say about the war. Kay urged me to meet him, and in spite of my reluctance to rake through old ashes I agreed. The three of us made a date for dinner.

Alex turned out to be a nice enough guy who looked very much the author, sitting in the restaurant booth wearing a tweed jacket and puffing on a pipe. I had resolved to keep the conversation purely professional but, in the end, couldn't resist digging into his private views about Vietnam. Although Alex himself had sat it all out comfortably in college, he felt that the war was wrong and allowed that, in his opinion, veterans had to share in the moral responsibility.

There was no trace of personal condemnation in his voice. In fact, he spoke with cool dispassion. Even so, I felt my limbs begin to tremble with anger. I watched him across the table, blowing soft streams of smoke through his nostrils, and suddenly, I wanted to jerk him out of his seat and hurl him into the jungle. I wanted him to hear the shriek of mortars, feel the earth shift on impact, listen to the screams, smell the blood, feel the electric fear in the pores of his own flesh, then hand him an M-16 and see what he would do.

But, of course, I couldn't do that. Instead, I proceeded to get quite drunk and lectured him for the better part of two hours, sounding no doubt like a berserk vet myself. I wasn't communicating anything more than a barely suppressed rage, and I knew it even as the words came spitting out. What's more, I also knew that I had no right to judge him. There was simply nothing in his prosaic, middle-class life that would allow him to relate to anything I was saying. It was all absolutely pointless.

Later, back in my cabin, I regretted the entire evening and fell into a torpor of self-pity over being a vet, especially in regard to Samantha. How had I ever been so deluded as to think she might love me—a girl so sweetly sensitive that even the six 0' clock news caused her pain? On the other hand, I could all too easily picture her with gentle Alex, and I envied him his innocence. What I wouldn't give to have mine back. Woefully, I recalled a few lines from the *Aeneid* which John Caputo had quoted in a *Playboy* article about vets:

> In me it is not fit, holy things to bear,
> Red as I am with slaughter and new from war,
> Til in some living stream I cleanse the guilt
> Of dire debate and blood in battle spilt

I was no longer "red...with slaughter and new from war," but I felt their indelible stains yet and wondered where I would ever find a living stream powerful enough to wash them away.

But I had other problems as well. Work was becoming increasingly difficult to handle. I would sit in Lewis's new, glass office with our business affairs executive, listening to the two of them plot deals, but I could hardly follow the figures anymore. Agents and producers were also courting me all the more avidly now. I would lunch with them at La Serre and nod knowingly at their chitchat about what restaurant had stolen which chef, or which studio head was schtupping what star, but none of it mattered anymore. All I could think about was *going home*.

One day Lewis made a wisecrack about the way I was dressed, and I realized that, by his lights, he was right. I certainly didn't look like the vice-president of a prosperous company. It had been a year since I had replenished my wardrobe, and my clothes were getting threadbare. Looking in the men's room mirror, I also noticed that I needed a haircut and got one that very afternoon. The next day I went to an expensive clothing shop and bought five hundred dollars worth of flannel slacks and conservative dress shirts. These would keep me going for a while, but my days in Hollywood were numbered.

Still, I had no idea what else to do. I had given up on my memoirs which, like my life, were as yet incomplete and must remain so until The Dream was fulfilled. I began to think of America as a latter-day Rome. We in Hollywood were the entrepreneurs of the Circus, mounting ever greater and more lavish spectacles to appease a fickle and disaffected public. What else was going on? Was there some new Christianity being born in the backstreets and ghettoes of the poor? I didn't know. But I was sure that if somehow I were to be transported back to that ancient city, I wouldn't spend the rest of my days promoting gladiator shows for the Arena; I would be prowling the catacombs and alleys, searching for the children of tomorrow. Where were they today?

It was in the context of these ruminations that I had the following, vivid dream, recorded in my journal. Although puzzling at the time, I reproduce it here because later it was to prove significant:

> Just awoke from a dream. I am to establish two companion magazines, one called *Here* and the other called *Now*. *Here* will be developed first; *Now* will come later. Eventually, there will be a merger of the two. I see this all from my shamanic spot with the words HERE and NOW being spelled out in giant letters on the hills across the canyon.

But what did I know about running magazines? All I had ever been trained for was films and war. Nevertheless, increasingly I felt the need to find some useful occupation for the future, and this problem also began to loom large in my thoughts.

Finally, there was Colette. Almost a year had passed since I left for Malta, and I had hoped that by now she would be starting a new life. One morning at work, however, a mutual friend telephoned to say that Colette had been deeply depressed lately and that he was worried. I was, too. I called her right away to make a date for dinner at our Japanese restaurant. She agreed to come but sounded listless and distant.

I arrived first, prepared for the worst. Even so, I was shocked by her appearance when she walked through the door. Her face was pale and gaunt, and she wore big, dark sunglasses, like some fugitive from the law. She was also letting her hair grow out, but in a haphazard, careless fashion, and the way she moved, almost stumbling toward the table, made me think of semi-catatonic patients I had seen in mental hospitals. Was this what I had wrought?

After she was seated and we had ordered drinks, I asked what she was up to. "Nothing," she replied, and I could see that it was literally true. Suddenly, right there, our whole life together came back to me in a flash — our first riding lessons; the day we were married; lavish Thanksgiving dinners with friends and relatives; the night we attended a swank Halloween party in elaborate, rented costumes; skinny-dipping in Tahiti; champagne at the Plaza — all good times, like pages turning in a family photo album. Why had I given it all up? Why couldn't I just be a normal, everyday person like everyone else, content with a solid job and a lovely, loving wife? I wanted it all back, to take her in my arms, beg her forgiveness, promise her that everything would be all right again forever. But I couldn't. The past was gone. The Dream had caught up with me and was cresting, about to break. Even now, I was being swept over into the abyss, and I certainly wasn't going to take Colette with me.

I began to wish I were dead, and the idea took root. On December 9th, I made this entry in my journal:

> All the Lords and Ladies of my soul are silent. In eleven days I turn 40 and it frightens me. This is a crucial period of my "career" — time to polish up the old charm, court the right people, exploit the skills I've acquired and secure a little dough for my old age. But the effort is too much and I've lost all ambition. What, then? Perhaps my life is over, after all. The green and virgin continent of my Dream could well symbolize death — "the native land" from which I sprang. Oddly, the thought doesn't trouble me as much as it should. I've lived a lot in forty years, more than most people pack into twice that time. Maybe this is all she wrote? I feel exhausted and boxed into a cul-de-sac from which, apparently, there is no escape.

There was one bright ray in all this gathering gloom, but even that seemed short-lived (though ultimately, it yielded an important insight for the future). This was a weekend workshop given by Dr. Moss at the Center for Healing Arts. I had decided to take it partly out of respect for Samantha's enthusiasm, but also because it promised to be a demonstration of practical, experiential techniques for transforming consciousness and not just a mere presentation of theory.

There were about thirty participants. We gathered in the Center's large, well-carpeted upstairs room, which was equipped with cushions for seating but was otherwise bare of furniture. Dr. Moss began by having us lie on the floor while he played tapes of classical music that we were supposed to "open up to," allowing whatever thoughts and feelings arose to surface without censorship. Later he talked about "honoring the moment" and "surrendering judgmental attitudes." At first, I was a bit irritated by all his New Age jargon, but I was determined not to let my own linguistic prejudices stand in the way.

After lunch, we continued with more exercises, such as chanting OM, energy exchanges, and free-style dancing—all of which Moss said were only samples of what could be experienced in a week-long conference. For myself, although nothing specific or spectacular happened, I did begin to feel quite expansive and radiant. By now, such states were easy for me to achieve alone in meditation, but here there were other people present, and I found myself interacting with them in a remarkably fluid and spontaneous manner. Moreover, Moss himself—whatever his lingual preferences—was obviously dedicated to this effort and won my regard on that score alone.

At the end of the day we gathered in a circle to share our experiences and hear Moss talk more about his work. Mostly what he talked about was *commitment*, which, of course, touched directly my own concerns. He quoted Jesus on the "lilies of the fields" and about the birds having their nests, the foxes their holes, but the son of Man having "nowhere to lay his head." He said that, in his own life, possessions were becoming less and less necessary, and he could imagine the time when he would be dispossessed of them entirely. He also talked about sexuality and how, although married, he was moving toward complete celibacy; and suddenly, I was really awed. I had never before met anyone who actually tried to practice *in detail* what Jesus and the other great spiritual masters had taught. Here was a man who not only talked about surrendering personal desire but was accomplishing it in fact! Then, like a bolt, it dawned on me: *Spirituality wasn't something you held as a belief or confined to specific periods of meditation, but something you lived day-to-day.* And although it was several months before I understood how to implement this insight in a disciplined way, eventually it was to become fundamental to my quest.

Finally, Moss concluded with a quote of Jesus' taken from *The Gospel According to Thomas*: "I shall choose you, one out of a thousand, and two out of ten thousand, and they shall stand as a single one." This was only meant as a general thought and not aimed at anyone in the room, but still, I held my breath. If he had looked at me at that moment, or given the least sign, I would have, like Peter and Andrew by the Sea of Galilee, "left my nets straight away" and followed him to Sky Hi or wherever... But, of course, he didn't.

When I left the workshop, then, it was with a touch of sadness.

I felt as though I had both found and lost a guru in a single day. Nevertheless, the following weekend I drove up to the Sky Hi Ranch just to look the place over. As soon as I pulled into the driveway, however, Athena appeared at my shoulder scowling belligerently to indicate that this was all a mistake, and I knew she was right. The moment had passed.

Someone came out of the house to see what I wanted, but I simply said that I had lost my way, which was true enough. I was on my own once again.

Driving back to the city, I wondered if I would ever have a bona fide guru. I suspected not and brooded, but Athena stayed with me and, in spite of my own state of depression, seemed to be in unusually high spirits. It struck me as strange at the time, and I wondered if she was actually capable of jealousy. In retrospect, I'm convinced she was.

For the next couple of weeks I existed in a kind of limbo.

Samantha was the crucial link between my Dream and waking life, but she hadn't called since the night outside the pizza place, and I was feeling too bloodied to call her. Thus, all further conscious action on my part was frustrated. My subconscious, however, seemed at least tentatively pleased with the way things were going, as the following dream, recorded on December 14th, indicates:

> I am in a plane that's out of control. We manage to land in the middle of a deserted city. The other passengers abandon me with just enough fuel to take the plane a few miles more, but unfortunately, I don't know how to fly. Still, I study the problem—contemplating possible angles for takeoff to clear buildings, flight paths between telephone lines, etc. Finally, I make a go at it, but it's unclear whether or not I am successful.
>
> I end up in a hotel. It's off season and there are only a few guests. Dr. Jung and his wife are there, bossing everyone around. Finally, I grow sick of his pompous attitude and tell him he is a sanctimonious idiot; also, that his wife is a bitch. Jung and his wife vanish and everyone else is immensely relieved.

> I am cuddling a baby—an infant who makes goo-goo sounds. I answer in its own language, and we are suddenly having the most marvelous communication. Dr. Moss appears and says, "You see, it's not the intellect." I think of logs bursting in a fire and have a new name— Popping Wood!

The first episode neatly summed up my present predicament. My guardians had abandoned me with my old life—the "plane" and "fuel," representing its conscious and subconscious aspects, respectively, which I would still need to take me "a few miles more."

The second episode confirmed my dismissal of worldviews as holding any ultimate answers, the last of which to attract me had been Jung's own model. No longer would I be tyrannized by metaphorical "truths," and this, of course, was a great relief to the other forces at work in my psyche.

Finally, the third episode foreshadowed what would eventually be required, for, in the words of Jesus, "Whosoever shall not receive the kingdom of God *as a little child*, he shall not enter therein." Exactly how to become as a little child, however, was not spelled out. I still didn't know "how to fly."

But Moss's workshop, and now this dream, strengthened my conviction that the answer must lie in experience, specifically the experience of higher states of consciousness. Consequently, I increased my efforts at yoga, doing exercises from Dr. Mishra's book both in the mornings and in the evenings when I got home from work; and slowly, I began to make a sort of dark progress.

On several occasions, one or the other of my hands would slip spontaneously into yoga nidra. After a while I learned to control this phenomenon and eventually could put both hands and arms into a feelingless state at will. Once, while concentrating on the "third eye,"[20] I fell into quite a deep trance in which my whole body seemed to disappear in a sea of blackness. Suddenly, there were rings of red light in my head, and I felt sucked through them into some other realm that was absolutely void.

Although such experiences were intriguing, they were not always pleasant. I began to develop mild headaches and neck pains, and one morning I woke up with a swollen eye. My secretary called her father, who was an optometrist, and he said it was probably caused by eye strain from reading in poor light, but I was convinced that it had something to do with the yoga sessions. Much of the time, too, I felt dammed up with "energy," and this was very uncomfortable.

Except for work, I spent these weeks alone, walking the hills behind my house, doing yoga, or simply mulling things over in front of the fireplace. My earlier intimations that I should be "serving humanity" now became obsessive thoughts, but I couldn't figure out what it was I was supposed to do.

One night I noticed two spiders scrambling around on a freshly placed log, trying to escape the flames. I took pity on them and rushed to the rescue. One, I retrieved; the other, I couldn't. He refused the proffered shovel. "No one can be saved who doesn't want to be," I thought gloomily, and mused on how I had once fancied myself Samantha's Knight and Protector. Now I had been reduced to Knight of Spiders, Protector of Bugs and was only half successful at that!

In the middle of December, Kay invited me to a party. I drove into Hollywood, parked the Audi, and started walking up the street toward her apartment building. On the way I suddenly began to *witness* a string of fantasies spinning full speed through my head. Like an athlete psyching himself up for the big game, I pictured myself at the party being witty, charming, and attractive. But what was I out to "win"? Did I want to impress people? Command their admiration? Score with a lady? I was shocked to find myself guilty on all counts. Here I was, the great nonconformist, preparing to shape the minutest details of my manner and speech in expectation of what others would think of me!

Even more disturbing, I realized that the entire process was beyond my control. These fantasy images arose in consciousness independent of my will, automatically molding my behavior to fit an external situation. Still, there had to be some inner impulse for their creation. Vaguely, I thought I discerned in them the workings of some unspecified sexual desire. But before I could be sure, the images vanished as abruptly as had my "combativeness" that time last summer with Samantha. My whole consciousness cleared, and I walked into Kay's apartment with a mind that was completely empty. It turned out to be one of the strangest evenings of my life.

Kay rushed over, grabbed my arm, and began introducing me to all her friends, but I had nothing to say to anybody. It was as though I had lost my script and forgotten my lines. I just listened to Kay's nimble banter and envied her dexterity with words, but couldn't participate. After a while she dashed off to greet someone else, and I wandered into the living room. Three guys were talking about something or other with their girls hanging on their arms. One of the guys was dominating the conversation, but the others didn't seem to mind. They were all having a good time, and yet, in some peculiar way, I understood that they were also all *asleep*. This wasn't a judgment, just an observation, and I didn't know whether to envy them or not.

Finally, I wound up in the kitchen, talking to a girl from Great Neck. She told me about her life working as a film animator and how she also enjoyed playing golf, swimming, skiing, traveling, etc. She made it sound rich and exciting, but to me her words mattered not at all. Suddenly, it was as though I could penetrate right into her soul, and what I felt there was an enormous loneliness. I was amazed, and my heart went out to her, but still I had nothing to say. I stayed with her just so she would have someone to talk to and I must have been a good listener, because she talked a lot. Then, halfway through, I realized something else. I could have taken her home to my bed right then and there, but I no longer had the impulse. It was simply gone.

When I left Kay's around midnight, I felt a new, curious freedom, but also terribly isolated. Everyone seemed to be dreaming the same dream except me. Although I didn't understand it then, the old familiar attachments—not just to externals but to internal desires as well—were being cast aside, one by one, like a ship casting off its hawsers before it sails.

I didn't do anything special for my birthday. I went to work, came home, walked Captain Blood, and cooked dinner like any other night. Nor, in spite of earlier misgivings, did turning forty bother me at all. I was even mildly awed that I had made it this far. Later, Colette called to wish me happy birthday, and I was glad to hear from her. Then Samantha called to say the same thing. I thought it kind of her to remember but had no illusions that it signaled any major shift in our relationship. At this point, we were just sort of estranged friends, and there was nothing to be done about it.

What is Truth?

A few days later I attended a Christmas show and party put on by our little theater group. Since breaking up with Elanore, I had stayed away from the weekly meetings, but now I felt the need for company. Everyone was in a festive mood when I arrived, and most of the performances were comedic, in keeping with the spirit of the occasion.

Midway through the program, however, a lone woman singer took her place in a single spotlight and, without fanfare or costume, treated us to a passionate, a capella rendition of the old Protestant hymn *Amazing Grace*. I had heard this hymn many times before, yet as I listened to the words,

> I once was lost, but now I'm found,
> was blind, but now I see...

they suddenly took on a new and unmistakable meaning. This was no cold and pious composition of some dogma-ridden clergyman but the direct testimony of a soul who had somehow found his way *home*. And through the medium of this song, he was telling us all that—yes, it *was* really possible, and oh, so unsurpassingly sweet! In the darkened theater, tears rushed to my eyes, for I too knew myself to be blind and lost, while everything in me ached to *see*. But how—*how?*

Two days before Christmas, I bought Samantha some Indian moccasins and dropped them off at her house. She had a gift for me, as well, but was in bed with a bad cold, so I didn't stay long. The next day I drove down to the Valley to get my car washed and shop for a Christmas Eve dinner. Carols blared from the radio, and all the shop windows were hung with decorations, but I just couldn't get in the mood. I saw a formation of geese against the steel-gray sky flying south on their way home, and I envied them. I too wanted to go home, but home was far away, and even my Dream now seemed distant.

Back at my cabin I tried to read, but thoughts of Colette kept popping into my head. What was she doing this Christmas Eve? Was she alone? sad? despairing? I felt overwhelmed with guilt.

After dinner I sat down with Captain Blood in front of the fireplace, and we opened our presents. I had bought him a big soup bone that he gnawed on contentedly. For me, there were a couple of bottles of liquor from the office and Samantha's package, but that was all. I saved Samantha's gift for last. It contained two books, *The Wisdom of the Heart* by Henry Miller and a slim volume titled *Rebel in the Soul* that I had never heard of. I gave it a quick glance-through. Apparently, it was a translation of some ancient Egyptian text, but I was too sad and weary to read anything. I went to bed early, hoping to get Christmas over with, but it was not to be so easy.

In the middle of the night I woke up with a verse from the song *Old Man River* running through my head. It told of a black dockhand who was tired of living but afraid of death—which might have reflected well my gloomy disposition, except for one thing: I was tired of living, all right, but suddenly I was no longer afraid of death.

I lay in bed in the dark and began to fantasize about killing myself. At first, it started the way most such fantasies do, where you see the pained reactions of others to your death or, better yet, imagine that no one will miss you at all, thus lending the ultimate in poignance to self-pity. I had had such fantasies before in my life and was not much disturbed, knowing that they usually ran their course and petered out on their own. This time, however, something quite different happened.

I started to examine the possibility of suicide from a completely rational standpoint. I thought of Norman Garey and how everyone seemed to recover from his death with remarkable ease, and I saw that the same would be true of most of the people I knew. No doubt Garey's immediate family had suffered deeply, and so would mine. But even if I lived, it seemed inevitable that they would suffer because of me—Colette, my parents, perhaps Samantha, too. Wouldn't it be better to get it over with in one fell swoop?

I wasn't hasty. I tried to examine the alternatives. One would be to stay in the film business and go back to Colette. By doing so, however, I would betray The Dream, and somehow, I was certain that this would bring a worse calamity than death. A second course would be to do nothing, just let my life wind down and flicker out. But this seemed rather weak and cowardly. The third alternative that presented itself was again suicide.

In this connection I remembered something Colette had said to me a month or so after I left her, "It's as though you were dead, but not dead," and I could see that this was true. How could she be expected to start a new life with me hovering in the wings? I was like an MIA (missing in action)—and perhaps I really was. Perhaps I was supposed to die in Nam. Perhaps the whole meaning of my Dream was not that I would escape death but only that it would be cruelly postponed. In any case, it was better to be a confirmed corpse, I thought, than a walking ghost.

With the other options discarded, suicide now began to seem truly the most rational and honorable course. No matter how I looked at it, life ended in tragedy, and once this fact was recognized, what could be the point of prolonging it?

I sat up in bed and opened the drawer of the little night table where I kept my .45 Colt Commander. I had bought the pistol during my days as a revolutionary back in San Francisco. It was black and spotless, and I picked it up in the palm of my hand, feeling its cold weight and admiring its flawless, functional design. Almost instinctively, I grasped the slide and jacked a round into the chamber with no idea of what I was going to do next, except that I was very calm and seemed to be moving toward some sort of final resolution. Then I heard a voice calling out sharply —"Stop!"

It was a woman's voice—either Athena's or Samantha's—I couldn't be sure which; nor could I tell if it was inside or outside my head. Quickly, I replaced the pistol in the drawer and looked around the room, but there was no one to be seen. Next, I noticed that my right hand was shaking very badly. For some reason this frightened me. I jumped out of bed, turned on the light, and began pacing in a kind of panic. I now knew I didn't want to die, but a struggle still seemed to be going on. Looking for some distraction, I picked up the first book at hand. It was *Rebel in the Soul*.

I started to read it mechanically, forcing my eyes to the page, at first hardly comprehending the words at all. Slowly, however, they began to form themselves into sentences, then whole paragraphs, and I was astonished by what I read.

The text was a spiritual treatise on suicide, cast in the form of a dialogue between a man and his soul. The man despairs of his life and wants to end it, hoping to find peace in death. His soul, however, argues that the quest for peace is a task of life, not death. The debate continues back and forth, but eventually the soul wins. The man relinquishes all thoughts of death, and by the time I finished the book, so had I.

I said a silent prayer of thanks to Samantha, then remembered that there was still a round in the chamber of my .45. I went back to the night table, removed the bullet, and never contemplated suicide again.

My commitment to The Dream was now complete. I had overcome the last temptation to avoid my fate, which was the temptation of death itself. But all freedom of action had been exhausted in this struggle. For better or worse, there was nothing left to do but surrender my own will, submit to The Dream, and live it out.

I had found my destiny at last.

The day after Christmas I walked out to my shamanic spot overlooking the canyon just to breathe the new air. My journal entry for that date reads,

> On the hill, a sudden change of perception—I don't know how to describe it. A touch of God. The world's suddenly *personal* and, at the same time, I feel as though a universal eye were peering through my skull.

During the following week, between Christmas and New Year, one of my assistant story editors brought his two-year-old son into the office. Moved by some sudden impulse, I put a Beatles tape on the stereo, swooped the child up, and began to dance. He laughed and bobbed in my arms, and we goo-goo-ed galore. Then I realized this was exactly the scene in my dream about learning to fly and felt washed away on a current of love.

Two days before the end of 1982 I was sitting at home in my cabin, thumbing through a magazine I had just bought. It was called *Communities* and contained a directory of spiritual and intentional communities scattered across the country. Each listing was accompanied by a paragraph or two describing the community's philosophy, population, location, etc. They ranged from Hare Krishna ashrams to Christian monasteries, from multiple-marriage families to middle-class co-ops.

As I read through this directory, the vague notion of a trip began to take shape in my thoughts. Perhaps I would write a book or make a documentary film? In the next moment, all my physical surroundings disappeared to be replaced by a startling vision. I saw myself climbing forlornly over the scattered ruins of our own decimated civilization. There seemed to be nothing left but bare rock and broken concrete. But then I noticed small rivulets of fresh water pouring out of the stones, all flowing together into a single torrent. And as I watched this torrent gather momentum, a voice, booming out of nowhere (masculine, for once) declared, "A thousand springs become a mighty stream!"

The vision dissolved, and I was back in my cabin, but with a sudden and clear understanding of the service I was to perform. I would start a magazine, after all, only it would be a visual one. I would buy some video equipment and haul it around to these various communities, letting them make a newsletter to be exchanged with other communities. I would call it *The Here and Now Video Newsletter*.

A few days later I asked the *I Ching* (the oracular Chinese *Book of Changes*) what it thought of the idea. The hexagram I threw was number 35—*Li K'um*, Clinging Fire, Receptive Earth. The Judgement reads as follows:

> PROGRESS. The powerful prince
> Is honored with horses in large numbers.
> In a single day he is granted audience three times.

and The Image:

> The sun rises over the earth:
> The image of PROGRESS.
>
> Thus the superior man himself
> Brightens his bright virtue.[21]

I took this answer to be an auspicious sign.

Eight:
Adventures in the Subtle Realm

By the end of January, I had written letters to some twenty communities asking if they would be interested in participating in a video newsletter. Within a few weeks replies began to trickle back, most of them favorable. I decided to leave in the spring, mostly for weather considerations, and figured the project would take me all summer to complete. What I would do beyond that, I had not the slightest idea. But just to be able to formulate these limited plans was an enormous psychological relief. It meant that my life in Hollywood had, at last, a definite termination point. Moreover, my thirst to perform some useful service would, at least temporarily, be assuaged. But I also knew that, although on one level this would be a temporal trek in time and space, on another it would be a spiritual journey inward, across the geography of my soul, and I had to prepare myself on both levels.

For the next several months, yoga meditation became the central focus of my life, affecting all other activities. In January I recorded this "typical day":

> I awake, but it is not yet true awakening. My head is still filled with leftover thoughts from yesterday, snatches of dreams, fantasies, and future plans. Groggily, I dress and take Captain Blood for a walk. Now my head starts to clear. Thoughts recede. I become aware of color, the warm wind, leaves, coyote chatter, the air-baked earth, twigs like pieces of modem sculpture strewn along the path.
>
> Back in my cabin, I meditate. Feeling prana is easy now, but I no longer try just for intensity. Instead, I experiment, playing with all sorts of subtle "energies," letting them swirl into patterns that liquify the flesh and rearrange the world. After 45 minutes or so I feel very light and high.
>
> This state lasts through the drive to work and well into the morning. Sometime before noon I start to come down, called back to the world by the demands of my job. But more and more I catch myself in the

midst of this mundane activity like a dreamer who partially awakens from a dream but can't quite pull himself free.

By 4:00 p.m. I'm watching the clock, starting to disengage again, longing to be home with my books, my meditations, my soul.

Evening on the Mountain. Build a fire. Stir-fry some meat and vegetables. Do a little yoga. Read the *Gita*, and *Gospels*, *Wisdom of the Heart*—wherever my instincts take me. Everything interlocks now, is cross-referenced; a hundred sign posts, like old friends, all pointing to the same verdant land that rises from the misty sea.

In his book, Mishra instructs the practitioner to listen for *nadam*, a sacred sound heard in the mind during meditation. I listened and heard it, a kind of steady, musical hum that drowned out all external noise. I was thrilled. I also continued to experiment with stepping through the red rings that appeared in my brain. Sometimes it was blissful, sometimes frightening, but I could never stay "on the other side" for more than a few moments. Actually, there was nothing there to stay for, and occasionally I wondered what the point was of all these psychic phenomena. But I persisted.

In February I recorded this entry in my journal:

All week I feel old structures crash and dissolve. Categories give way to tidal flux; thoughts evaporate in violet light and subtle fire. I go deeper into meditation and end up higher. I extend this liquidity into other areas of daily life. Morning exercises become a dance; music forms a language. Even reflexive business decisions can be seen against a broader field, like electric arcs leaping from pole to pole.

This morning during meditation I felt emptied of mass, born aloft on a wave of pure movement, then catapulted into a space between "me" and the "world." But unleashing such energies exacts a price. Once again my eyes look like someone has smashed a fist between them, and I am developing a sty. Oddly, I am not worried by this disfigurement. I look in the mirror and see my bruises as somehow honorable; purple hearts in the campaign to free the soul.

This period of intense yoga meditation climaxed in the following experience:

This morning while doing yoga I slip into an easy trance, almost too easy. I am filled with orange light that swirls freer than ever before. Nadam, usually only a hum, now sounds like a small roar. I stay here for some time, shuffling in and out of the mirror of my mind. Finally, I decide to come down, but the thought occurs to me to try one last experiment. I open my eyes while still extremely high.

The world looks a shade brighter but otherwise the same: a mosaic of greenery beyond the window; the raw, wet wood of the sun deck; the white, white of the window frame—too white! I start to slide out through my eyes and suddenly I am swept away on a thunderous wave of energy which rushes through me, body and soul.

I panic, hold tight to the floor, and the wave rolls on, but I also remember Castaneda's injunction not to give in to fear. I grit my teeth and let go. The wave comes again, but more gently—swoosh! I break off meditation and go into the kitchen to do the breakfast dishes. As I look out the kitchen window, the wave comes once more, but gentler still. Then it is over.

I feel tired, physically drained, but somehow washed clean. All morning my mind is clear and empty, and I am aware of sounds, sights, smells in sharp relief. I try to notice some fundamental change in myself—a greater wisdom perhaps, but there seems to be none.

But four days later I recorded this:

Since my "wave" experience, meditation—indeed, my life-has shifted into a higher gear. A mild samadhi state is now easy to achieve. Every day I experiment with different aspects of this realm. Sometimes it's sounds, sometimes smells, sometimes visions—but these are just the sensory games I play. Deeper is a growing awareness of my own thought processes, much influenced by reading Krishnamurti, who stresses attention to thoughts and emotions. This *witnessing* now carries over into my work-a-day world and makes life both more difficult and more interesting: *difficult* because the actual details of the job are harder to keep track of, but *interesting* because I am more aware of my interactions with other people. Even when I am alone, like driving to and from work, my thought-flow is now constantly interrupted by this witness, watching thoughts come and go and making them all seem less significant.

Last night, lying in bed, I played with "knowledge." I began by recognizing that I was envious of people who are very knowledgeable, but what makes them so? They are obviously easy talkers and have good recall of facts and figures, but do they actually have this knowledge present in their heads at all times? To see how it works, I slowly and repeatedly summoned a single fact into consciousness, "Columbus discovered America in 1492," and realized that this knowledge was only present *as I summoned it*. In the times between thinking about this fact, I was completely ignorant of it.

Although seemingly trivial, this little discovery presaged a fundamental shift in my approach to meditation and even the whole spiritual path. For one thing, in the past *witnessing* had been largely a spontaneous occurrence. Now, for the first time, I had consciously used and directed it toward a specific phenomenon. But far more importantly, in all my previous experiences witnessing had been limited to an awareness of mental activity itself—never before to the space *between* that activity. In touching ignorance, I had inadvertently touched emptiness—or consciousness itself, which is the real value and fruit of Attention.

At the time, however, I was still much too dazzled by the more spectacular production of subtle sights, sounds, and energies engendered by Mishra's yogic techniques to appreciate the true significance of this discovery. After all, to someone who so recently had been a thorough skeptic, such subtle phenomena seemed to provide incontrovertible evidence that spiritual transformation was really underway. Thus, for a while I was more than content to bask in the glow of these psychic fireworks, much like the man in the famous Sufi story who, having lost his keys in the dark by his doorstep, nevertheless searches for them under the lamp post because that's where the light is. And, to the extent that this light kept me searching, it played its role. Moreover, as these new experiences served increasingly to detach me from the old conditions of my life, changes—if not a transformation—were inexorably and indeed being wrought.

A journal entry on March 8th reads,

> Yesterday I buy $1,000 worth of video equipment from a guy at work: camera, recorder, cables, tripod, etc. In the evening he comes over to my house to show me how it works. We set it all up in the living room and run some tests. I ask him to leave the equipment assembled and, when he goes, I sit alone with my new "electronic friend," feeling quite thrilled. This is the passport to my future, unborn life. Only twelve weeks to go, and as we used to say in Nam, "I'm short!"

Although I hadn't yet told Lewis I was leaving, the fact that I knew I was made a difference. With no personal future in the business to worry about, I actually became a better executive. If a project required that such-and-such be done, I no longer cared whose toes I stepped on as long as the decision was the right one for the project. I also began to see through other people's games more clearly. I learned to read fear and insecurity in moist palms, tapping fingers, and dry throats, and I noticed that the more arrogant and overbearing someone might appear, the more terrified that person was inside. The whole industry seemed to be fueled by fear, and realizing this, the last of my own envies and jealousies of more "successful" colleagues fell away.

For the first time, too, I felt the iron grip of guilt over leaving Colette loosen its hold somewhat. Dimly, I was beginning to perceive that this inordinate self-induced suffering masked an equally inordinate conceit, that behind my very eagerness to shoulder *all* responsibilities for what had happened lurked a secret and egotistical belief in my own God-like autonomy. But it was this very belief that was being undermined by the whole course of my journey, forcing me to confess my essential impotence and, thus, throwing me into the arms of God, or Fate, or whatever Power ruled the cosmos.

Finally, I invited Colette up to Topanga for dinner one night so that she could see what my life had become. I didn't expect her forgiveness, but at least, I thought, if she knew I hadn't abandoned her to go chasing starlets, it might help. I tried to tell her something of what I was going through— my own confusion and helplessness, and indeed, she seemed to understand a little more. I was also relieved to learn that she had gotten a job. At the very least, it would get her out of the house and mixing with people again. Besides, I had been sending her money regularly, but this would end in a couple of months, and eventually, she would have to fend for herself. Then all I'd be able to offer her would be my prayers.

Even my relationship with Samantha finally stabilized, but only after a couple more frustrating months. Throughout most of January and February, she maintained a cool distance in spite of occasional attempts on my part to bridge the gap between us. Every once in a while, however, the barriers would come down. Suddenly, she would call out of the blue, all warm and effervescent, and we'd end up having dinner together, which usually went well. Yet, within a few days she would inexplicably retreat once more, and when I'd ask for another date, she would put me off with vague excuses. Knowing her fragility with people, I tried to be patient, but eventually, my patience began to wear thin.

One morning during just such an exasperating conversation, I told her off and figured that was the end of it. Several hours later, however, she phoned me at work to complain that I had sent her solar plexus into an uproar. We argued some more, and I hung up, but now my own solar plexus was churning so badly that I could hardly concentrate on the day's business. Finally, I sent her a dozen roses, and the next day she called again, this time gushing words of love and tenderness. I felt sure we had been reconnected, but it was not to last. A week later she was as cool as ever, and I got really pissed off.

The whole pattern of our relationship seemed to have become nothing more than a prolonged and childish flirtation, and I was as annoyed with myself for succumbing to it as I was with her for perpetuating it. What's more, through all this Athena had remained uncharacteristically silent, thus depriving me of her counsel. I began to think that Samantha's relevance to my life had run its course, but this proved to be premature.

The turning point came in the beginning of March during a terrific rainstorm. Much of the power in L.A. was out, and when I arrived at work the building had been shut down. On my way home I heard radio reports of tornadoes in the area. Then I heard something else as well—Athena's silky, familiar whisper informing me that Samantha was stuck in her house and urging me to drive by there. This time I didn't bother to argue.

The narrow road that threaded its way up through the rain-soaked hills to Samantha's apartment was flooded in places and strewn with debris but by no means impassable. Nevertheless, Athena had been right. I found Samantha sitting alone in the dark, wrapped in blankets, cold and depressed. Nor did she resist when I told her to get dressed and come with me.

I took her back to my cabin and built a fire. After a while she started to talk, mostly about her feelings of isolation—her own "dark night of the soul," and all I did was listen. I already knew something about her history of disappointing relationships, and slowly I began to understand how these past hurts and fears stood sad guard over the gateways to her soul. She talked, too, about how hard it was trying to live up to Moss's concept of unconditional love, which had become her great spiritual hope and goal. And whereas in the past I had dismissed such talk as vague idealism, the phrase suddenly acquired a specific and illuminating meaning for my own life.

I saw that unconditional love had nothing to do with hugging strangers in workshops, or meditating on the heart chakra, or throwing oneself open to the world in a general way; but rather it was the most fundamental moment-to-moment demand of the very love that already existed in and animated my immediate and concrete relationship with Samantha. From the beginning, this love had been wholly unearned and itself unconditional—a spontaneous gift, a wild wave of divine energy that rushed into my life, turning everything upside down, transforming and reshaping all its elements toward its own righteous ends. Yet here I was, trying now to impose upon this sacred process my own thoroughly personal and petty conditions: I would go on loving Samantha only *if* she ceased flirting, only *if* she confided in me, that is, only *if* she responded in kind. My real task, however, was precisely to ignore all this, to love her *in spite of* all this—in a word, *un*-conditionally—so that this love would be free to continue working its mysterious alchemy unconstrained in the depths of my being. This was Samantha's true meaning and purpose for my life, the koan of Amor, the path of Bhakti by which, in Campbell's words, the kingship of my own proper Castle would be won.

Later, when the electricity came back on, we returned to her place, cooked dinner, and watched *That's Entertainment* on TV. Afterwards, she played a record of Walt Disney songs that someone had given her for Christmas. We sang *Zippity-Do-Da, Zippity-Day*—which, as unromantic as it sounds, I'll always think of as "our song"—and laughed and joked that it seemed to take Fire and Flood to bring us together.

In the end, however, what was really unusual about this day was that, except for the flood, nothing unusual happened—no ESP, no weird mystical tensions, no intimations of other realms—we simply had fun. After that I gave up all fantasies of the future and took each day as it came. We continued to see each other regularly until I left in June, and it was the first real stretch of time we had ever spent together relaxed and happy.

Back in February, I had also signed up as a volunteer at The Center for Healing Arts, which meant helping out with such menial chores as setting up chairs for lectures and workshops, collecting donations, passing out fliers, and cleaning up afterwards. The program was designed to allow people with limited incomes to attend these various events at reduced rates in exchange for their labor, but this was not my motive. It was through the Center that I had been exposed to people like Joseph Campbell and Richard Moss, and I just wanted to contribute something back. Consequently, I never volunteered for events based on my own interest but on the Center's need for bodies, so when I got a call asking if I could lend a hand at a Saturday workshop entitled *Rebirthing*, I said yes without any idea of what rebirthing was.

The morning I was due at the Center I woke up late and had to skip meditation in order to get there on time. I had also been out with a friend the night before and was feeling the effects of a little too much wine, so I was not in the best of moods. What the hell is rebirthing, anyway? I thought. It sounded flaky, and for the first time I almost regretted having volunteered.

When I arrived at the Center I tried to perform my duties cheerfully, spreading cushions around the main room and checking people in at the door downstairs. Eventually, I got into the swing of it, but only after the last person checked in did I remember that I was actually supposed to participate in this nonsense. Skeptically, I trudged upstairs to join the group—fourteen participants and our rebirthing instructor, Marsha Sheldon.

Marsha was a big woman in her early thirties with a generous and earthy manner that bespoke her Southern roots. Rebirthing, she explained, was a process of deep-chest breathing designed to evoke traumatic childhood experiences extending back to and including actual physical birth. The theory was that, by reliving one's birth, a rebirthee could be released from emotional and physical blocks incurred at that time. Marsha warned, however, that other phenomena might also occur, such as the channeling of higher energies, visions, or merely heavy emotional states unrelated to specific memories. The idea was not to try to anticipate anything in particular but work with whatever came up. The rebirther's job, on the other hand, was simply to sit close by, monitor and encourage the rebirthee's breathing, and be available for moral support. An average session lasted two hours.

After demonstrating the breathing technique and giving us each a chance to practice, Marsha asked us to divide up into pairs for the afternoon's work. An Armenian girl named Miranda picked me and, during lunch, explained that she had some personal problems involving her husband that she hoped to work out. I was delighted. Although I instinctively liked Marsha, I had little faith in the whole procedure and decided to dedicate the day to helping Miranda.

When lunch was over Miranda and I retired to a large, high-ceilinged room downstairs. The room had no windows, so the only illumination came from the half-open door. Miranda asked me to go first, and again I was pleased. I resolved to make mine a quick session and give Miranda the lion's share of the afternoon.

I stretched out on my back and closed my eyes. Miranda massaged my limbs to relax the muscles, then covered me with a blanket. I began breathing: long, deep inhalations that became equally long and deep exhalations, all without interruption—a technique called the *connected breath*. After half an hour I felt very relaxed but not much else. Marsha stopped in to check on us, commented that my breathing was excellent, and left. Still nothing was happening. Then, quite suddenly, a kind of dream image appeared in my mind. It was of a pregnant, naked woman —the Madonna of the Apocalypse—who looked a little like Samantha, and I realized that I was the new life she was carrying. This was followed by two other images, or series of images. In the first I was a child wandering around my own childhood searching for something. In the second I was a very old man lying on my deathbed with Miranda's hand on my forehead, but I felt quite all right. It was okay to die. I wanted to tell Miranda this but found the effort to speak too great.

In spite of the fact that these images were very vivid, and I could observe them with all my waking cognitive powers intact, I didn't consider them particularly profound. Perhaps after my White Heats and the Great Man Dream I was a bit jaded. In any case, I began to try to conjure something more awesome.

As I mused thus, Miranda's face appeared in my sight, and for a moment I thought my eyes must have inadvertently opened. Quickly, however, I realized that this was not the case. That's funny, I thought, I must be seeing Miranda through closed lids. The next thing I knew I was looking at the ceiling which, however, appeared to be impossibly close—in fact, in some way I seemed to be *on* the ceiling! Then suddenly it dawned on me that I had *left my body*, my sole connection to it being the steady sound of my own breathing heard far below.

Miraculously, I was free of all fleshy bonds. I soared. I romped. I expanded and contracted into all the various nooks and crannies of the room, like a child let loose on a sunny day. I was intoxicated by my disembodiment, and the only words I could think of to describe it were *at play in the fields of the Lord*. Mind had parted from matter. The genie was out of the bottle. I seemed to have become pure consciousness, and it was one of the most blissful experiences I had ever had.

I don't know how long I continued in this state, perhaps for half an hour or so. Eventually, however, the effort to maintain respiration became increasingly difficult. I sensed that if I stopped breathing altogether, I could travel farther afield, maybe even beyond the walls of the room and out into open space itself. It would be so temptingly easy. But I also remembered Marsha's instructions that whatever happened we were to continue breathing. I decided not to chance it. Now the problem became how to return to my body. It seemed like such an arduous task to stuff all this gaseous consciousness back into the compact hunk of flesh below, nor was I really sure how to go about it.

Finally, I got an idea. With great effort, I activated my voice and asked Miranda to count backwards from ten to one. At first she could barely hear me, my words were so weak; so I repeated the request, forcing distant throat and tongue to work harder. This time she understood and began counting. I imagined myself an airplane coming in for a landing... 9, 8, 7,... I swooped lower... 6, 5, 4,... hit the runway... 3, 2, 1,... I was down, back in my body, and it was exactly the sensation of slipping a hand into a glove.

When I opened my eyes, there was Miranda hovering over me, smiling. I smiled back and told her all that had happened. I was elated and giddy, and when I tried to walk, I felt unsteady, like a sailor who has been at sea trying to readjust to dry land.

This euphoria lasted the rest of the afternoon during which Miranda and I switched roles, I becoming the rebirther, she the rebirthee. But her session was much less dramatic and not nearly as pleasant, full of troubling, dream-like images and ineffable anxieties. Later, when we all gathered upstairs again to share our experiences, Miranda's proved the more typical. Marsha, of course, was quick to point out that out-of-body experiences were not the primary goal of rebirthing, whose full therapeutic effects usually couldn't be realized in less than ten to twenty sessions. For me, however, this was unimportant. What the experience had done was to unequivocally demonstrate the plasticity of consciousness and hence, by implication, Reality. But it was also, paradoxically, the beginning of the end of my fascination with *experience* itself as a means to, or condition of, Gnosis. Still, I had a way to go before I fully exhausted this approach.

Three weeks later I had another, equally powerful experience at the Center, though of a slightly different order. This one involved Samantha. She, too, had become a volunteer, and we both signed up for a Saturday workshop given by a psychic healer named Valerie Hunt. As with rebirthing, the actual subject matter of the workshop was of only peripheral interest to me—a kind of smorgasbord of psychic techniques involving crystals, energy sharing, experiments in telepathy, etc. During a guided meditation, however, I had another vivid "conscious dream" similar to the images I had seen just before my out-of-body experience, only here the imagery was woven into an extended "story." Later I recorded it in my journal as follows:

> I am on a path headed for the sea. I descend onto the beach and start to swim. I know there are sharks in these waters and I'm afraid I'll run into one. What will I do? Suddenly, a great, dark shape swims before me, and I recognize instantly that it must be a shark. I think of turning back but am out too far.
>
> The shark swims closer, menacingly. Just then I realize what it is I must do and chuckle out loud. I grab onto the shark's back, letting it carry me. We take off full of terrible energy across the open sea. Then the shark plunges into the deep, zooming down, down to the very bottom. Here, there is a ruined city full of dead soldiers from Nam. We linger for a moment, but I realize I can't stay.
>
> The shark moves on, rising up toward the surface with incredible speed. We pass through a cloud of suspended plasma spheres, glowing white, each containing a human embryo, and I understand that these are the future generations waiting to be born. As we zoom through, I grab one and stuff it in my pocket.
>
> Breaking the surface I can see the New World, green and lush on the horizon. We start toward it. Now Samantha appears, sitting forlornly on a drifting raft, knees drawn up to her chest with arms wrapped around them, staring into space. I call her name, but she doesn't hear me. There

> is a line from the raft floating in the ocean. The shark snaps it up in his teeth, and we race forward with Samantha in tow.
>
> Between us and the horizon I can now see a string of archipelagoes stretching out like stepping stones to the virgin continent. I know I must stop at each one before proceeding on, but I can't imagine what will happen on these isles, and the dream ends.

There was nothing obscure about the symbols in this visualization, nor did they provide any startlingly new revelations about the course my life was already taking; therefore, as with the images prior to my out-of-body experience, I didn't regard them as particularly significant. While driving home after the workshop, however, Samantha described the visualization she had had during the same exercise, which meant that it had occurred simultaneously with mine. Later I recorded hers, too:

> Samantha walks down to the sea and starts to swim. She grows tired and reaches out for a raft that is floating by but is too exhausted to grab it. She sinks to the bottom and continues on through the earth's core to the other side. There she is surrounded by dolphins and becomes one of them. With great energy they dash through the depths, visiting a crystal palace. Then she zooms up out of the sea and off into the vast silence of outer space. She is tempted to stay there but can see the earth below—green and full of life-and is drawn back.

This exercise had started with us being asked simply to imagine we were walking along a path. There was no mention of where the path would lead—whether to mountains, or desert, or forests, or sea. In this light, the parallelism between our two "dreams" seemed quite remarkable—both of us swimming in an ocean, I with sharks, she with dolphins; the image of the raft; a visit to the depths; and the final goal of a continent or planet drawing us on. Could such correlations really be written off to pure chance? I just couldn't believe it. By every definition this was telepathy, and a rather vivid demonstration of it, at that.

Although these two experiences—being out-of-body and telepathic dream-sharing—occurred spontaneously and without any conscious effort on my part, there was one project during this period that I undertook very consciously which proved of great benefit. This was a six-week Dream Workshop conducted by Marsha who, I learned, was into other things besides rebirthing. It was attended by seven other participants, all of them women.

What is Truth?

The object of this workshop was to record and discuss our dreams to see what sort of guidance they might be providing for whatever transitions were going on in our lives. Marsha had recommended that we keep paper and pencil beside our beds so that we could transcribe our dreams immediately upon waking. I used a pocket-sized tape recorder instead. What Marsha had predicted, and what I found to be true, was that recording dreams not only made them easier to remember but actually seemed to encourage the production of more dreams with more meaningful content.

All in all, I had eight dreams that related directly to my quest. Here I'll describe only three of the most significant. The first is dated March 23rd.

> I am in a large warehouse-type building like the Oakland Army terminal (through which I processed on my way to Nam). I used to be a powerful emperor, but I am losing my sight and have to be guided by a woman, and I have to trust her. There are a lot of other people in the warehouse—mostly younger—and we seem to be going through long lines as part of an initial processing for something. No one seems to recognize that I am an emperor, but I understand. Such titles don't mean anything here.
>
> The first line leads to some kind of physical test that the younger people must undergo. I realize, however, that this isn't for me. Standing in another line I become restless. I zoom ahead, bypassing all sorts of checkpoints. Because I am older I know all the tricks and can get away with this easily, but my woman guide stops me. Gently, she suggests that we should do the endurance test. I realize that she is right and follow submissively.
>
> In the endurance test everyone has to pick an affliction and live it out. As we go through the line, I see that the people ahead of me have chosen to be crippled, or crazy, or hunchbacked, etc. When my turn comes, I choose to be mute. Now we must pass through a gauntlet of people who make fun of us and the afflictions we've chosen. The idea is to make us give it up by mocking us until it becomes unbearable. As I go through this gauntlet, people ask what my affliction is. I sign to them that I am mute. They begin to laugh and taunt me with such words as, "You think *that's* an affliction? That's not an affliction! Look at the people who have leprosy and such. Now there's an affliction!" But inside I'm frustrated and think, if you only knew how terrible it is not to be able to talk. Still, I keep my vow of silence.

The second dream I had on April 4th:

127

What is Truth?

I am standing on a rampart overlooking a canyon (much like Topanga) with hills beyond. There are several other people with me from my childhood. We are waiting to witness a demolition across the way. Suddenly, there is an enormous explosion and half the mountain crumbles. For a moment I think it's over, but then there is another series of explosions that topple houses and a large tower on the other side of the canyon. The explosions continue, and I start to get scared. Where will they end? Will they engulf *everything*? Finally, the explosions cease, and I can now see the ocean beyond where the hills used to be. I look down and notice the chief of the demolition crew standing in a box with headphones on and an electronic detonator panel in front of him, only he is wearing a tuxedo and looks more like the conductor of a symphony orchestra. He glances up at me with a sly, self-satisfied smile, then takes a very formal bow.

The third dream, which took place on April 18th, unfolded in two parts:

Part I: I am a commander in a war, in a trench behind some kind of barricade. But this is not Vietnam. It's some sort of modem, abstract war, A voice says, "Look!" and I look across the trenches, across this muddy, dark field and hilly countryside strewn with tangled barbed wire and pock-marked with shell holes. Rising up into the night is a fabulous, huge, glowing, temple-like Taj Mahal structure that reminds me of the spaceship at the end of the movie *Close Encounters*. I am at once awed but also a little suspicious. Then I notice a figure standing on one of the Temple's ramparts, and he is standing over us at such an angle that we are no longer protected by the trench and barricade, because he can fire right down into it. I start to rally my troops, urging them to take better cover, but a voice says, "No! He's not a malevolent soldier, not a malevolent being." I stop and look up, and sure enough, the figure hasn't moved or made any threatening gestures, so we cease trying to take defensive action...

Part II: Again I am in a war, the Second World War this time, and I am commanding a company or a battalion. We have surrounded a German stronghold and can wipe them out to a man. Indeed, there are cogent political reasons to do so—to prove our strength and make an example of them, and this seems to be what my superiors want. But suddenly, I feel an intense distaste for this realpolitik cynicism and rebel. Seizing a bullhorn, I call to the Germans and explain the situation, the logic of killing them all. But, I add, *for the love of a woman* I want them to surrender and put an end to this bloodshed.

It is probably obvious that the theme of all three dreams was surrender or submission. As the first dream opened, I had already surrendered my status as emperor, which is clearly a designation of *temporal* as opposed to *spiritual* power. The action of the dream, however, was still to take place in the temporal realm (the Oakland Army Terminal), but the tasks would now be different. In contrast to the "younger people," I was no longer required to undergo the physical tests that are a prelude to the supreme worldly trial of youth, which is war; yet the fact that these tests were conducted in the same arena implied that they would lead to an equally supreme but *spiritual* trial, or the spiritual equivalent of war. Nor would my worldly knowledge — knowing "all the tricks" — help me get through these tests. Instead, I had to submit to the guidance of a woman (Athena), because I was spiritually blind (as in the hymn *Amazing Grace*), and also as a test of my ability to keep silent. In other words, my discipline was to be the opposite of what is normally required in the temporal world: I had to refrain from action — or more properly, reaction (*vis-a-vis* Samantha, for example) — in spite of provocation. In worldly terms, such passivity would be seen as a weakness or an affliction. Here, however, it was a virtue. Thus, this dream defined my proper field of action — the temporal world — but also the new discipline required in it, i.e., the surrender of all personal will and action.

In the second dream I had to submit to a demolition, but here there was not even the suggestion of choice. I simply had to stand and watch fearfully as my Topanga hideaway (and all that was old, solid, and stable) was totally destroyed. The conductor's bow at the end, however, hinted that such wanton ruin had a larger purpose, namely, that destruction was necessary in order to reveal the open sea and, by implication, the way home. This dream, then, was really nothing more than a statement of a basic spiritual fact: The old must be cleared away before the new can enter, or as Jesus said, "Men do not put new wine into old bottles."

In Part I of the third dream I was in an actual war (not just a test), but again, it was clearly not any temporal conflict. It was an abstract, or spiritual, war, and I was in the midst of a classic *wasteland* (*a la* Parzival) when, suddenly, something awesome and *not of this world* appeared. My initial instinct — the instinct of temporal power — was to take defensive action. The dream, however, warned that this would be a mistake. Once more, I was required simply to do nothing, to cease reacting and thus allow the greater, spiritual power to manifest. This, too, is a fundamental principle of all spiritual paths.

Part II was more personal in that it dealt with my own specific burden of guilt. But although guilt is experienced as a temporal problem, its solution is ultimately spiritual, and the dream pointed a way to bridge this gap. Here, I was engaged in what was evidently a war against a temporal Evil symbolized by the Germans. This was significant, because I had always regarded World War II, unlike Vietnam, as socially and morally necessary and envied the moral shield carried by the Allied soldiers who liberated Europe from German occupation. In Vietnam, on the other hand, I had often felt more like a German storm trooper than a liberating ally. Thus, the war in this dream was really the continuing conflict of Good and Evil in my own heart—a conflict in which I had already shed so much emotional blood (as in the band-aid dream with Dr. Mark). Now, however, I realized that to press the fight further would only result in more bloodshed, but how was the conflict to be resolved?—a resolution necessary before the final stage of the quest could begin. The answer given was through *the love of a woman*. In the words of Virgil, I had found my *living stream* in Samantha Jones and was now *fit to bear holy things*.

Although none of these dreams radically altered the direction of my path, they did provide quite specific instructions for proceeding along it. What's more, as a result of working so intensely with them, I gained a new perspective on how to interpret dreams, in general. In the past (at least up until my Great Man dream), I had always regarded dreams as potential servants of my conscious interests. That is, by acquiring an understanding of my dreams, I assumed I would acquire greater understanding and, therefore, control over my conscious life. This, of course, is the standard psychotherapeutic motive for dream analysis.

Now, however, I began to view this relationship in reverse; it was "I" who was the servant of my dreams, or the subconscious Realm from which they issued, and my purpose in analyzing them became to understand better the tasks required of me by that Realm *even if these tasks seemed to run counter to my conscious interests*. Ultimately, the distinction between *conscious* and *subconscious* was seen to be an illusion and could be dispensed with, but as long as self-identification rested exclusively with

What is Truth?

"I" and the illusion persisted, I found that adopting this stance rendered dreams a virtually infallible source of spiritual guidance.

The actual format of the workshop was also interesting in that it provided an arena in which to test the instructions I had received in my first dream, namely, to keep quiet. I had never been timid about speaking my mind, but now, by restraining an impulse to babble out elaborate interpretations of the other participants' dreams and simply listening to them with an empty mind, I found I could experience them as if they had been mine. Consequently, I rarely entered into the discussions. Instead, I would just continue in this state of "empty listening." At some point, however, the dreamer herself would almost invariably make a secondary comment that answered a riddle posed by her dream. All I had to do then was draw her attention to this fact, and immediately, there would be gasps or blushes of recognition and delight.

After a while I developed something of a reputation among my fellow workshoppers for being particularly intuitive when it came to dreams—an ability I think they were especially surprised to find in a man. The truth is, this was really an application of Athena's first Commandment—Pay Attention—and thus something I myself had learned from a woman. In fact, I realized that ever since the beginning of my journey, I had been a student of the Feminine, starting with the Moon Goddess of Malta and then Athena and Samantha. It is in this light that a fourth dream I'll describe (which I actually had after the workshop) was significant:

> I am driving through a valley in a wilderness park with a friend from my San Francisco days named J.S. We spot a huge, silver-back bear and stop to follow it up a mountainside. At one point I am reluctant to go further, because it is a steep and dangerous climb and reminds me of an actual event in my youth when I almost fell off a mountain to my death. J.S., however, forges ahead, and I finally follow him. We end up in an Alaskan wilderness where we get lost. It turns out that this wilderness is Russian territory, and the Russians come to rescue us in a small plane. In all the commotion we've lost sight of the bear, and I comment to J.S. that I've been tracking this bear for twenty years but always lose him on this side of the mountain.
>
> As the Russian plane comes in for a landing at the airport, I find myself behind the controls. This is my first time handling a plane, but I'm getting the feel of it pretty good. The plane begins to drift a little, but I bring it back on course, and we make it to the terminal just fine. In the

waiting room I notice that J.S. is dressed like a shaman with a juju-bead necklace. We get a report about a movie being made somewhere on a foreign location where everything is going wrong—fighting on the set, misunderstanding among the crew, etc. In any case, it no longer has anything to do with me. At the terminal J.S. and I are joined by two other male friends from my youth whom I used to be very close to.

Finally, I am on my way back to Russia alone to find the bear, and there is an injunction that, this time, I must not get lost or give up.

Aside from clearly indicating that I was making progress on my quest (i.e., I had now "learned to fly") and that the quest itself was an adventure that I had been pursuing, in one form or another, for the last twenty years, this dream was unusual in its markedly masculine character. No women at all appeared in it, and the bear hunt is a primordially male endeavor. My tutelage at the knee of the Goddess, then, seemed to be drawing to a close. The journey was shifting back into masculine spheres, and soon I would need again all the male prowess I possessed.

The final workshop was held during the last week of April. We sat around Marsha in a semi-circle in the large basement room of the Center, each giving our appraisals. It was evening, and the room was lit by flat, artificial light reflecting smoothly off the bare, white-brick walls. I was situated near the middle of the semicircle, facing Marsha. A woman I'll call Esther sat on Marsha's right, both of them leaning against one of the walls. Suddenly, I noticed a kind of halo surrounding Esther's head and shoulders—a very distinct band of black and magenta light about one foot wide. I looked at Marsha, and she, too, had a halo, but hers was a dense, uniform gold. I thought it must be some kind of optical illusion. I blinked my eyes several times, then looked back at Esther. The black and magenta light was still there. What's more, it seemed to have a *meaning*. I knew from previous workshops that Esther was seriously ill, and the black and magenta light appeared to be a reflection of this condition. Again, I looked at Marsha, sitting serenely in her envelope of gold, and this too seemed expressive of her own, obvious tranquility. I had never believed in auras before, but I was seeing something now to which I could give no other name.

I mark this incident as the culmination of that stage on my path that might be called my Adventures in the Subtle Realm. This stage included all my yogic meditations aimed at raising higher energies, entering yoganidra, trying to open the Third Eye, listening to nadam, etc., as well as my out-of-body experience and the telepathic dream with Samantha. Taken together, they had served to further demonstrate and confirm what the Great Man Dream had already shown me, namely, that consciousness was not confined to any conventionally defined states, and reality superseded the limits of all purely materialistic metaphors. As such, these adventures had proved useful. But I was also starting to suspect that they were not going to bring me any closer to Gnosis. Could I have been wrong in assuming that Gnosis was a matter of *experience?* This was the prevailing New Age view, but I began to wonder if it was true.

When I listened to the conversations of people involved in workshops, they all seemed to be wrapped up in *process*—a favorite New Age word. The implication was that a spiritual path consisted in acquiring greater and greater openness to higher and more subtle realms of consciousness in what appeared to be a gradual, but also endless, progression, with all sorts of ups and downs in between. Even Samantha, whom I had thought on the brink of some revolutionary transformation after her first visit to Sky Hi, had settled into a more or less cyclic pattern of expanded and contracted states with no specific end in sight. Where was it all leading? Most people seemed unconcerned. To them the process *was* the transformation, and the transformation *was* the process.

Recently, however, I had begun to delve directly into the classics of mystical literature, and these sources did not confirm this popular opinion. According to the mystics, the spiritual path had a definite if ineffable goal that produced an abrupt and permanent transformation of one's whole life. Moreover, this transformation—or better, this *transcendence*—would obviate the necessity for all further processes, paths, and disciplines. Indeed, the very insistence that such a Gnosis was the real aim of all spirituality was the crucial difference that separated the mystics from their more conventional fellow religionists.

Furthermore, by now I had run across passages scattered through the literature that specifically warned against the type of phenomena I had been experiencing as either relatively unimportant or even a positive hindrance. After empowering his disciples to tread on serpents and drive out evil spirits, Jesus admonished them, saying,

> Notwithstanding in this rejoice not, that the spirits are subject unto you; but rather rejoice, because your names are written in heaven.[22]

and adds four verses later,

> For I tell you, that many prophets and kings have desired to see those things which ye see, and have not seen them; and to hear those things which ye hear, and have not heard them.[23]

An even more severe warning about *siddhis* (psychic powers) is given by Krishnamurti in his *Explorations into Insight*:

> I say in the process of clearing the house, this house [mind], there are a great many things that are going to happen. You will have clairvoyance, the so-called 'siddhis' and all the rest of it. They will all happen. But if you are caught in them, you cannot proceed further. If you are not caught in them, the heavens are open to you.[24]

What exactly would happen when the heavens opened? If it wasn't a matter of either concepts or experience, what else could it be? My mind boggled, and I began to think Gnosis must have more to do with *meaning* than with any specific phenomena, such as trances, telepathy, or states of consciousness. I suppose I had come to regard this world as a vast dream (as, in fact, it was often described by mystics) and to believe that in Gnosis one would suddenly be able to read all its symbols clearly and discern their meanings in relation to the whole. Perhaps I imagined, too, that the phenomenal world itself would become transparent, and I would actually see, standing behind all the multiplicity of things, an entirely different configuration to reality—something like Schopenhauer's *Harmonia Praestabilita* or Plato's *Universal Ideas*. But because Gnosis is prior to all images, it cannot be *imagined* beforehand. In the end, like Parzival, I would have to pierce "right through the middle" of both experience and concept, in all their forms, to find out.

Nine: Images of Light

At the end of the last chapter, I mentioned a shift in my reading toward the more classical works of mysticism. So far during my quest I had been influenced primarily by such renowned authors as lung and Campbell as well as a host of New Age scientists and thinkers like Fritjof Capra, David Bohm, and Ken Wilber. In order to support their sometimes differing points of view, however, virtually all of these contemporary writers made reference to or quoted from the world's great religious scriptures-the Buddhist sutras, the *Bhagavadgita*, the Gospels, etc., along with many lesser known teachings by Zen roshis, Taoist sages, and Christian saints. Up until now I had avoided these ancient and often monumental texts, partly out of a conceit endemic to our age-that whatever is old is perforce obsolete, and partly out of sheer laziness. As my disillusionment in contemporary interpretations of spirituality—especially the emphasis on *experience*—grew, however, my attitudes began to change. Now I wanted to find out for myself what the old masters had had to say.

But conceit and laziness were not the only obstacles I had to overcome before tackling the classics. Anything labeled *religious* aroused in me an almost subconscious aversion, for I had always associated the very idea of Religion with puritanical morality and intolerant dogmatism. Yet, whatever its outward excesses and abuses, religion was obviously the primary cultural vehicle through which the spiritual impulse in humanity had been carried and communicated. In the beginning I had thought of my own quest as principally philosophic or psychological. But The Dream had profoundly changed that. By becoming both personal and transcendent, my quest had undeniably assumed an essentially spiritual character. Thus, to continue to ignore religious literature—especially, the great classics—because of an old prejudice would be foolhardy.

Moreover, I was becoming increasingly aware that almost every religious tradition had two aspects: one formal and exoteric, as embodied in its social and political institutions; the other informal and esoteric, represented by its mystics, who were often themselves canonical outlaws but nevertheless claimed a true or Gnostic understanding of their respective traditions. It was the latter, of course, that intrigued me, and I based my investigation on trying to discriminate between the two aspects. The question I began with was whether or not there were some central truths, or insights, that crossed all cultural and historical boundaries (as Campbell had demonstrated was the case with mythology) and from which the various religions arose. In other words, did the mystics of different traditions agree as to their own experience or understanding, and if so, could a composite picture be drawn of what this experience or understanding was and how it could be achieved? Many of the authors I had read asserted that this was so. Hoeller had called it the Great Tradition, and Wilber (borrowing from Aldous Huxley) referred to it as the Perennial Philosophy, but again I wanted to find this out for myself.

It was (and is) my habit to read several books at a time, alternating a chapter or two of one with a chapter or two of another. This was never an intentional methodology on my part, but as a way of pursuing the spiritual classics, it proved to be very revealing. Often I would put down a Buddhist sutra and pick up the *Bhagavadgita*, or one of the Gospels, only to find I was reading the exact same idea, though expressed in a different cultural idiom. What follows is a summary, in highly condensed form, of how my own thoughts were influenced by this reading over the next few months.

Webster's defines *mysticism* as follows:[25]

> 1: the experience of mystical union or direct communion with ultimate reality reported by mystics 2: a theory of mystical knowledge, the doctrine or belief that direct knowledge of God, of spiritual truth, of ultimate reality, or comparable matters is attainable through immediate intuition, insight or illumination and in a way differing from ordinary sense perception or ratiocination.

And just because this insight or illumination differs from ordinary sensory or rational perception, the first obstacle any investigator of mysticism encounters is that it is pre-eminently mysterious. Almost immediately, I began to run into a series of baffling, paradoxical statements, such as this from *The Gospel According to Thomas*:

> Jesus said to them: When you make the two one, and when you make the inner as the outer and the outer as the inner and the above as the below, and when you make the male and the female into a single one, so that the male will not be male and the female (not) be female, when you make eyes in the place of an eye, and a hand in the place of a hand, and a foot in the place of a foot, (and) an image in the place of an image, then shall you enter [the Kingdom].[26]

And similarly, from the Buddhist *Surangama Sutra*,

> Accordingly the Tathagata's Womb becomes the clear intelligence of the true and mysterious Mind of Intuition that throws its perfect reflection and insight into all the phenomenal world. Therefore, in the Tathagata's Womb Oneness has the same meaning as Infinity, and Infinity has the same meaning as Oneness, the minimum is embraced in the maximum and the maximum in the minimum.[27]

Or, negatively stated by the Christian mystic Meister Eckhart,

> But as he [God] is simply one, without any manner and properties, he is not Father or Son or Holy Spirit, and yet he is something that is neither this nor that.[28]

Most sources agree that the necessity for stating things in paradoxes results from the inadequacy of words to convey the kind of knowledge being communicated. Thus, the Buddha says of his own teachings,

> They are intended for the consideration and guidance of the discriminating minds of all people, but they are not the Truth itself, which can only be self-realised within one's deepest consciousness.[29]

And in the *Bhagavadgita* Krishna tells Arjuna,

> Just as filling a water jug in the midst of a universal flood is superfluous, so adherence to the Vedas is to the knowers of Brahman.[30]

Perhaps this is most tersely put by the Chinese sage Lao Tzu:

> Those who know do not talk. And talkers do not know.[31]

But even Lao Tzu went on to write eighty-one verses about the subject, so in spite of the difficulties, the urge to communicate remained.

According to the mystics, however, the problem with words only reflects a much deeper and more profound problem in our fundamental perception of reality, and this is an almost universal tendency to see the world as a collection of opposites, or dualities.

In the *Bhagavadgita* Krishna declares,

> O Slayer of Enemies, all creatures are deluded at birth by the conflict of opposites, arising from desire and malice. But when people cultivate merit, and their impurities are exhausted, they are freed from the delusion of conflict. They serve me steadfast in their practice.[32]

Or, listen to Meister Eckhart:

> And if we will see things truly, they are strangers to goodness, truth and everything that tolerates any distinction,...They are intimates of the One that is bare of every kind of multiplicity and distinction.[33]

Of all the traditions Buddhism perhaps deals with this problem at greatest length and in the most thorough detail. Here is but one sample from the *Lankavatara Scripture* in which Buddha says,

> False-imagination teaches that such things as light and shade, long and short, black and white are different and are to be discriminated; but they are not independent of each other; they are only different aspects of the same thing, they are terms of relation not of reality. Conditions of existence are not of a mutually exclusive character; in essence things are not two but one....All duality is falsely imagined.[34]

On first encounter this principle, at least, seemed subject to purely rational comprehension. I could well see how opposites were interdependent. If the sun never set, not only would we have no concept of "night," we wouldn't even have the notion of "day," because there would be nothing to contrast it to. Just so, we never speak of "long" basketballs, because there are no "short" ones. Moreover, it was easy to extend this proposition into subtler areas of life. Obviously, the enjoyment of food depends on a certain degree of hunger. Few people are eager to tackle a full turkey dinner right after polishing off a five-course meal in an Italian restaurant. Even the eternal conflict between Good and Evil could be viewed as a series of mutually dependent relationships. Without murders, there would be no martyrs. Without disease, we couldn't enjoy health. Without war, no one would appreciate peace.

On the surface, then, there seemed to be nothing particularly mystical, or even mysterious, about this principle of interdependence. Indeed, it has formed the basis of most of the world's great rationalist philosophies from Aristotle to Confucius. Its watchword was *moderation*, and its goal a more balanced, harmonious life, which is also the goal of most modern-day psychotherapies. Was this the message of Mysticism as well? Many New Age writers seemed to think so, suggesting a synthesis of techniques from spiritual and therapeutic disciplines designed to balance such things as rational and emotional faculties, masculine and feminine energies, etc.

But no matter how rosy the language, essentially what such wisdom counseled was acceptance and compromise. One had to take the 'bad' with the 'good', these philosophers argued, and learn to live with the World's Shadow in a kind of cheerfully stoic but still fundamentally unresolved truce until death brought a categorical end to it all. Thus, I felt for a while that I had run into a frustrating dead end.

On closer examination, however, I began to realize that this was only a superficial interpretation of what the mystics were really trying to communicate. To them, the opposites were not merely dependent on each other, they didn't exist at all! The *Bhagavadgita* had called them "delusions." Eckhart said that, if we saw things "truly," they would be "bare of every kind of multiplicity." And Buddha preached that all duality is "falsely imagined." Thus, the aim of mysticism was not a life that "balanced" the opposites (though this might be a by-product of the teachings) but one that abolished or transcended them. And this I could not achieve conceptually. No matter how hard I tried, when I looked out the window, it was still either day or night. Although I might accept a little hunger as the price for enjoying a good meal, I still preferred that meal. And if Good and Evil were only relative, they still seemed very much to exist in the world. In short, a conceptual understanding of duality might ameliorate suffering somewhat, but it could never carry one beyond it.

The mystery of Mysticism remained, yet somehow it had to be penetrable, for as Krishna says,

> (The ocean of) ignorance made of the three primordial tendencies (that bind the self) is divine and difficult to cross. Yet those who take refuge in me cross it.[35]

And just what lay beyond this ocean of ignorance? It was often described as *emptiness,* or *silence,* or *formlessness,* or *immovability.* Thus, Krishna continues,

> My form is ineffable, yet I pervade this world. All beings reside in me, but I do not reside in them.[36]

Meister Eckhart declares,

> In the innermost part, where no one dwells, there is contentment for that light, and there it is more inward than it can be to itself, for this ground is a simple silence, in itself immovable, and by this immovability all things are moved.[37]

And Lao Tzu tells us,

> The Way is a void, Used but never filled:
> An abyss it is, Like an ancestor
> From which all things come.[38]

And the Buddha says,

> Thus, O Sariputra, all things having the nature of emptiness have no beginning and no ending. They are neither faultless nor not faultless; they are neither perfect nor imperfect. In emptiness there is no form, no sensation, no perception, no discrimination, no consciousness.[39]

But lest we mistake this "emptiness" for a cold, indifferent nothingness, the Sixth Patriarch and founder of Zen warns,

> When you hear me speak about the void, do not fall into the idea that I mean vacuity. It is of the utmost importance that we should not fall into that idea, because then when a man sits quietly and keeps his mind blank he would be abiding in a state of the "voidness of indifference." The illimitable void of the Universe is capable of holding myriads of things of various shapes and form, such as the sun and the moon, and the stars, worlds, mountains, rivers, rivulets, springs, woods, bushes, good men, bad men, laws pertaining to goodness and to badness, heavenly planes and hells, great oceans and all the mountains of Mahameru. Space takes in all these, and so does the voidness of our nature.[40]

Likewise, the *Tibetan Book of the Dead* says,

> Now thou art experiencing the Radiance of the Clear Light of Pure Reality. Recognize it, O nobly-born, thy present intellect, in real nature

void, not formed into anything as regards characteristics of colour, naturally void, is the very Reality, the All-Good.

> Thine own intellect, which is now voidness, yet not to be regarded as the voidness of nothingness, but as being the intellect itself, unobstructed, shining, thrilling, blissful, is the very consciousness, the All-good Buddha.[41]

Note the reference to emptiness of "color" in the first paragraph and listen to Eckhart, writing centuries later in a totally different culture:

> The authorities say that if the eye had some color in it when it was observing, it would recognize neither the color it had nor the color it had not; but because it is free of all colors, it therefore recognizes all colors. ... And as the powers of the soul become more perfect and unmixed, so they apprehend more perfectly and comprehensively whatever they apprehend, receiving it more comprehensively, having greater joy, becoming more united with what they apprehend, to the point where the highest power of the soul, bare of all things and having nothing in common with anything, receives into itself nothing less than God himself, in all the vastness and fulness of his being. And the authorities show us that there is no delight and no joy that can be compared with this union and this fulfilling and this joy.[42]

Note, too, that in both these descriptions a new melody of words is being introduced to characterize what lies beyond the veil: *shining, thrilling, joy, delight*; for as Buddha says,

> Highest Reality is an exalted state of bliss, it is not a state of word discrimination and it cannot be entered into by mere statements concerning it.[43]

And chiming in with a description of his own Gnosis is this unknown author of a second century manuscript, *The Discourse on the Eighth and Ninth*:

> Rejoice over this! For already from them the power, which is light, is coming to us. For I see! I see indescribable depths. How shall I tell you, O my son? ...How [shall I describe] the universe? I [am mind and] I see another mind, the one that [moves] the soul! I see the one that moves me from pure forgetfulness. You give me power! I see myself! I want to speak! Fear restrains me. I have found the beginning of the power that is above all powers, the one that has no beginning. I see a fountain bubbling with life. I have said, O my son, that I am Mind. I have seen! Language is not able to reveal this. For the entire eighth, O

my son, and the souls that are in it, and the angels, sing a hymn in silence. And I, Mind, understand.[44]

But in addition to incomparable and unspeakable joy, bliss, and delight, the seeker who pierced the veil would find something else as well — something perhaps even more valuable — freedom. Eckhart declares,

> This man lives now in utter freedom and a pure nakedness, for there is nothing that he must make subject to himself or that he must acquire, be it little or much, for everything that is God's own is his own.[45]

Krishna concurs:

> Having overcome all attachments his actions no longer bind him. This man is free.[46]

And Buddha explains,

> The Bodhisattva's Nirvana is perfect tranquillisation, but it is not extinction nor inertness; while there is an entire absence of discrimination and purpose, there is the freedom and spontaneity of potentiality that has come with the attainment and patient acceptance of the truths of egolessness and imagelessness.[47]

Or, as Jesus said so simply but eloquently,

> And ye shall know the truth, and the truth shall make you free.[48]

But Jesus also promised his disciples something even more astonishing, which orthodox Christians have ever claimed as the exclusive gift of their own redeemer:

> Verily, verily, I say unto you, If a man keep my saying, he shall never see death.[49]

Yet, hear the words of Lao Tzu:

> But when you know
> What eternally is so,
> ...
> Then, though you die,
> You shall not perish.[50]

And Krishna's admonition to Arjuna:

> Never did you or I or these kings not exist,
> nor shall we ever cease to be. [51]

And Buddha to his followers:

> I am is a vain thought; I am not is a vain thought; I shall be is a vain thought; I shall not be is a vain thought. Vain thoughts are a sickness, an ulcer, a thorn. But after overcoming all vain thoughts one is called a silent thinker. And the thinker, the silent One, does no more arise, no more pass away, no more tremble, no more desire. For there is nothing in him that he should arise again. And as he arises no more, how should he grow old again? And as he grows no more old, how should he die again?[52]

Of course, orthodox Christians do not interpret Jesus' promise in quite the same way. For them, the resurrection takes place only after physical death when the soul separates from the body. Not so for Christian mystics; at least, not for Meister Eckhart. See how closely his words parallel those of the Buddha:

> And I have often said that there is a power in the soul that touches neither time nor flesh ....If the spirit were always united with God in this power, the man could never grow old; for that now in which God made the first man, and the now in which the last man will have his end, and the now in which I am talking, they are all the same in God, and there is not more than the one now. Now you can see that this man lives in one light with God, and therefore there is not in him either suffering or the passage of time, but an unchanging eternity. For this man, truly, all wonderment has been taken away, and all things are essentially present in him. Therefore nothing new will come to him out of future events or accidents, for he dwells always anew in a now without ceasing.[53]

A *shining emptiness, above all dualities,* full of *radiance* and *bliss* and *joy, ineffable* and *beyond compare, complete freedom* and *spontaneity,* and, finally, *eternal life*—according to the mystics this is what lies beyond the veil of delusion, this is the fruit of Gnosis, or Enlightenment. And as the children of exiles sit at their parents' knees, listening eagerly to tales of the "old country," so I too eagerly read these passages as glowing accounts of my own native land. But were there any clues as to how one might return there? Clues, yes, but no clear map, and all of them hidden in the language of paradox. Nevertheless, I began to discern some broad outlines to the course.

What is Truth?

Almost all of the literature confirmed that the journey involved a death of sorts — a tradition that stretched back to the earliest explorers of the spiritual realm, the tribal shamans. Listen to what Autdaruta, a Greenland Eskimo, says about his initiation:

> Some time afterwards, he [an older shaman] took me on a journey again, and this time it was so that I myself might be eaten by the bear; this was necessary if I wished to attain any good. We rowed off and came to the cave; the old man told me to take my clothes off, and I do not deny that I was somewhat uncomfortable at the thought of being devoured alive. I had not been lying there long before I heard the bear coming.
>
> It attacked me and crunched me up, limb by limb, joint by joint, but strangely enough it did not hurt at all; it was only when it bit me in the heart that it did hurt frightfully.
>
> From that day forth I felt that I ruled my helping-spirits. After that I acquired many fresh helping-spirits and no danger could any longer threaten me, as I was always protected.[54]

And here is what Don Juan tells Carlos Castaneda:

> On the other side [of the spirit world], the man will have to wander around. His good fortune would be to find a helper nearby not too far from the entrance. The man has to ask him for help. In his own words he has to ask the helper to teach him and make him a diablero [shaman]. When the helper agrees, he kills the man on the spot, and while he is dead he teaches him.[55]

But Buddha too speaks of a spiritual death, though in somewhat more philosophical terms:

> There has been an inconceivable transformation-death by which the false-imagination of his particularised individual personality has been transcended by a realisation of his oneness with the universalised mind of Tathagatahood,...[56]

And, of course, spiritual death and rebirth are central to the teachings of Jesus:

> Verily, verily, I say unto thee,
> Except a man be born again,
> he cannot see the kingdom of God.[57]

Buddha called this death-rebirth a "turning about" that takes place at a certain stage of spiritual development.

> But with the Bodhisattva's attainment of the eighth stage there comes the "turning-about" within his deepest consciousness from self-centered egoism to universal compassion for all beings,...There is an instant cessation of the delusive activities of the whole mind system; the dancing of the waves of habit-energy on the face of Universal Mind are forever stilled, revealing its own inherent quietness and solitude, the inconceivable Oneness of the Womb of Tathagatahood.[58]

And Eckhart called it his "breaking-through":

> Then I received an impulse that will bring me up above all the angels. Together with this impulse, I receive such riches that God, as he is "God," and as he performs all his divine works, cannot suffice me; for in this breaking-through I receive that God and I are one ....then I neither diminish nor increase, for I am then an immovable cause that moves all things.[59]

According to Eckhart, however, there was no way this could be achieved:

> Whoever is seeking God by ways is finding ways and losing God, who in ways is hidden.[60]

And the Buddhist sutras agree:

> All sentient beings are ever abiding in Nirvana. Nevertheless, the thing called Enlightenment is nothing that can be attained by practising, nor can it be created by human hands;...[61]

Lao Tzu, too, points away from any effort:

> By letting go, it all gets done;
> The world is won by those who let it go![62]

Still, the promise of success remains for those willing to tread the path. As the Tibetan Buddhist Gampo expresses it,

> It is great joy to realize that the Path to Freedom which all the Buddhas have trodden is ever-existent, ever unchanged, and ever open to those who are ready to enter upon it.[63]

And as Krishna assures Arjuna,

What is Truth?

> Give up your mind to me. Be my devotee. Worship me. Bow to me. I love you. I promise you in truth that you will come to me.[64]

And Jesus assures us,

> Ask, and it shall be given you; seek, and ye shall find; knock, and it shall be opened unto you: For everyone that asketh receiveth; and he that seeketh findeth; and to him that knocketh it shall be opened.[65]

Finally, all agree that the secret of this Gnosis is not to be found somewhere out in the objective world, but lies hidden in one's own self. Here is the Buddha:

> ...if they [ordinary people] only realised it, they are already in the Tathagata's Nirvana for, in Noble Wisdom, all things are in Nirvana from the beginning.[66]

The Sixth Patriarch:

> Our very self-nature is Buddha, and apart from this nature there is no other Buddha.[67]

Meister Eckhart:

> Everything good that all the saints have possessed, and Mary the mother of God, and Christ in his humanity, all that is my own in this human nature.[68]

Lao Tzu:

> It is wisdom to know others;
> It is enlightenment to know one's self.[69]

The *Gnostic Book of Thomas the Contender*:

> For he who has not known himself has known nothing, but he who has known himself has at the same time already achieved knowledge about the Depth of the All.[70]

Krishna:

> Knowledge, the end of knowledge, enlightenment, dwells in everyone's heart.[71]

Jesus:

Neither shall they say, Lo here! or, lo there! for, behold, the kingdom of God is within you.[72]

Even Dr. Mishra, author of my meager Yoga manual, wrote,

> Supreme consciousness, supreme Brahman is your self.

and touched my own heart by adding,

> Now, you are in your native land.[73]

But, of course, I wasn't.

In some ways it all sounded so tantalizingly close; yet in others, almost impossibly out of reach. It also sounded quite mad — especially sitting in my office with several new films in the works, contracts to be negotiated, budgets prepared, producers dealt with, scripts written, actors hired, phones ringing, and all the other general frantic business of modern life pressing me from every side. There were times when, in the middle of a meeting with some writer or director, I'd glance out my tinted-glass windows across the parking lot to the low, smoggy hills in the north, over which I would be traveling come spring, and wonder if I was really, here in twentieth-century America, going to give it all up to go chase a wild and ancient vision of eternity? Perhaps all this talk of Enlightenment and Gnosis, of radiant bliss and supreme consciousness and life everlasting was, at best, a fantastic exaggeration and, at worst, the collective delusion of demented minds. If so — if this vision was as insane as it sometimes sounded — then to forsake the worldly success I had struggled so hard to achieve would, indeed, be an eternal mistake, and one from which I might well not recover.

In point of fact, the accusation of madness is one that has dogged the heels of mystics since time immemorial. In *The Gospel According to John* we read this about Jesus' contemporaries:

> And many of them said, He hath a devil, and is mad;
> why hear ye him?[74]

There is also a story that Mohammed, on first receiving the Koran, was accused of being berserk. In fact, he himself was in such doubt about his own sanity that it took a dream from Allah to convince him of his own spiritual legitimacy.

I don't know of any reference to the Buddha being denounced as a lunatic (though the first man he tried to preach the Dharma to is supposed to have muttered, "Let it be so," and quickly taken another road), but plenty of later Buddhist and Taoist sages were considered mad. Here is what the seventh century Chinese hermit, Han-shan, says about himself:

> When men see Han-shan
> They all say he's crazy
> And not much to look at
> Dressed in rags and hides.[75]

And, of course, Han-shan would have fared even worse today. The trouble with dismissing mysticism as pure pathology, however, is that, although mystical descriptions of reality are often extravagant, bizarre, and self-contradictory, they are nonetheless consistent from culture to culture and age to age. That is, as a community of witnesses to the existence of a Transcendent Reality not accessible to reason, mystics constitute an amazingly homogeneous group. This stands in striking contrast to the world's renowned rational philosophers who, in spite of achieving high levels of consistency within their own systems, widely contradict one another. Thus, where rational men have failed to agree on the true nature of reality, "madmen" apparently have succeeded. What's more, this "madness" has been historically so persuasive that it has formed the well-spring of virtually every great human civilization, including the Judeo-Christian one to which we "sane" citizens are the inescapable heirs. In short, if Buddha, Lao Tzu, Jesus, and Mohammed were mad, then the history of our most sublime cultures is a history generated by insanity.

In the end, however, it was not the force of logic that convinced me. As this journal entry indicates, I became a mystic by default:

> Tonight I wrestle with cynicism. Perhaps the rationalists are right: There is no God, no meaning, not even consciousness—just this billiard game of bouncing atoms in the dark. Nothing to do but go for the pleasures of the moment: Get rich! Get drunk! Get laid! The trouble is all such pleasures have turned sour on me. I am driven to God not by reason, not for pleasure, not for virtue, not even for love. I simply have no other choice. My only consolation is that if, indeed, it is all meaningless, then my own life won't be one jot more meaningless than anyone else's!

During the next several months I would continue to have such moments of doubt, discouragement, and even fear. My guardians were gone forever, and Athena, too, seemed to have temporarily faded again. But the worst had passed with Christmas Eve when all true resistance to my destiny had crumbled. I was alone now, but also stronger, no longer torn between conflicting desires and contradictory ambitions. Deep in my bowels I felt everything being honed and refined for a single purpose—the journey home.

One night I attended a lecture on Buddhism by a scholar named Roger Weir at the Philosophical Research Society and discovered a name for this new sense of resolve. It was *sotapanna*, or "stream-entered," which is to say there was no going back. Nor did I want to. In *The Gospel According to Thomas*, Jesus said,

> The images are manifest to man and the Light which is within them is hidden in the image of the Light of the Father.[76]

I was determined to find some way to crack that image and let out the Light.

What is Truth?

Ten:
Enchanted but Unchanged

I have already described the kind of yogic meditation I was attempting, based on Dr. Mishra's manual, which might best be characterized by the word active. That is, I was trying to produce certain psychic effects and altered states by an active concentration and manipulation of the mind. As I grew more and more dubious about the value of these effects and states, however, my meditation began to change as well. This shift was also influenced by such passages as the following from the Buddhist *Surangama Sutra*. Here the Buddha is analyzing the nature of perception for the benefit of his favorite but somewhat dense disciple Ananda:

> When I was looking at you as sentient beings do, it was your head that was moving about but my perception of sight did not move, and when you were looking at me, it was my hand opening and closing, not your "seeing" that moved. Ananda, can you not see the difference in nature in that which moves and changes, and that which is motionless and unchanging? It is body which moves and changes, not Mind. Why do you so persistently look upon motion as appertaining to both body and mind? Why do you permit your thoughts to rise and fall, letting the body rule the mind, instead of Mind ruling the body? Why do you let your senses deceive you as to the true unchanging nature of Mind and then to do things in a reversed order which leads to motion and confusion and suffering? As one forgets the true nature of Mind, so he mistakes the reflections of objects as being his own mind, thus binding him to the endless movements and changes and suffering of the recurring cycles of deaths and rebirths that are of his own causing.[77]

Like Ananda, however, I had trouble understanding exactly what the Buddha was talking about. What *was* the difference between that which "moved and changed" and that which was "motionless and unchanging"? What was the *true nature of Mind*? In order to find out I began to use meditation more as a kind of laboratory in which to observe ordinary, everyday thoughts and perceptions. A journal entry at the time reflects this shift in technique:

What are the fundamental perceptions of consciousness, i.e., sights, sounds, the senses, thoughts, and feelings, and how do they arise? My meditation follows this track. I no longer try for states of "bliss" except, occasionally, just for fun. Far more interesting has become the investigation of the very soil out of which consciousness itself arises. I also heed Krishnamurti's advice to "stay with" feelings, thoughts, pain, etc.

The ultimate objective of this kind of meditation, according to both the Buddhist sutra and Krishnamurti, is to produce, or *realize*, a still mind, a phenomenon the Buddhists compare to waves subsiding on an ocean. But there was a problem. As Krishnamurti pointed out, as long as the mind was being "observed," it wouldn't hold still:

> But when the brain, your mind, is completely still, you don't see your still mind. There is no knowing that your mind is still. If you know it, it is not still, for then there is an observer who says, 'I know.' The stillness which we are talking about is non-recognizable, and non-experienceable.[78]

There is a story in Buddhism that illustrates this same idea. Subhuti, one of the Buddha's greatest disciples and famed for his understanding of emptiness, was sitting under a tree not thinking about anything. Suddenly, the gods started showering him with flowers. What's this for? Subhuti asked. We are praising you for your teaching of emptiness, the gods replied. But I haven't said a word about emptiness, Subhuti exclaimed. You haven't said a word about emptiness, and we haven't heard a word about emptiness; this is true emptiness, the gods declared.

And yet, according to Buddha, the solution to this paradoxical predicament is not to be found in trying to suppress all mental activity and making the mind blank:

> But, Mahamati, as earnest disciples go on trying to advance on the path that leads to full realisation, there is one danger against which they must be on their guard ....They may sometimes think that they can expedite the attainment of their goal of tranquillisation by entirely suppressing the activities of the mind-system. This is a mistake, for even if the activities of the mind are suppressed, the mind will still go on functioning because the seeds of habit-energy will still remain in it. What they think is extinction of mind, is really the nonfunctioning of the mind's external world to which they are no longer attached. That is, the

goal of tranquillisation is to be reached not by suppressing all mind activity but by getting rid of discriminations and attachments.[79]

If all this sounds contradictory and confusing, it was for me as well. What seemed to be required was something that was neither an effort at awareness nor complete laxity. If no effort at all was made, I found myself becoming completely involved in fantasies and daydreams from which nothing was gained. Consciously trying to still the mind, on the other hand, marred the very stillness I was attempting to achieve. Eventually, I settled on a kind of stop-and-go technique recommended in the sutras and similar to the exercise I had performed in examining how 'knowledge' was held (i.e., "Columbus discovered America in 1492."). The idea was to keep alert and *mindful* enough not to become "lost in thought" but at the same time not to try to direct the flow of thought itself. With only some minor alterations, this became the form of meditation I practiced for the duration of my journey. Athena's first Commandment—PAY ATTENTION—had finally become refined into an actual discipline. Moreover, I found that I could (and did) apply this discipline at any time of the day or night when my mind wasn't otherwise occupied with practical tasks. One immediate and delightful effect was that "waiting" disappeared from my life. I always had something fascinating to do, and I could do it anywhere.

The real value of this shift in meditative technique, however, was to bring back into sharp, and now acutely detailed, focus the fundamental question—*Who am I?* By carefully observing my own perceptual and mental processes, I began to realize fully and completely something I had only suspected before: I was not my thoughts, feelings, memories, or even sensory perceptions. These were independent "events" that arose and faded in consciousness quite spontaneously. Although by an act of will I could temporarily interfere with them or change their direction, I was definitely not their creator, nor could I even stop them from being created for more than very short periods of time. Inevitably, the whole chaotic stream would bubble up and race off again under its own steam, quite apart from any control I tried to exercise. But the more I came to understand the independent nature of this stream's activity, surprisingly, the less power it had to carry "me" away with it. A painful memory concerning Colette, for instance, which in the past would have been capable of sparking a whole melodrama of guilt and anguish, could now be recognized and let pass without much ado. Slowly, I was learning Athena's Third, and most important, Commandment—DETACHMENT, for in order to see who we *really* are, we must detach from everything we *think* we are. Thus, although detachment doesn't directly answer the question *Who am I?* by showing us who we are not, it narrows the field of possibilities.

As my readings in the classics deepened, I began to see that detachment might also be the key to understanding another important but much neglected aspect of spirituality, the practice of virtues. Nowadays one hears little talk of such time-honored disciplines as celibacy, humility, poverty, charity, even among people who are trying once again to pursue the spiritual life. I, too, had never been particularly interested in such matters, assuming them to be more in the nature of moral precepts appropriate, perhaps, to bygone ages but no longer applicable to a modern liberal society. In the literature, however, I found that these virtues did not vary much from one culture or age to another, nor were they presented, by mystics, at least, primarily as social standards; rather, they were espoused as specific requirements of the esoteric path—requirements designed to help the seeker detach from his or her biological impulses and desires. Such detachment was considered necessary, because virtually all traditions regarded the misidentification of self with desire (or clinging, craving, lust, etc.) as the great obstacle to Gnosis and in some cases the actual cause of suffering and death. The Buddha's Second Noble Truth of the origin of suffering, for example, reads as follows:

> Thus, whatever kind of Feeling one experiences—pleasant, unpleasant or indifferent—one approves of and cherishes the feeling and clings to it; and while doing so, lust springs up; but lust for feelings means clinging to existence (upadana); and on clinging to existence depends the (action-) Process of Becoming (bhava, here kamma-bhava); on the process of becoming depends (future) Birth (jati); and dependent on birth are Decay and Death, sorrow, lamentation, pain, grief and despair. Thus arises this whole mess of suffering.[80]

And the Buddha's Third Noble Truth of the end of suffering makes clear that the antidote to this self-perpetuating process is detachment:

> What now is the Noble Truth of the Extinction of Suffering? It is the complete fading away and extinction of this craving, its forsaking and giving up, the liberation and detachment from it.[81]

Moreover, five of the eight steps outlined in the Buddha's Fourth Noble Truth (the Eightfold Path to Liberation) enjoined practices of virtue, namely: Right Mindedness, Right Speech, Right Action, Right Living, Right Effort. Thus, in Buddhism practices of virtue were quite evidently exercises in detachment, which, in turn, was seen as the fundamental principle of attaining liberation, or enlightenment.

In the *Bhagavadgita* desire arising from the senses was also seen as a major barrier to wisdom, and detachment from desire (as a means of attaining liberation) constituted almost the entire message of the poem, as the following verses indicate:

> Wisdom is covered by this constant enemy of the wise. It appears in the form of desire and is insatiable, like fire.[82]

> Concentrating on sensory objects, people become attached to them. From attachment arises desire, and from desire, anger. Anger leads to delusion; delusion leads to distortion of memory; distortion of memory distorts understanding. As understanding perishes, so perishes the person.[83]

> Therefore, fulfill your obligations, always without attachment. People who act without desire attain the highest.[84]

Although writing in an entirely different milieu, Meister Eckhart was saying essentially the same thing when he spoke of the necessity for eliminating all desires from the heart in order to make room for God to enter therein.

> If I want to write on a wax tablet, it does not matter how fine the words may be that are written on the tablet, they still hinder me from writing on it. If I really want to write something, I must erase and eliminate everything that is already there; and the tablet is never so good for me to write on as when there is nothing on it at all. In the same way, if God is to write on my heart up in the highest place, everything that can be called this or that must come out of my heart, and in that way my heart will have won detachment. And so God can work upon it in the highest place and according to his highest will. And this is why the heart in its detachment has no this or that as its object.[85]

In reading the Gospels it was clear that practices of virtue formed the bulk of Jesus' teachings, and, like most people, I had assumed that they were primarily ethical. But now, in the light of other traditions, I began to wonder if this had been Jesus' main intent. One episode, in particular, seemed to hint strongly that it was not. This concerned the rich young man who asked Jesus what he should do to attain eternal life. Jesus replied that he should keep the ten commandments. The young man, however, insisted that he had done so since his youth and demanded to know what he still lacked. At this point Jesus answered,

> If thou wilt be perfect, go and sell that thou hast, and give to the poor, and thou shalt have treasure in heaven: and come and follow me.[86]

My own reading of this story was that Jesus was making a clear distinction between exoteric, or social, virtues and an esoteric practice. Thus, his initial advice to the young man to keep the ten commandments was exoteric and ethical, meaning that the ten commandments would suffice for ordinary secular life. If, however, the young man aspired to be *perfect* (i.e., enlightened), it would be necessary for him to surrender all worldly attachments. What's more, by taking detachment as the heart of Jesus' esoteric teaching, passages that had previously seemed almost irrational now began to make sense; for example,

> Therefore I say unto you, Take no thought for your life, what ye shall eat, or what ye shall drink; nor yet for your body, what ye shall put on. Is not the life more than meat, and the body than raiment?[87]

A full understanding of the esoteric use of virtues as *disciplines of detachment* took time to jell. Nevertheless, the more I read, the more intrigued I became. I started to see the practice of virtues as a means to consciously embody the insight I had had at Dr. Moss's workshop—*spirituality wasn't something you believed in, but something you lived*. Here was a concrete way to do just that. Consequently, I began to experiment with a variety of specific virtues, albeit in a random fashion. And although these experiments overlapped, for the sake of clarity I'll discuss them here separately.

Celibacy. In spite of what might be supposed, the permanent and complete cessation of all sexual activity is not given unanimous priority in mystical tradition. Jesus said of this discipline, "He that is able to receive it, let him receive it," and spent much more time preaching against the corrupting influence of *inner* lusts than any actual physical acts. Buddha also pointed to sexual desire as a prime cause of suffering and illusion, but the Fourth precept of the Eightfold Path enjoins only purity of mind and sexual self-control, not total abstinence.

Except for my brief affair with Elanore and an occasional evening with Samantha, I had, in fact, been physically celibate for the past nine months. But this didn't mean that I hadn't "lusted after women in my heart," as an American President once so quaintly put it. I had, however, been restrained from acting on these desires for practical, not spiritual, considerations. Because of Samantha's place in my life, I knew that all such entanglements would be doomed, and the mess caused by ending them was not worth the fleeting pleasure in between. Yet now I decided to try to turn this frustrating state of affairs to advantage: What if I could stop desire from arising in the first place, or at least become detached enough from it so that it would no longer be a source of distraction? Remembering how my desire had vanished spontaneously with the girl from Great Neck, I made a vow of celibacy to try to achieve this consciously.

Since sexual desire does not usually arise by a conscious effort of will, the first thing to do was to try to observe it in action to see just how and when it *did* arise. In my own case, I learned that the process worked something like this:

Whenever I came in contact with a woman, I discovered that my mind would sort her into an eligible or ineligible category, based primarily on age and attractiveness. This happened so automatically as to be almost subconscious. If the woman fell into the eligible category, the first flicker of desire would be felt in the form of a question, Is she also attracted to me? Again, the question was practically subliminal, but it would prompt a special alertness on my part. I would catch myself studying her body language and trying to make eye contact for an answer. If the answer was yes, then a second question would emerge, Is she available? This second question would lead to a subtle inquiry aimed at discovering whether or not any objective obstacles, such as a husband or boyfriend, prevented an actual consummation. If no such obstacles could be detected, desire might now swell into full consciousness and provoke an open flirtation. If at this stage the woman responded favorably, my own reluctance to get involved would usually intervene, and the desire would fade out on its own. Nevertheless, I would still have enjoyed an imaginary, psychological conquest, and, what's more, I realized that this psychological conquest was actually more important than the assuagement of any purely biological impulse.

On the other hand, if at any point in this chain I received a negative response from the woman, frustration would ensue. But this frustration itself was also primarily psychological, often accompanied by a perceptible drop in self-esteem and, sometimes, even a distinct sense of failure.

Furthermore, this whole process happened so quickly and so habitually that I had never really been aware of it before. In fact, I was amazed, after observing my reactions for a while, at how enslaved I was to such a subtle and fundamentally imaginary pursuit. Thus, the effort to break this pattern became not a burden but an act of positive emancipation. Nor was the solution difficult. The instant I became aware of desire arising in any situation, I simply reminded myself that I was celibate, so, whatever the outcome, further pursuit would be fruitless. Thus, remembering the vow itself became the means of its accomplishment, and eventually, even this formal procedure proved unnecessary; merely becoming conscious of desire was enough to cause its natural dissipation.

I maintained this discipline for the rest of my journey, with two exceptions. One was Samantha. From the beginning I held her exempt from the vow, though I still tried to be vigilant about observing any desire she evoked. Actually, by now the novelty of sex with her had worn off, and our occasional lovemaking had become more the expression of a friendly intimacy than any overwhelming physical passion. Moreover, it happened so sporadically as not to constitute any continuous outlet for sexual energy, which would, of course, have largely negated the value of the discipline.

The other exception occurred months later while I was on the road making the video newsletter. The lady in question was so attractive and alluring that I simply chucked my discipline for a night; nor, I must say, did I have any regrets. In fact, the interesting thing about this incident was that I had a choice. Previously, in such seductive circumstances, there would have been no question about my response. By then, however, sexual impulses no longer controlled me, I controlled them. In the long run, this was perhaps the greatest practical benefit of the whole experiment.

A more immediate result of practicing celibacy, however, was an increased ease and tranquility in the company of women. As it ceased to matter whether or not they found me sexually attractive, I found I no longer felt I had to make an effort to be attractive. I could just be myself. A corollary to this new sense of tranquility with women was a lessening of tension with men, because I had stopped competing with them for feminine favors. In a word, I had become a little freer in all my relations.

There is one last, rather ironic note to add to this entire experience, and that is, the more inwardly continent I became, the more outwardly attractive I seemed to appear to women, in general. Never in my life have I received so many sexual invitations, both implicit and explicit, as I did during those pre-spring months of 1983. Unfortunately for those who might be tempted to try celibacy as a strategy of sexual pursuit, it is by definition, of course, self-defeating.

A virtue that *is* given considerable import in almost every spiritual tradition is *humility*. Lao Tzu says,

> If I can be the world's most humble man,
> Then I can be its highest instrument.[88]

And Krishna tells Arjuna,

> People who are humble and without illusions, who have conquered all attachments, who are firm in the knowledge of the inner self, desireless, free from the conflicts of joys and sorrows, from ignorance, they attain the Absolute.[89]

And Jesus declares,

> For whosoever exalteth himself shall be abased;
> and he that humbleth himself shall be exalted.[90]

Humility, however, is extremely subtle and, therefore, can be easily counterfeited, even with the best of intentions. The Devil's favorite sin, according to Coleridge, "is pride that apes humility." But in the poet's caution there is also a clue to humility's nature, for if pride can so readily masquerade as humility, there must be a close connection between the two. What is pride?

Webster's tells us that *pride* is

> inordinate self-esteem; an unreasonable conceit of one's own superiority in talents, beauty, wealth, rank, etc., which manifests itself in lofty airs, distance, reserve, and often in contempt for others.

And conversely, *humility* is

> freedom from pride and arrogance.

Genuine humility, then, is not so much an action or a feeling as the cessation of actions and feelings or, more specifically, the elimination of conceit, superiority, and contempt—all of which I had in abundance, except, of course, during those spells of deep self-pity that I've already described. But wait. Here was another curious relationship: could pride and self-pity have anything to do with each other? As I examined my own emotions, I found that they did indeed. In fact, they were two sides of the same, imaginary coin. In regard to Samantha, for instance, I had once imagined myself her Knight-Protector. But because I had identified so strongly with this image, when she rejected it, I felt she had rejected me and so suffered the consequences. Yet, really, it had all been caused by an attachment to a fantasy in my own head.

Intellectually, at least, I came to understand that as long as I based my identity on such images of myself *vis-a-vis* the world, my identity would be dependent on the world's corroboration and, likewise, vulnerable to its rejection. Pride preceded a fall not by any abstract moral law but through inevitable psychological necessity. This was the Tarot's ever-turning Wheel of Fortune, and the question became how to break the cycle.

As with celibacy, the first task was to pay attention. By observing myself in business and social situations, I realized that my mind was constantly engaged in making a stream of judgments, all based on a certain prideful image I had of myself as being smarter and more talented than my associates. Sometimes during a conversation, in my eagerness to make a point that would reinforce this image, I wouldn't even hear what the other person was saying. The key, then, to diffusing this syndrome was to surrender my image. In practice, however, I found this very difficult to do. There always seemed to be the ghost of an image lingering somewhere in my consciousness. Yet, by cultivating the kind of "empty listening" I had learned in the dream workshop, I did manage to suspend the flow of internal judgments somewhat. This, in turn, allowed me to become more appreciative of the people around me, particularly my subordinates at work who, in the past, I had often "not had time for." Consequently, my suite of offices became a refuge for exasperated secretaries and disgruntled gofers, earning Lewis's sarcastic designation, "the Left Wing." But I no longer cared. The people had become more interesting than the job.

Finally, although I can't claim any great success in actually achieving humility, the whole undertaking convinced me that the source of my own unhappiness could always be found within myself and not in any external situation. If I became annoyed or upset with others, it always could be traced back to an attachment I had to a certain image that I wanted others to confirm. Thus, I began to see that we are always and only the victims of our own imaginations, and this was an invaluable lesson.

The one virtue, of course, that is still very much in vogue today (almost to the point of becoming a cliche) is *love,* or *compassion*. Usually, this is conceived in terms of a feeling for humanity as a whole and sometimes for all sentient beings, as well. In the name of love, we demonstrate against nuclear war, abstain from eating meat, protest the killing of whales, meditate for world peace, and try to be nice to minorities. In New Age workshops we are given exercises designed to open our hearts or make us feel the oneness of life—all of which is supposed to produce more love on the planet in much the way plants produce oxygen that then floats benignly around the atmosphere giving life to all creatures. Not that I found anything wrong with these rituals—indeed, I have already described some euphoric experiences in such workshops—but that was the trouble: they remained *experiences* whose glow inexorably faded with time. Was there a kind of love that did not rise and fall in the flux of ordinary emotions? A love beyond the grip of temporal circumstances? A love in which one could permanently abide? The spiritual literature affirmed that there was and gave hints as to how it might be approached.

In the *Bhagavadgita* compassion is associated with self-control leading to equanimity:

> One who is without envy toward any creature, is friendly and compassionate, unselfish, not egotistical, with equanimity toward happiness and suffering, is merciful, always satisfied, self-controlled, assured, whose heart and mind are directed toward me—such a one is my favorite devotee.[91]

The Sixth Patriarch of Zen also equates compassion with a certain self-control:

> Even in time of dispute and quarrel, we should treat intimates and enemies alike and never think of retaliation. In the thinking faculty, let the past be dead. If we allow our thoughts, past, present and future, to become linked up into a series, we put ourselves under restraint. On the other hand, if we never let our mind become attached at any time to anything, we gain emancipation. For this reason we make "non-attachment" our fundamental principle.[92]

Of all the masters, Jesus spoke the most about brotherly love and, in the following passage from *Matthew*, gives us a concrete and detailed description of what he means:

> Ye have heard that it hath been said, An eye for an eye, and a tooth for a tooth: But I say unto you, That ye resist not evil: but whosoever shall smite thee on thy right cheek, turn to him the other also. And if any man will sue thee at the law, and take away thy coat, let him have thy cloak also. And whosoever shall compel thee to go a mile, go with him twain. Give to him that asketh thee, and from him that would borrow of thee turn not thou away. Ye have heard that it hath been said, Thou shalt love thy neighbor, and hate thine enemy. But I say unto you, Love your enemies, bless them that curse you, do good to them that hate you, and pray for them which despitefully use you, and persecute you; That ye may be the children of your Father which is in heaven: for he maketh his sun to rise on the evil and on the good, and sendeth rain on the just and on the unjust. For if ye love them which love you, what reward have ye? do not even the publicans the same? And if ye salute your brethren only, what do ye more than others? do not even the publicans so? Be ye therefore perfect, even as your Father which is in heaven is perfect.[93]

I had heard these words before but had never taken them as a literal guide to conduct for the simple reason that the kind of love required seemed impossible for ordinary mortals to achieve. Certainly, if someone sued me for, say, ten thousand dollars, I wasn't about to go to court and hand him twenty! But then, that was when I was content to be an ordinary mortal. Now, however, I was after something else.

As with his advice to the rich young man, I asked myself if Jesus' teachings about love weren't really designed as a spiritual discipline for the attainment of Gnosis, or perfection? I thought they might be and began to see love not so much as some mysterious force to improve the world but as a specific practice to be attempted in everyday life just like celibacy and humility. Indeed, as a discipline, it was closely related to the demand for unconditional love that had become the central task of my spiritual relationship to Samantha, only here it was being extended as an all-embracing compassion. What's more, it could only be realized in the same way, namely, by giving up any attachment to the expectation of reward or reciprocation. But, then, wasn't that its purpose?

Comprehending the nature and goal of this virtue, however, did not in any way lessen its awesome magnitude nor make it seem any easier to achieve. I was having enough problems with Samantha, and she was only one person! Moreover, in Samantha's case I already had the decided advantage of being in love with her from the start, which was far from true of the rest of my relationships. Consequently, I hardly knew where or how to begin. As often happens on spiritual paths, however, I found an answer in the least likely of places.

Recently, our company had been approached by a producer, whom I'll call Caligula, with a silly tits-and-ass screenplay that, nevertheless, had commercial potential. The trouble was that Caligula, like his pseudo-namesake, had such a reputation for mercurial temper and blatant rudeness that even as thick-skinned a businessman as Lewis was reluctant to get involved with him. Since I would be the executive responsible for day-to-day dealings with Caligula, Lewis asked my opinion. I told him we should go ahead with the project. In the past I had worked with some pretty notorious people and had never had any problems. Caligula, however, proved to be the exception.

Almost from our first meeting I realized we were fated to lock horns. Caligula was the ultimate challenge to any discipline of compassion. If I could simply learn to tolerate the man, let alone love him, this would be an accomplishment of note.

The method here was in part the same as in my practice of humility, i.e., *listening*, but it required an additional and strenuous effort to understand Caligula himself. What made him tick? I soon realized that most of his rudeness was not inherent but a calculated tactic to manipulate people through intimidation. Moreover, I observed that those who allowed themselves to be so manipulated were not entirely blameless. They submitted to his tactics because of their own desires for and attachments to the things they imagined Caligula could provide, whether it was a job on the crew or a place in the cast.

Although being a vice president exempted me from Caligula's personal abuse, occasionally he would threaten to tell Lewis that I was too intractable to work with, thereby hoping to get me to back down from a decision. I never did. Instead, I would simply offer to withdraw from the picture anytime Caligula requested it. Although such a move might well have been considered an admission of failure on my part, it could also have jeopardized the whole project, and Caligula was never willing to take that risk. He had some attachments of his own. Thus, I managed to stay more or less personally clear of Caligula's games.

On one occasion, however, he did get to me by insulting my story editor. In spite of my discipline, I became furious and insisted that Lewis demand an apology. Lewis called Caligula's agent, and before the day was out our producer showed up with a basket of expensive cheeses, ready to make amends. I felt a surge of vengeful triumph but also found it disappointingly ephemeral. It was not that I regretted forcing Caligula's apology, but only my own motives. I had acted out of anger and a desire to retaliate and had paid for these emotions the whole day with a churning stomach. Now, with victory in hand, I discovered it hadn't been worth the price.

I was also a little surprised at how easily Caligula had knuckled under, but then it dawned on me that a man who chooses intimidation as a strategy for dealing with the world must have an inordinate fear of being intimidated himself. This threw a new light on Caligula's character, and I came to regard him not so much as a tyrant but as a rather desperate individual.

In any case, to win a battle is not to win a war, and for the next four months Caligula and I fought over almost every aspect of the film. Several writers came and went, and the original director was fired even before the cameras rolled. My primary concern, however, was to protect the screenplay, which had deteriorated with every rewrite. Finally, we got a marginally acceptable script and set a start date, but there was no guarantee that Caligula wouldn't continue rewriting on the set, which is almost always disastrous.

It all ended for me on location in a plush Florida hotel. I had joined the crew for the first week of principal photography. The project was launched on schedule, but I could see that under Caligula's capricious command it was clearly sailing into trouble. Now, however, there was nothing more I could do.

Just before returning to L.A. I went to Caligula's room to say goodbye. The air-conditioning had failed during the night, and our Captain had succumbed to an allergy attack. What I found in the darkened suite, with the hot Florida air wafting through the opened windows, was straight out of Tennessee Williams—a lonely, ailing, overweight, little man, sliding past his prime down the gray corridors of time toward old age and death; friendless, loveless, isolated, and driven; a man too smart not to know how fleeting and fickle success can be but who nevertheless clings to it with all his ruthless power simply because there seems nothing else to do in the face of oblivion. Nor did I pity Caligula, for wasn't he just a slightly more bizarre example of our common human condition? I felt, rather, that we were kindred souls in this vale of tears. I also felt I had learned at least something of compassion.

The greatest boon of all these experiments in detachment (both in meditation and in practices of virtue), however, was not to make me more compassionate or appreciative, nor even to free me from the bonds of fantasy and desire: It was to tangibly demonstrate what the mystics reiterated over and over—*that I truly wasn't the life of this body or its mind.* The very fact that I could observe physical impulses, feelings and desires, thoughts and images proved absolutely that I could not simultaneously be them. They were all "objects" in my consciousness, just like trees, or mountains, or thunder storms. Thus, the *subject* to consciousness—the "I" who witnessed them—had to be something else...something different. But what?

I still seemed somehow to be attached to this body-mind. I looked out through these eyes and no others. I could command my own hands to move but not anyone else's. I knew my own thoughts but was generally not privy to the thoughts of those around me. Was I, then, a "soul" or a "ray" of the Divine trapped in this capsule of flesh? If so, it would appear that the orthodox interpretations of religion were correct, and I could be finally released only in death. But the mystics insisted otherwise. According to them, my own self-nature was already the Buddha; the Tao was present everywhere, or as Jesus said about the Kingdom of God,

> It will not come by expectation; they will not say: "See, here," or:
> "See, there." But the Kingdom of the Father is spread upon the earth and men do not see it.[94]

That was precisely my problem. I still couldn't *see* this Kingdom.

In April I gave Lewis notice that I was leaving the company, and we fixed the date for June 3rd. By now I had received many more replies from various communities to my letter outlining the video-newsletter project and was beginning to make concrete preparations for the trip. As the actual departure date drew closer, I found myself thrilled but also increasingly anxious over my eventual fate. How would I make a living in the future? And what about on-going expenses, like medical insurance, car coverage, Writers Guild dues, credit card payments? — things I had come to regard as necessities of life.

Such thoughts led me to consider another aspect of spiritual life that, in virtually all the traditions, is given the highest praise but has today fallen into almost universal disrepute, namely, *poverty* and its close twin *homelessness*. Most of the great sages, however, had lived just this sort of existence and demanded it of their followers. Thus, Lao Tzu wrote about himself,

> Lazily, I drift
> As though I had no home.
> All others have enough to spare;
> I am the one left out.[95]

And Krishna gave this description of his true devotee:

> The silent sage, indifferent to praise or blame, who is content with little, who has no home, whose mind is steadfast in devotion, is dear to me.[96]

Buddha was even more explicit about what he expected:

> A man who wishes to become my disciple must be willing to give up all direct relations with his family, with the social life of the world and all dependence on wealth. A man who has given up all such relations for the sake of the Dharma and has no abiding place for either his body or his mind has become my disciple and is to be called a homeless brother.[97]

This was, of course, exactly what Jesus had recommended to the rich young man who wanted to be *perfect* when he told him to sell all that he had, give to the poor, and follow him. Moreover, anyone who reads the Gospels cannot fail to be impressed with how often and forcefully Jesus enjoins his disciples to a life of poverty and homelessness, as in this verse:

> And everyone that hath forsaken houses, or brethren, or sisters, or father, or mother, or wife, or children, or lands, for my name's sake, shall receive an hundredfold, and shall inherit everlasting life.[98]

As a film executive, of course, I was not yet in a position to undertake such a discipline, but I soon would be, so I began to give it considerable attention. Ironically, it had been poverty that I was so anxious to escape when I first came to Hollywood ten years before. Was I really willing to return to that estate now, and to what end?

Like other practices and virtues, poverty was obviously an exercise in detachment—in this case, it seemed, from physical possessions. Actually, for the last year or so I had not thought of myself as particularly attached to "things." I felt as though I could take them or leave them. Was the discipline of poverty, then, unnecessary for me? As I pondered my upcoming trip, however, something convinced me otherwise.

Originally, I had conceived of this trip as marking a definite termination of my old life. But slowly, slyly, my thinking began to change. Instead of a clean break with the past, I started to view it as nothing more than a long, summer vacation—a well-deserved breather from ten years of steady career building.

This shift in perspective was so subtle I almost didn't notice it—almost. In point of fact, I had trained myself too well to be seduced by such mental gymnastics. It was clearly motivated by a dread not so much of losing any specific possessions but of living without any plans or prospects for the future, of surrendering all sense of physical security. As I moved closer to this abyss of the unknown, my mind filled with dire scenarios of deprivation, sickness, and death. But what kind of real security could I, or anyone, erect against such terrors? In the end, whether rich or poor, weren't we all subject to the vagaries of accident and illness? And wasn't wealth itself intrinsically ephemeral, ever threatened by war, depression, and changing economic fortunes? Finally, didn't we all live under the certain and inexorable sentence of death?

But if death was inexorable and security illusionary, it would be a fool's game to waste my life in a vain attempt to fend off the one and cling to the other. Yet this was exactly what I had been doing—pursuing money and position as though they held some magic power to exempt me from the inevitable fate of all biological beings. It was not so much the desire for actual possessions, then, that had spurred my ambition and trapped me in a thoroughly futile life but what lay behind them—the fear of death. If I was ever to be free, I knew I would have to face this fear squarely, once and for all. This had been the task "left undone" in Nam. There I had met death and even won a partial victory. Still, I had been unable to conquer it completely, because I had been thinking only in terms of physical survival. But such a victory, if it could be won at all, had to be done so *spiritually*.

This was the wisdom of the mystics and the new task I had set myself. To balk now was impossible. I had gone too far. "You can't negotiate with God!" Hoeller had declared, but that's just what my rational mind had been stealthily trying to do. Whether this journey was to be merely a temporary pilgrimage or a total commitment was the difference between a token sacrifice and complete surrender. I did not want to appease God, I wanted to find him. And the only way to do this would be to accept poverty—to take no thought for my life, what I ate, or what I drank, or what I put on. Thus, I began to divest myself of my possessions.

I paid off several-thousand dollars worth of debts and signed over the house and Audi to Colette, who had kindly agreed to care for Captain Blood during the summer. Another two thousand went to purchase a used VW camper, which I dubbed the Old Gray Mare. I figured gas, food, and lodging for the trip would come to two-thousand dollars more and bought traveler's checks in that amount. In the end, I had five thousand left in the bank, and this was to be my sole cushion against the future. Given the rate of inflation over the last decade, I was almost back where I had started when I first came to Hollywood a decade before. Of course, this wasn't as complete a renunciation as Jesus had required of his disciples, but still, it was enough to make me gasp.

I have described the above thoughts, feelings, and experiments of this period of my life in a highly organized fashion, but in truth, it is a false picture of how I actually experienced it. Everything moved in fits and starts, blended together, overlapped, and swirled in confusion. I was like a man in the pitch of night, feeling his way up a staircase without railings, and what little light I could see filtering down from above came through a dark glass indeed. In all the workshops and lectures I had attended, people talked about their "transformations," and it was the subject of innumerable books, pamphlets, and tapes, but I had so far failed to find the magic key. I had certainly altered my worldview, even my very thought processes. I had dabbled in shamanism, practiced yoga, meditated, and tried to be virtuous. I had felt expanded and contracted, dreamed incredible dreams, heard nadam, seen auras, been charged with higher energies, had visions, even traveled out of my body, and yet, ultimately, it all seemed to have made little difference. I always came back from these psychic forays to the same old self I had begun with, an isolated and mortal entity bobbing on the black sea of time. As a friend later so succinctly expressed it, I had been enchanted but unchanged.

In the final weeks before leaving I began to relinquish the hope of ever really attaining Gnosis. How many people in all history had actually achieved it? Instead, I lowered my sights, wishing only to find some satisfying and useful task in life.

In May Samantha and I drove up to Ojai, fifty miles north of L.A., to attend a seminar at the Ojai Foundation. One of the Foundation's main purposes was to host talks and programs given by leading thinkers in philosophy, religion, and the sciences who were breaking new ground in their respective fields. The day we went, Rupert Sheldrake and Fred Alan Wolf were presenting their revolutionary, non-causal views of biology and physics, but I was more interested in the people who ran the Foundation than the theories being expounded. They seemed to live simple, idyllic lives, dedicated to service, true midwives to a New Age. Could I be happy in such a place? I put them down on my list of communities to visit for the newsletter.

On May 19th, Lewis issued a memo announcing my departure. My journal entry for that date reads as follows:

> All day various people in the company stop by to express their reactions —shock, dismay, curiosity, best wishes, etc. Most disturbing to them seems to be that I have no long-range plans. It makes me think plans have less to do with the future than the present. They help us bridge the uncertainties of the moment. Without them we are dancing over an abyss. I feel it, too. While everyone else's life continues along in well-cut grooves, mine is grinding to a halt. Freedom and Fear are the twin angels of this death.

After that everything started happening very fast. On May 29th, with just a week to go, I recorded this:

> Already my little cabin is half stripped, as is my soul. Funny, but I have no regrets about leaving this place—no unfinished business here. It was truly a cocoon, a hermitage, a nest for incubating the spiritual egg. Now it's time to hatch. What did I expect? A new "shining" self? But it's not like that at all. On the contrary, I see all my faults unclouded by any vanity. ...Friday, Samantha comes over to peruse my goods and decide what she wants. In spite of a rough day at work she is in good spirits and talks forcefully about her life. This is the best going-away gift of all, to see her coming out of a long, wintery soul funk, flexing her feline, feminine mind. She is so warm and supportive it's hard to believe we'll be apart, and in a way we won't. As we talk, little parallel incidences in our lives fall into place like meshing gears, so that at one point we laugh and joke that pretty soon we won't need to talk at all!

On Friday, June 3rd, my last day at work, I got a letter from a young man aspiring to a career in films and writing to me for advice. Ironically, it was exactly the kind of letter I had written ten years before trying to break into the business, and here it was, crossing my desk on the very day I was giving it all up. Supposing I wrote back the whole story of my life, would it make any difference to him? I doubted it would and, instead, asked my secretary to send him a nice note wishing him luck.

There was little time, however, to muse on life's ironies. I spent the weekend in hectic, last-minute packing and saying goodbye to family and friends. On Sunday I loaded the Old Gray Mare—clothes, books, typewriter, more books, video equipment, guitar, sleeping bag, and still more books. It was like choosing what to take on a one-way trip to a desert island.

By five in the afternoon it was finished. My cabin was empty with only a few lighter-shaded patches of rug where furniture had once sat to indicate anyone had ever lived there at all. I took a final, fond look around and walked out the door. Another chapter of my life had come to a close.

I spent my last night in L.A. at Samantha's. She had prepared a lovely feast with lots of wine and, after dinner, gave me a present for my journey. It was a gold-plated questing cup. Everyone else had bidden me goodbye with anxious hugs and worried looks. She alone never questioned what I was about or showed the least sign of concern but had remained the serene accomplice of my fate. Now she had given me this crowning token of encouragement, this symbol of the Grail, and as I slowly turned it over in the palm of my hand, I finally understood why she had come into my life. Some men, like Joyce himself, dared an *eternal mistake* for the sake of art; some men for their country; others out of ideological conviction or religious belief; but I had none of these. All I had was Samantha; and as with Parzival and Condwiramurs, it was her love that would sustain me in this quest. We had come full circle, back to the starting point of our original legend. I would be her Knight, after all. I had explored and exhausted many conventional spiritual techniques, but none had produced more than relative and transitory results. Now there was nothing left to do but surrender myself, body and soul, into Samantha's hands. For her, I would find the True Grail or die. It was as simple as that. My Destiny was sealed, and with this silent vow I finally retrieved my honor, as well.

My last journal entry was dedicated to her:

> A final word for you, Sweet Samantha: I remember Hoeller quoting the French magician, Eliphas Levi:
>
> "Our intelligence is made for truth and our hearts for love…That is why the honor and happiness of those we love imparts to us divine grandeur and bliss. When we love, we see the infinite in the finite, we find the Creator in the creature; and when we are objects of love, we are the representatives of God, His ambassadors to a certain soul, fully empowered to grant it happiness on earth."
>
> —and so it is with you, Samantha. God be with you.

Thus, I learned Athena's Fourth and last Commandment—SURRENDER and SACRIFICE. It had begun as the surrender of philosophical beliefs and cosmological assumptions, became the surrender of self-interest and personal will, and finally climaxed in a readiness to sacrifice life itself, if need be, to win the Grail—all in the name of Amor. But one other sacrifice would ultimately be required—a sacrifice I never would have been able to make of my own free will. This remained for Athena to accomplish in her good time. Meanwhile, there was nothing more for me to do but obey the law of all journeys and quests—*walk on!*

Eleven:
Hand on the Plough

> And another also said, Lord, I will follow thee; but let me first go bid them farewell, which are at home at my house. And Jesus said unto him, No man, having put his hand to the plough, and looking back, is fit for the kingdom of God.[99]

Nor did I look back that morning I left Samantha. I shoved a Mose Allison cassette into the dashboard stereo, pointed the Old Gray Mare north, and bent myself to the Great Adventure with a sense of joy and freedom I hadn't felt in years. But this did not mean my journey would be made without discipline. I had rules:

1. Although I would ask free room and board wherever I videotaped, I would accept no money, nor would I sell the tape at a later date. I wanted the newsletter to be a true service to which I had no financial attachment or expectation of reward.

2. I would travel with a low profile, asking no preferential treatment, participating in whatever tasks were at hand, and generally making myself useful. Specifically, knowing that many of the communities I visited would be vegetarian, I resolved to obey Jesus' instructions to his disciples when he sent them forth to preach, "And into whatsoever city ye enter, and they receive you, eat such things as are set before you." And I resolved to do this without secret disdain or concealed complaint.

3. While traveling between communities I looked forward to spending some time by myself, but I would not stay in motels. I would camp out whenever possible and shun all luxuries. Further, I would adhere to no fixed schedule and remain flexible in my route, allowing time and fate to work their will in guiding me.

4. Finally, and most important, I would not judge the people I stayed with. I would keep inner silence and outward humility, as I had been instructed in my testing dream.

By now my conception of the newsletter itself had taken on a definite form, but it was a form designed for maximum freedom. Each community would be allotted a ten-minute "column" in which they could present whatever they wanted. I would act only as cameraman and technician and make no editorial decisions or commentary. Nor, except for removing camera stops and starts, would there be any editing, so everything would have to be shot in sequence. I would volunteer suggestions for maintaining continuity but, even here, I would leave the final decision up to each community. If their segment made no sense, that would be their problem, not mine.

At the end of the summer I would undertake to make copies of the newsletter for each of the communities that had participated and send them out. I would also donate the original to a community I felt could handle future distribution, but that would be the end of my involvement.

I started with a list of some twenty-five communities and, by picking up names along the way, ended with fifty. There would only be room for ten or twelve communities to participate without making the whole thing an unwatchable epic, but I decided to let Fate determine who ultimately would be in it. I did, however, begin with a few broad guidelines. For personal reasons I wanted to avoid cities, so the communities would be largely rural. Where four or five communities had a similar focus-say, yoga—I chose one at random and ignored the rest. I also decided not to visit communities that already enjoyed some notoriety, figuring they needed my services the least. Finally, I set geographical limits on my travels. I would not venture south of L.A., cross the Canadian border, or go east of Denver. Thus, my journey would be confined to the western United States.

Before starting out I had marked each community on a map with a number that corresponded to an index card containing pertinent information, like address, local directions, brief descriptions, etc. When all the communities were marked, I examined the map. They tended to fall in clusters, primarily in central California, Oregon, northern Washington, and central Colorado, with the rest strung out between. These constellations determined my general route—first heading north up to Washington, then east to Montana, then turning south again, but otherwise I was flexible. For me personally, there was an additional advantage to this system. Since only numbers were noted on the map, not names, I would have no way of knowing which community I was going to visit next unless I looked it up in the index cards. This I resolved to do only at the end of my stay at any given community. In this way I would be locked into whatever was going on at the moment as much as possible and could keep my mind from wandering off into fantasies of the future. It was a conscious exercise in living here and now.

My attitude toward the trip as a whole was perhaps best summarized in a poem that came to me from Athena before I left:

> waste no time
> chasing new lovers;
> who can compare with my daughter,
> mirror of your heart?
> and seek no guru
> on your travels;
> is there any more severe than me?
>
> I gave you this solitude
> as a sacred gift,
> and blessed you with emptiness;
> abuse them no longer
> with tears of self-pity:
> have you not heard?
> all that is surrendered
> shall be returned
> a hundredfold.
>
> now gather in the four directions,
> the lords and ladies of your soul:
> set the tune and call the measure
> of the mystic marriage
> to your moon-begotten queen,
> the Shining One of a thousand names!
>
> she will bear you a child
> but you must carry him to term,
> the infant king,
> whose womb is memory,
> whose sign is mercy,
> whose star is mercury,
> whose name is morning—
>
> he walks the royal road
> naked through the gate

careless of his safety
mindless of his fate:

don't stand in his way
nor try to guide his steps,
with all your worldly knowledge;
such knowledge is useless
to him who walks this path,
and now, who walks this path is you.

It was in this spirit, then, that I set out with Samantha's cup tucked among my clothes, following at last and in fact her "plaintive north star song of old"—and I was not without hope that, somewhere along the way, I would find the Pearl Beyond Price, the True Dharma of the West, the Holy Grail itself. Now, however, I tried to shut this hope from my mind. It was enough to be Samantha's Knight, seeking some worthy adventure in which to prove myself.

Such were the extravagant flights of fancy that accompanied me that first day of driving leisurely north via the hilly inland route toward Ojai, which was to be my first stop. I arrived mid-afternoon and gallantly presented myself to Leon, who was in charge of the office, offering my services for "whatever tasks were at hand." What was at hand was a shovel and a field full of rocks to be cleared in preparation for planting corn. To my flabby, desk-bound muscles the rocks felt more like boulders, and soon I was well baptized in soil and sweat.

By dinnertime I needed no biblical injunction to "eat what was set before me," which turned out to be a strange but nourishing macrobiotic buffet. And later, when I crawled into my sleeping bag in the back of the Old Gray Mare under a canopy of stars, I felt the last vestiges of my former existence fall away like a snake's dead skin. It seemed almost incredible that a mere three days before I had been a motion picture executive, hobnobbing with the stars. I had done what I set out to do in Hollywood and, except for Colette, had no regrets. But now I had no regrets about leaving it either. I was going home.

I stayed nine days at Ojai, most of it spent gathering wild sage, clearing brush, laying pipe—hard physical work that I gradually grew accustomed to and even started to enjoy. Excess pounds stored up in a sedentary life of rich business luncheons and pasta dinners began to melt in the heat of bodily exertion. I could feel muscles tighten, and my skin started to brown. Moreover, this work had a decidedly different quality than that found in the panicky world of pictures. There were hassles and frustrations, to be sure, but also, underneath, a real sense of love and commitment. Instead of the endless anxious chatter about careers and possessions, conversations here were spiced with dreams, rituals, psychic recipes, folklore, and spiritual teachings from an eclectic array of traditions. Nor were these Ojaites pious puritans, much to my delight.

After a particularly heavy day of clearing brush to meet a fire inspection deadline, a beer-and-pizza night was proclaimed. The pizza was homemade, vegetarian but zesty. The beer was store-bought and arrived in great quantities. After dinner we sat around the smoking terrace, drinking and laughing. Soon guitars emerged, then drums and flutes. It reminded me of San Francisco in the sixties, when people still made their own music, and even I, a complete musical idiot, beat out the rhythm with a stone on my beer bottle.

But neither was life at Ojai all just work and play. Most of the community members were engaged in some form of spiritual practice. In the evenings there was a Zen meditation held in a large yurt, and one morning I participated in a Native American pipe ceremony. It was conducted in an open field just after dawn with coastal mists still swirling in the grass. When my turn came to puff the bloodstone pipe full of smoldering herbs, I related the dream I had had of hunting the silver-backed bear. I said I thought it was the inner bear of courage and hoped we all might hunt him successfully, and surprisingly, no one laughed.

A few nights later I drove down to La Canada with several people, including Joan Halifax, the Foundation's director, and Robert, who was a kind of father figure to the community, giving advice and smoothing out the rough spots. The occasion was an Indian sweat to be held in the suburban backyard of a medicine man named Harley Swiftdeer. We arrived too late for the sweat but joined everyone in the tepee for a dream ceremony afterwards. Harley's vision had come from a Grandfather and prophesized the unification of the four races of Man. I paid close attention to the ceremony, smudging myself with the smoking sage and dropping a dime and a penny into the old syrup bottle (which carried the vision) when it came my way. Harley was a heyoka, or trickster, shaman, full of earthy humor and practical jokes. The reason for the sweat was to celebrate his birthday, and I had brought him a six-pack of Dr. Pepper and some clove cigarettes, which Robert had told me he virtually lived on, as a present.

Returning to Ojai, everyone slept in the rear of the Old Gray Mare while Robert and I sat up front talking about the difference between monastic communities and social alternatives, the essential unity of all paths, and the tasks ahead. He saw the Foundation as a kind of crucible where various traditions and teachers could meet, mix, and enrich each other: Tibetan Lamas came to powwow with Native American Medicine Men who conversed with Zen Masters who, in turn, held discourse with modern scientists like Rupert Sheldrake and David Bohm. It made my head buzz with excitement.

When we finally rolled into Ojai at 4:00 a.m. and roused our sleeping passengers, Joan said to me groggily, "I'll bet a couple of years ago you never thought you'd be sitting in on an Indian Dream Ceremony in the San Fernando Valley." I laughed and thought about the time when Samantha was still my secretary, and I used to give her fatherly advice about facing the "real world." How far away that world seemed now.

After a while I discovered that Ojai, too, had its Shadow—the shadow of petty, personal interests that the Ojaites themselves called the "I-me-mine syndrome." Sometimes it would express itself in playful ways, like the time I drove into town to do my laundry and found half the community at the local hamburger stand gobbling up greasy cheeseburgers and sugary ice-cream cones. Actually, there was no official rule against breaking the Foundation's macrobiotic diet, but everyone felt guilty just the same. It was the age-old lure of forbidden fruit. More seriously, there were complaints about the heavy workload, lack of time for oneself, community burnout, and Joan's sometimes domineering persona as an authority figure. All these, I learned later, would be common gripes wherever I went, but I took them in stride and held to my vow not to judge. It wouldn't always be so easy.

One day, while scrubbing down a large canvas yurt used for conferences, a strange thought occurred to me. We had been working for several hours under a hot sun and now sat around the yurt's wooden deck, smoking cigarettes, and watching the sky turn fiery red when suddenly I felt I was back in Nam—only this time the "war" was righteous and bloodless, and I was perfectly content. I mentioned this to my fellow scrubbers who were surprised to learn that I was a vet. "But you're so normal!" one woman protested. I laughed and explained that there were probably a dozen people in Hollywood at that very moment shaking their heads, convinced that I had gone totally bonkers. One person's madness was another person's sanity, and I felt right at home. Anyone who thought I was *normal* was my kind of crazy.

But humor aside, my sense of *deja vu* was quite profound. It *was* like being back in Nam—the physical work, the Spartan living, the strangeness of different places, diets, customs, etc., and I began to feel again that quickening sense of some ultimate task "left undone." Would I really get a second chance? The possibility, at least, seemed closer.

I finally also got around to videotaping the first column in *The Here and Now Newsletter*, and it went exactly as I had envisioned it. The community planned the format, taking my advice on technical matters and continuity, but the message was all theirs. It took us three days to complete, and when I played it back for them I was showered with compliments. At last, I felt that in some small way I was doing something useful.

Several people asked me to stay, or at least return when my journey was over, and I was tempted. I liked the community, their style, their vision, and the focus of their work. But it was still far too early to make any decisions, and, although I was sad to leave them, I was also eager to be on my way. I said goodbye and in the morning drove on with Athena silent and gentle at my shoulder.

That night I camped on the Kern River, just north of Lake Isabella. My next stop was Lone Pine where lived Franklin Merrell-Wolff, a ninety-six-year-old mystic who in 1936 had a Gnostic Realization that fit in almost every detail the classic descriptions I had read of enlightenment. Actually, it was Samantha, true to her role, who had turned me on to him, lending me *Pathways Through to Space*, the book in which Dr. Wolff described his Awakening. Naturally, I was anxious to meet a flesh-and-blood human being in whom such a transformation had been wrought.

I had not kept a journal since leaving Los Angeles, but I wrote to Samantha regularly. In a letter dated June 17th, I described my journey there:

> A restless night with the Kern River pounding in my ears. In the morning, it's hard to meditate, mind keeps wandering on vagrant, shifting paths. Where is it going? Where am I going? I am anxious to

move. I smudge the Old Gray Mare with dried sage and head east along 178. For an hour or so I coast down the barren back of the El Paso Mountains and hit 395 which runs due north to Lone Pine, but something tells me to continue on 178 which makes a great arch eastward up the Panamint Valley, rejoining 395 a few miles south of Lone Pine. This is high-desert country, scorching and desolate. For a hundred miles there's not a sign of human life, not a gas station or telephone pole, only the rough, gray macadam road snaking through the steely sage. So, too, do my thoughts grow desolate. On the one hand, I berate myself for keeping too much in the way of goods and money, so that I don't really have to beg my sustenance day-to-day like the old wandering Bodhisattvas. On the other hand, I am ruffled by anxieties as to what will happen when what money I do have runs out. At first, I try to free myself from such clingings, but the heat and effort combine to cloud my brain. Finally, I give up and just let them rise and fade.

Now the road seems to have no end and the desert is certainly endless. Then the old snake starts to curve back toward the west—direction of magic and introspection according to the Indian Medicine Wheel—and I pick up 190, a smoother, better road. Slowly, we climb out of the valley, the Old Gray Mare and me chugging along, and are rewarded with cooler breezes. Still, the land is a moonscape of rock and sand, lizards and brush. Then, coming over a rise, my first glimpse of the Sierras—two snowy peaks floating on the horizon!

The road dips, but soon the mountains come into view again and hold, and I'm running toward them, a line of giant ice-crowned magi holding sagely congress over the ages. Then everything turns miraculous. A cloud of dust and mist blows up from the foothills, obscuring the base of the mountains so that the peaks now seem to be suspended in the finest azure. I look again, and the cloud is glowing with blue light and rainbow tints, but still the mountain peaks shine through with a light of their own as clear as I've ever seen. I feel I am approaching some holy place. Holy Lone Pine. And now, too, I feel Dr. Wolff's presence, as though he were summoning me, and press on into town, where every tree, every store, every person looks, to my desert-dazzled eyes, sacred.

Although he entertained a steady trickle of visitors, Dr. Wolff lived alone in a modest ranch house with a devoted young student who helped take care of his personal wants. In spite of his advanced age—which had slowed his memory and made him, at times, a bit wobbly on his feet—Dr. Wolff was in remarkably good shape, both mentally and physically. After a few hours of conversation, I chucked the idea of trying to include him in a ten-minute column on the video newsletter and instead decided to do a full-length interview.

In the meantime I hiked halfway up the eastern face of the Sierras to visit the ashrama that he and his students had built back in the thirties. It was an impressive granite structure, blasted out of the native rock and built in the shape of a balanced cross. Seeing it perched among the pines over a deep ravine, I thought of films I had seen of Ethiopian monasteries hewn out of mountainsides so inaccessible that visitors had to climb rope ladders to reach them. Dr. Wolff's sanctuary was not quite so formidable, though wandering through the now-deserted rooms under a partially collapsed roof, I felt the awe of all that labor performed not for profit nor any worldly gain but simply as a monument to the spirit.

That evening, after a few more hours of conversation with Dr. Wolff, I was equally impressed with the man. In stature he was rather short and thin with something ascetic in his manner despite the fact that he smoked a pack and a half of Pall Malls a day and enjoyed a glass of white port now and then. He sported a gray, Van Dyke beard, and I never saw him without a tie and jacket, though these were always old and hopelessly out of fashion. Nevertheless, the over-all impression he made was one of immense dignity and integrity which might even have seemed austere but for his wry sense of humor. As for his thoughts, I could only absorb their surface meanings, and it wasn't until months later when I returned to sit at his feet and learn the true secrets of philosophy that I began to appreciate their true depth and scope—but that, perhaps, is the subject of another book.

What I did come away with, however, was a kind of unspoken standard to be applied throughout the rest of my journey. As far as I could tell, Dr. Wolff was a genuine Gnostic, and yet he was also and proudly a product of Western culture. He wore Western-style clothes, spoke with a Western twang, and kept to the habits and customs of Western rural life (even to the point of refusing to set his clock by daylight saving time); his table was laid with such traditional fare as fried chicken, potatoes and gravy, beans, apple pie, ice cream, and coffee. More importantly, although he had been heavily influenced by Eastern ideas—particularly those of the great Vedantic sage Shankara—his own thinking was a rich and purposeful grafting of Eastern concepts onto the preeminently rational branches of Western philosophy, whose roots could be traced back through Kant and

Spinoza to Plato. "It is true," he was fond of saying, "that Realization is beyond the grasp of the rational mind, *but*" — he always added gravely — "that does not make it *ir*-rational." In this man, East and West had met to the glory of both.

Ever after, I found it impossible not to look upon the imported accouterments of Eastern traditions — such as, dress, diet, chants, and prayers — with a critical eye. It was not that I was averse to this cultural cross-pollination — indeed, I enjoyed the often colorful results as much as anyone — but I always had to ask myself if adopting this or that mode of dress or diet was really a necessary condition of spiritual attainment. This was Dr. Wolff's legacy to me on that first visit, and I treasured it dearly during the rest of my travels.

From Lone Pine I continued north up the back of the Sierras, following the spring-choked streams and camping in alpine meadows. At a place called Tuttle Creek I met a fellow vet with two wooden feet that looked like Dutch clogs. He was heading east with his dog, hoping to get to India and a place called the Palace of Peace. He was broke, so I gave him twenty dollars and a pack of cigarettes and wished him well. I also spent a day meditating on *The Sutra Spoken by the Sixth Patriarch* and got a sudden whiff of what that old master had meant by "Our very self-nature is Buddha." I was sitting on a rock in an open field, and as soon as I thought of these words, my mind went blank. It just seemed to disappear, and for a moment I couldn't tell the difference between myself and the rock or the field. It was only a split-second flash and happened so fast that I hardly knew what, if anything, had occurred. Nevertheless, I felt somehow I had touched Reality and settled into a wonderful calm that lasted for several days.

Somewhere north of Sacramento I turned west again, heading for the coast where my map was clustered with numbers, but I stopped at several communities in between. As at Ojai, I was warmly received and tried to integrate myself into their daily routines. At a place that featured hot springs I soaked naked for hours surrounded by pines under a mercurial moon. At the Ananda Cooperative Village I was generously invited to join an intensive workshop in Kriya Yoga. In a letter to Samantha dated July 4th, I described it as follows:

> At 5:30 a.m. the gong rings out over the forest, alerting everyone that sadhana begins in half-an-hour. From 6:00 to 8:00 we do hatha yoga and

meditation. There is an hour for breakfast (eaten in silence), then classes until noon. We get two hours for lunch, more classes, and another sadhana from 4:00 to 6:00 p.m. Dinner lasts until 7:30, and there's another class until 10:00, followed by herb tea and sugarless cookies (I'm becoming a connoisseur of herb teas!). At 11:00 I crawl into the Old Gray Mare, body stretched like a rubber band and mind singing with psychic fireworks. This lasted for three days during which I earnestly tried to get the hang of Kriya meditation. It involves chanting a mantra—*Hong Sau*—combined with a complicated technique for raising and focusing energy. I got pretty spacey and heard some strange sounds but didn't feel I was progressing toward anything more than a new form of mental light-show. Okay, I get the message: Reality isn't what it seems—but what is it? On the third day I went back to my own brand of quiet, attention meditation. ...That night I woke up from one of the strangest dreams I ever had—almost indescribable. It was more of a physical sensation than a dream. I felt as though some sort of circle had been completed, and a space was opening up inside—huge, unknowable, but at the same time absolutely concrete and grounded. With it came a single word: *Reality*.

As with the flash I had gotten back at Tuttle Creek, what was different about this dream from all my previous spiritual experiences was a kind of solidity that was very unspiritual in one way but somehow more profound in another. Both seemed to involve a sort of Totality in which the sense of "I" was, for the briefest moment, lost. But as I was to discover later, this is the very essence of Gnosis, and these "flashes" were actually tiny foretastes of the Revelation to come. I was, indeed, drawing closer.

In the meantime I continued sticking to my rules and practicing my disciplines. I avoided all luxuries and accepted without complaint whatever fell to me in the way of chores and accommodations. In particular, my little injunction about food was proving highly effective. I learned to detach from virtually all taste preferences with the result that the simple experience of eating itself became an unassailable pleasure, because it no longer depended on *what* was being eaten. Perhaps the hardest discipline was restraining myself when it came to the actual videotaping. My "producers" and "directors" were by and large amateurs, and I was constantly tempted to jump in and "show them how it should be done." Eventually, however, I conquered even this vestige of professional pride, not so much by repressing it as by discovering the fascination of letting events unfold of themselves. It was, after all, not *my* newsletter but belonged to the communities who participated. I was merely their instrument.

I also added a new discipline to my repertoire which started off almost as a penance. Everywhere I went there was communal dining and its inevitable aftermath, a huge stack of dirty dishes. Again I was reminded of the Army and how much I had detested K.P. while still stateside. When I got to Nam, however, things changed. In fact, in the midst of a mortar attack one night I had actually vowed never to complain about doing dishes again. Now, fifteen years later, I had an opportunity to test that vow.

Wherever I stayed I volunteered to wash the dishes, and in the end managed to transmute this, too, into a kind of meditative delight. Usually, there would be people hanging out in the kitchen making conversation, or someone might have music playing on a tape deck, but even when I was left alone with nothing but the crickets for company, I learned to take attentive pleasure in the feel of steaming, soapy water, the cool smoothness of porcelain, the lightness of aluminum and plastic, or the sheer density of cast iron. It was positively sensual!

In short, a month into my journey, everything seemed to be going surprisingly well, both in terms of the external service I had hoped to perform and in the inner detachment I sought to effect. By now I had lost another ten pounds and acquired a rich tan. I felt young again and full of optimism, but it was premature. Almost imperceptibly, the old Shadow of the World began to steal across my travels. The first hint of this was reflected in a letter I wrote to Samantha on July 8th:

> Wednesday I came down out of the mountains into the hot, flat Sacramento Valley, through huge tracts of farmland being tilled by giant tractors that cast great clouds of dust into the windless air, then crossed into the hills at sunset, and the cool Napa Valley beyond with its neat little rows of vines glowing emerald green in the gilded light... Spent the night in a funky trailer camp, drinking beer with a bunch of boozy young farmhands traveling here and there with their fat wives and snotty-nosed kids all lost and sad under the stars. It breaks my heart to feel the emptiness of their lives beneath all the pool-game bravado and schemes to make a little extra money and dreams of a three-bedroom home in some suburb with barbeque pits and power lawnmowers.

Thursday I take 101 north to Geyserville, then cut towards the coast over a tiny, winding road, C-1, that meanders into the coastal range through tawny grass hills covered with scrub oak and brushed by billowy clouds. Higher up I run into great stands of redwoods filtering light into golden pools and filigree patterns. There are no houses here or any sign of human life, but the forest is alive with fat, gray squirrels, who greet me at every turn, and graceful, scampering deer. Finally, I take a side road up to the Starcross Monastery, a Catholic refuge from the world. A sister comes out to talk to me in front of the old, white Victorian house that is their home. No, they aren't interested in being videotaped or attracting visitors, she says, and ponders aloud the relevance of Christianity to the society below. She suggests, however, that I might want to check out a Tibetan Buddhist monastery some six miles farther up the road. Having just received my first rejection, I thank her and leave, but before I have time to absorb my feelings about this, I am rounding a curve and am struck by a bizarre sight—an enormous, copper-domed temple glistening majestically on a hillside of redwood and pines! The grounds are surrounded by a high, barbed-wire fence and the large, covered gate is securely padlocked. No one seems to be about, but then I spot a guy working in the garden and, after I introduce myself, he scurries off to find someone to talk to me. ...In a little while a well-dressed young woman comes out to the gate, wearing a suede coat and stylish sunglasses. When I explain to her I'm making a video newsletter, she frowns and asks me a lot of questions: Who's paying for it? What's the purpose? I tell her it's a free service, but she doesn't get it. She's up from Berkeley (apparently the headquarters of this sect) and full of sophisticated suspicions. Coincidentally, I have just finished reading *The Life and Hymns of Milarepa*—a famous Tibetan saint and severe ascetic— and thought of explaining my existence as a "homeless brother," a "wandering Bhikshu," but then I look at her suede coat and expensive shades and, instead, bid her a polite goodbye.

Two rejections in one day! What does it mean? Nothing. I have no attachment to this work, not even love. It is a meditation on Arising Phenomena, all of which pass equally away back into the sea of creation. For me, material things are the easiest to give up. I miss practically nothing in the way of goods from my old life—not house, nor bed, nor diet, nor car, nor places, nor routines. Next in line to fall are those activities associated with my *persona*; clothes, titles, career, social power. To be stripped of them is to be stripped of pretenses, and the result is an initial sense of exhilaration and freedom. The exhilaration, however, is wearing off as I face the much harder task of confronting and surrendering personal judgments (as with the girl from Berkeley and even the farmhands). Such judgments form spontaneously and without my conscious volition but seem less and less logical. I used to think I was growing wiser, but now I think I am growing less wise. Certainly, I have less to say to anyone...

I am staying with a woman who takes people out into the wilderness on vision quests. She is into politics, both in terms of society at large—antinuclear demonstrations, etc.—and the inner politics of the New Age—false prophets; power-tripping therapists; mind-fucking gurus; problems of organization, leadership, egos, etc.—much of it is a replay of the sixties dressed up in eighties jargon, but she herself is a good lady. Still, I don't think anything can be done without a "turning about in the seat of consciousness," as the Buddhists say. Actually, I'm not sure anything really needs to be done. After all, the Cosmos has run itself pretty good for the last umpteen-million years or so. Then again, we are just as much a part of the Cosmos as anything else, so...the wheel turns.

For me the wheel was turning slowly from enthusiasm to disillusionment. As I mentioned, I had packed the Old Gray Mare with books and continued my studies at every opportunity, but even reading began to turn sour, as this excerpt from a letter to Samantha bears out:

So many words, millions and millions, spilled out, passed on, scribbled down, transcribed on tablets and papyrus, on rice paper and in stone, copied over and over by innumerable scribes, rolled into scrolls, bound into books, painted on walls, hidden in jars, typed in manuscripts, spewed forth from a thousand presses to grace the most prestigious libraries, the bookshelves of scholars, the tote-bags of students, even bookracks in supermarkets; to be pondered over, thumbed through, underlined, memorized, folded, discarded; to be left in bus stations and bathrooms, on airplanes and beaches, in classy hotels and mountain campsites—wherever Man goes he carries these words, in songs and poems, mantras and dissertations, in voluminous philosophical treatises and in one-line koans—an endless supply of maps penned in every language, and where do they all lead? To the same locked gate, the Gate of Silence, the Door to the Void, The Abode of the Unspeakable. What is the use of all these words? I feel their weight as cumulative and oppressive. The babble of a thousand sages rings in my ears like the chatter of coyotes. I feel crushed by all this mindless cacophony, this absurd but persistent chorus of nonsensical wisdom.

As I continued north, visiting more communities, I also found that not everyone was as dedicated and serious as the people at Ojai and Ananda.

This vignette, reported to Samantha, was not atypical of some so-called "spiritual" communities:

> A couple of girls—one American, one Australian—are trying to talk an Iranian guy into coming to the Bahamas with them in the winter. It's too rainy and cold here for their taste. The Iranian guy wants to know what they'll do in the Bahamas. The Australian girl shrugs, "Swim, hang out. It's warm." The Iranian guy isn't satisfied; it all seems too amorphous to him. The Australian girl suggests they could go to Bolivia instead. It's not as warm, but there's good coke there. The Iranian guy is into vipasyana meditation. The American girl says, "Gee, I should come meditate with you sometime." The Iranian guy tells her it's easy. You just sit and don't think about anything. "Yeah," the American girl says, "I tried that once, but I just fell asleep." The conversation switches back to the relative merits of places to winter; the Bahamas, Australia, South America, Canada—and I leave.

In fact, the very word *spiritual* had, in many cases, become so diluted as to include virtually any activity and an amazing range of beliefs. Sometimes, when I inquired about a person's particular practice or discipline, all I'd get was a puzzled expression. If I pressed the question, they'd often respond with something like "Oh, everything I do is spiritual." Others felt that accumulating material wealth was, if not the goal of spiritual life, at least a sign of progress. Shades of Calvin. At one community I ran across a group of people who believed they could achieve physical immortality. At first, I thought it was a joke—a New Age parody, but they were quite serious. What's more, anyone who doubted their doctrine was labeled a "deathist" and treated with scorn and derision. In the face of such bizarre creeds, it was difficult to maintain my non-judgmental attitude. Finally, I encountered a community where it became impossible.

In its literature the community portrayed itself as a paragon of New Age morality, but in reality the place was organized like a feudal fiefdom. The owner and his inner circle of friends lived in relative luxury, devoting their time to yogic disciplines and cultivating effete diets, while the heavy labor was done primarily by young, working-class drifters up from the south in search of jobs. The latter lived in shacks or tents, were paid sub-minimum wages, and worked without benefit of any kind of pension, medical insurance, or even workmen's comp. Nor was any attempt made to include them in the social, spiritual, or educational functions that the community professed to provide for humanity at large. I spent many a night with these boys, pitching horseshoes and getting drunk in the woods. Their souls were adrift on a sea of apathy and steeped in despair.

This whole brave new structure was built on such a primitive system of capitalist exploitation that it roused the ghost of Marx in me. I was tempted to stay and organize a revolt. Mentally, I even began to map out a strike strategy, and the more I thought about it, the more feasible it seemed. Perhaps this was what I was meant to do? I had the skills and experience, shouldn't I try to put them to use? Wasn't *justice* also a virtue worthy of my efforts?

In the end, however, Athena stayed my hand. I knew I couldn't presume to lead anyone unless I was willing to settle in and become a worker there myself. But this would entail a long-term commitment, and once the struggle was engaged, I would have to see it through. The whole process could take months, even years, and what would happen to my quest? As formless and ephemeral as this quest sometimes seemed, I knew I couldn't abandon it. It had become the thread upon which my whole life hung. Still, I couldn't just walk away without saying a word, either.

Finally, I compromised with my conscience. I made friends with a young worker who was very bright and whose uncle had been a labor organizer. I told him my idea for a strike strategy and why I thought it could succeed and left it up to him to do with it what he liked. I knew he might well think my intrusion arrogant, but in point of fact, he seemed rather intrigued. We shook hands and said goodbye, and I never did find out whether anything came of our conversation.

I was now six weeks into the journey and had continued to write Samantha faithfully—long, detailed letters that usually ended with heady and extravagant declarations of cosmic love. But since I never knew where I would be next, it was impossible for her to write me back, and I began to brood over the situation. She had said that she loved me, but neither of us had made any promises for the future. What if her feelings had changed? Perhaps my letters were becoming an embarrassment? I decided to telephone her and see.

The instant I heard Samantha's resonant voice, I knew my worries were unfounded. She bubbled with enthusiasm for my letters and said that her own life was rich with new, radiant experiences which she promised to remember in all their specifics and tell me about later. I had called from a pay-phone, so we couldn't talk long, but afterwards, I felt jubilant. I leapt back into the Old Gray Mare and pushed north once again, refreshed and brimming with hope.

On July 21st, I crossed into Oregon, but the Shadow followed. The next community I visited had gone bust sometime during the spring. I wandered around the deserted houses and overgrown fields trying to imagine what had happened. A caretaker told me they had been embroiled in factional disputes and had had trouble with drugs, all of which finally led to their demise.

At another long-standing farm community I found the members depressed and uncertain about what lay ahead. In the past year they had lost the only two couples who had children, and almost everyone remaining was over thirty. "It's one thing," a bearded guy told me ruefully, "to pool your economic resources, but when you have to throw your kids into the pot, that's the real test." A woman I talked to had a slightly different perspective on why the two couples had moved. According to her, they had wanted more of a spiritual focus. "Hell, I guess spirituality is just something up to the individual," she said. "I dunno—me, I just wish people were more up front about their emotions. Still, we ain't gettin' any new blood. Without children, how long we gonna last—ten, maybe twenty years? Anyway, for better or worse, this is my community, but I dunno about the future."

Personally, I had no complaints. Everyone treated me with kindness, but the general atmosphere was heavy with a contagious gloom. Still, I didn't get discouraged. Every so often there would be a sign that I was on the right track, and meditation continued to yield glimpses of insight. This one, which I described to Samantha, happened late one afternoon while I camped under a tree:

> Out in the long-shadowed field a brown pony neighs to no one; the little stream sings to no one; the summer insects hum to no one; the wind sighs in the pines to no one, and suddenly, for an instant, there really is NO ONE! That is all. All...just *that*. It was only a momentary glimpse, but in that moment God took something from me, and maybe that's the way it will be with me. He'll come in moments like this, and each time he'll take a little something, until finally there is nothing left—no one but Him.

At one place I visited, I accompanied some of the folks to a big party at their neighbor's farm deep in the Oregon woods. The scene looked like a cross between a hippie gathering from the sixties and Fourth of July in the Old West. Bearded, blue-jeaned long-hairs and women in ankle-length calico skirts danced to live rock 'n' roll, roasted joints of lamb and chicken over open fires, and swigged down great jars of home-brewed apple wine. As I meandered through the crowds I heard a voice call my name, but who could possibly know me in this wilderness? It turned out to be none other than J.S., the guy in my bear dream, whom I hadn't seen or heard from since leaving San Francisco. What's more, I realized, this part of Oregon had actually once been the province of Russian fur trappers! It was spooky. Apparently, this dream, too, was coming true, and I felt the bear himself could not be far ahead in time.

I passed through Eugene, where I stayed three days with a nice, middle-class, poly-fidelitous family (two men and a woman) who had devised a marriage contract to govern almost every aspect of their lives, then moved on into the Oregon heartland to a community called Breitenbush. Here all my disciplines seemed to ripen, and I feasted on their fruits, but these days of felicity were to be the last of my old life. Perhaps a fetus, happy in his nascent consciousness and unable to imagine any reality beyond the womb, feels the same just before the painful cataclysm of birth. At any rate, this is how I described it to Samantha:

> Breitenbush! As bright and lovely as its name! There is a weeklong Communities Conference in progress here at this beautiful hot-springs healing center, with its peaked-roof lodge and miniature, geothermally-heated cabins where the steam comes right out of the earth into old-fashioned radiators. As the Old Gray Mare and I approach, the sun explodes through the billowing clouds, and you can feel the human energy vibrating miles away. "Something special is going to happen here," Athena whispers, as of old. "Pay attention." And I do.
>
> The meadow in front of the lodge is filled with milling folks in states of colorful dress and undress. They come from a dozen or so communities on the West Coast to exchange ideas on everything from biodynamic farming to interpersonal relationships. Musicians play flutes and mandolins in the lush grass, mothers bare their breasts to nurse squirming infants, older children scamper underfoot bathed in radiant light. Adult, serious types sit in the shade, heads bowed together, discussing the fate of the planet. I pass through them all, making

everyone smile, find a few people I know from previous stops, catch up on gossip, and feel utterly at home.

The next two days swirl together in a seemingly endless cycle of workshops, work projects, meditations, festivities, food, and just lazy soaking in the hot tubs. At 7:00 a.m. I'm up for yoga classes given by Nitae (whom I met at Ananda) and his wife. It's a familiar routine to me, and I'm glad they've come. Later they give a workshop on Spiritual Marriage which is heart-warming and well received. They talk about meditating together, dedicating their lovemaking to God, and spending days in silent, nonverbal communication. I want to hug them both.

After lunch—a meal of Mexican-type veggies served from an outdoor kitchen in a very friendly but orderly manner—I join a work crew digging ditches for geothermal pipes. It's blistering work in the afternoon sun, but I love it, swinging my pick up and down the trench and jumping in to dig out stones with my fingers. Finally the dinner gong sounds, but I stay behind to finish up a section of trench I've started. My fellow workers think me odd, but I don't mind. I'm happy!

At night there's a talent show with singers, acrobats, even a stand-up comic who parodies health foods and gurus. Between all this activity there's still time for soaking in the small, hot pools, followed always (as I've grown accustomed to) by a quick dip in the ice tub! The exhilaration lasts for hours. Also, there are slow, contemplative walks back and forth from where the Old Gray Mare is parked to the main lodge building along a path that winds under thick oaks and crosses a slurpy brook.

More profoundly—and not always pleasantly—I am exposed to old attachments still clinging to my soul. They hurt when suddenly lanced but then drain away like pus from infected wounds. A suave guy—New Age suave, of course—charms everyone with his chic—New Age chic—red tunic, matching pants, and winning self-confidence. He's witty and has a way with words and alternately chides and strokes his audience as he shows slides from various communities around the world. It turns out he's a "Networker" trotting the globe—a dashing and glamorous role!—and I find I am envious. Walking back to the Old Gray Mare that night I go slow and feel the envy simmer, but now at a kind of distance, the way one can look at a stubbed toe, feel the pain, but not identify with it. Actually, I'm a "Networker," too! All I have to do to compete is develop a style and announce myself as such. But do I really want to give in to my own envy and court the envy of others only to see myself reflected in their eyes? Or do I continue on this path of anonymity and see things as they are, just so, without any expectation of reward? I laugh, because there really is no longer any choice.

During the days I mingle with the rest of these dreamers, listening but not talking (you would be amazed at how mellow the old warrior has become!), and hear the most naive and outrageous theories about what is and what is to come. One guy in a loincloth and flowing gray hair insists that we must all return to the cities. "I don't know how much longer they can last without our input," he says seriously. Another community is manufacturing fuel-efficient stoves to save the Third World from a firewood shortage. I admire their impulse to service, but this effort seems like spitting in a hurricane, and their political savvy appears to be nonexistent. Although silent, I feel myself growing contemptuous, but what do I have to offer? Nothing, really. No geopolitical theories, no global strategies, no grandiose schemes. I am bankrupt of such ideas, and thus my cynicism. But I am also genuinely frustrated. I want to help. I want to have answers. I want to serve, too. I despair—more importantly, I *allow* myself to despair, another form of humility. Now, only one notion arises. I must seek God first. "Cast out first the beam out of thine own eye," the Gospel says. Mankind has gotten along without my input for the last 100,000 years, it can survive for a year or two more. I also remember that the Buddha's last temptation to quit his search for enlightenment was the appeal to Social Duty. Needless to say, he resisted. In the meantime, tiptoeing through this gypsy throng is like wading through an ocean of human wildflowers bursting out of winter.

By mid-week all but the most die-hard community conferencees have left, and life at Breitenbush slips back to relative tranquility. Gone are the throngs from the lodge rooms, and the meadow is empty of celebrants. A little band of Christ-conscious vagabond musicians hangs in for a few days more, camping out of their VW van which is twice as old as the Old Gray Mare. They are a colorful group, but ragged and barefoot, and have absolutely no money or prospects; they just wander from community to community playing flutes and guitars and picking up free meals where they can. I am intrigued but feel guilty in their presence and overloaded with possessions. Two of them befriend me in the "smoking area," and I offer them cigarettes. They talk about surrendering into Jesus and "going with the flow," but back at the lodge one of their brothers gets into an argument with a Breitenbush woman over responsibilities. I just hear the end of it. "Come down to earth," the woman says. "Wow, you're so attached to *things!*" the vagabond snarls and walks away muttering about "hangups" and "attachments" and what a drag everything is. His attitude doesn't strike me as very saintly. In *fact*, I have just been reading these words of Inayat Khan,

"In all forms of life he sees God, and thereby he has toward everybody that attitude which a lover of God, a worshipper of God, has toward God. Therefore, the Sufi complains no more, has no grudge against anyone, has nothing to grumble about...for complaint comes to a person who thinks of himself most of the time."

Soon my two friends begin to show up miraculously at the smoking area just when I'm about to light up. Naturally, I continue offering them cigarettes, but it grows embarrassing. One of them has a healing wand — a plastic tube filled with water and ashes from India. "Hold it to your heart," he insists, "and you'll see all the colors of the chakras." I try it but see nothing. That evening I pass their campsite and hear them arguing over various schemes to make money. It seems they, too, still have some attachments from which the mere fact of poverty has not released them.

In the morning I am greeted by an olive-green snake slithering by the Old Gray Mare. I jump back with a start, then grow fascinated, and the instinct of revulsion vanishes. It is so beautiful and graceful, going about its way in the world. I follow until it disappears in the bush, enthralled. Still in a mild state of awe, I sit for morning meditation on a bumpy log. I close my eyes and pass quickly through all the warm-up phases. Then suddenly, I'm hardly there at all! I open my eyes. Only the barest ripple of thought seems to separate me from Creation...

Saturday there is a wedding at Breitenbush. The bride and groom have visited here before and know some of the community members, but still it is a business affair. Everyone pulls together to organize it. My job is to sweep down the lodge decks, covered with pine cones and needles. In the Fireplace Room the musicians who will play at the ceremony practice — two long-hairs on piano and mandolin playing Celtic reels. Soon my broom beats out the rhythm on the wooden planks, and I am no longer working but dancing. My next job is bartender. As I set up the champagne glasses for the reception (wearing, by the way, my blue blazer and gray slacks, which I brought along thinking, "maybe I'll run into a wedding somewhere down the line"), the wedding guests do a Sufi dance in the meadow before me. It's so beautiful I begin to cry, and not a few guests later get a glass of champagne flavored with my tears.

After the reception, dinner is served on the deck. I help carry the dirty dishes back to the kitchen. Everywhere I look there are stacks and stacks of grungy pots and pans. Poor dishwashers. I strip off my jacket and shirt and dig in. Again, people passing thank me for my extra help, but it is undeserved. They don't get it. Work *is* life, and I am really in ecstasy. All these disciplines, renunciations, and services which the Holy Ones perform and which others admire so much because they imagine them to be difficult and austere are in reality joys and privileges to the performers. This is one of the great sacred Secrets, and it will always be secret, no matter how many people give it away, because no one will ever believe it who has not tried it.

Later I go back to the lodge. The musicians are playing their jigs and reels, but I don't dance tonight. I have drunk a few glasses of champagne myself and have forgotten the effects of alcohol. My body is a bit unstable, but mind continues to be clear. I sit in a corner for hours, trembling with each note that seems to link me with my own Irish ancestors, and I see all their misty, emerald lives stretching into the melancholy past—we are a race of sentimentalists, lovers, poets, and balladeers, and I am not ashamed of loving you outrageously and forever...

—Your Knight of the New Dharma

Breitenbush, too, had its Shadow, its tensions and frustrations, but it no longer seemed to matter to me—at least, not as much. There was even a dispute as to whether they should participate in the newsletter, but through it all I remained detached and tranquil. By the time I left, I felt something pivotal had happened, not an illumination but a dissolving of distinctions, an absorption of matter into spirit.

It was with a light heart and easy smile, then, that I drove down out of the mountains into Oregon's central plateau without the slightest premonition that I was headed for the Wasteland—a psychic desert, barren beyond anything I had ever experienced before or could possibly have imagined.

Hand on the Plough

Twelve:
The Discovery of Gnosis

That evening I made camp on the banks of the Metolius River. The next morning I drove to the river's source a few miles away where it springs full flood from a fault in the earth, then flows briskly eastward through a valley of lush grassland and stately pines. On my way back to camp I stopped at a little country store to stock up on groceries. Outside, there was a pay phone, and although I had just mailed off a letter to Samantha, it was such a lovely day that I decided on impulse to call her.

There was nothing extraordinary about our conversation. In fact, on the surface it was quite mundane. I told her a little about Breitenbush, and that I had written more at length, and asked how she was doing. "Oh, fine," she answered, then added more obliquely, "I've made some new friends. My life's changing." That was all. But it was too late for any secrets between us. I could tell by the tone of her voice that this "new friend" was really someone she had fallen in love with. It made my heart go numb, and I could feel a great darkness descend, slowly extinguishing all the lights of my life.

After we said goodbye, I stumbled out of the booth and drove back to camp. The sun was still shining, but all beauty had fled the world. It was August 8th, 1983.

I don't remember the rest of the afternoon. I must have gone to sleep early. In the morning I trekked listlessly on to Rajneeshpuram, the controversial commune founded by Indian guru Bhagwan Rajneesh in the center of Oregon, where I spent the day. In a final letter to Samantha, written from a trailer park on August 10th, I described my visit as follows:

> Driving in on a long dirt road, you are greeted by humorous signs like:
>
> *Essentially a One Lane Road*
>
> and:

Blind Curves
No Shoulders
Big Trucks
Good Luck!

Later you pass Krishnamurti Lake and Gurdjieff Dam. Yellow school buses grind up and down the raw, newly cut roads with black letters painted on their sides that announce, Buddhafield Transport. At the reception trailer everyone is stopped and searched for weapons (because of a recent bombing incident in Portland) by mauve-uniformed Peace Officers, themselves sanyasins (disciples). There is a slight paranoia in the air, but our red-clad hosts are as uncomfortable about these security measures as everyone else. Once past this checkpoint, everyone seems open and friendly. No private vehicles are allowed in the town, so I am taken by van to the Mirdad, or Press Office, to discuss my video project. Along the way there is evidence of tremendous amounts of money and energy being invested in all kinds of construction. (Later I am told they are a sixty-million-dollar-a-year operation and proud of it!) The place swarms with red-clad sanyasins dashing hither and thither—they certainly seem to know where they are going—smiling and necking. It is a city of smiles.

The people at the Mirdad Office don't quite know what to make of my project. I have to talk to a woman named Sunshine who is about to take a half dozen mid-western tourists for a guided tour of the "city" (town, really) in a large air-conditioned bus. She invites me along.

Sunshine and the English bus driver are a delight, full of humor and charm, as they point out various projects: commercial farming, water reclamation, hen breeding, experiments in introducing natural predators to balance out native coyote, snake, and mosquito populations; housing projects (all air-conditioned); Rajneesh Airfield; etc. Woven into their commentary is a subtle but effective defense of what they are doing designed to counter the anti-Rajneesh propaganda of the local Oregonians who are trying to oust them.

Downtown Rajneeshpuram looks like a budding resort town (they get up to 200 tourists a day) with a modern shopping mall that houses such establishments as the Zen Boutique and Zorba Bookstore. There is also a discotheque and an excellent Mexican restaurant (whose cuisine I sampled later). They have only been at it for two years, and everything appears raw and new, but one can see a kind of Spiritual Acapulco blooming in the Oregon hinterlands.

Back at the Mirdad I learn my video newsletter has run aground on an unbreakable policy: No one can stay on the property for free, and the only hotel, The Rajneesh, costs $50 a night—a price I am unwilling to pay. The people at the Mirdad have grown to like me, but there is no way around this rule.

I have dinner on the restaurant terrace—chile relleno and two bottles of Dos Equis—and chat with the blonde waitress in a scarlet mini-skirt as a storm builds over the mountains in the east. Like the rest of the sanyasins I've met, she too is smiling, happy, and dedicated, and I'm almost tempted to take the vows myself. Of course, there must be a shadow Rajneeshpuram (there always is), but that's not what stops me. It is, suddenly, that I see no difference between the inside and the outside. This is true not just of Rajneeshpuram but of all the communities I've visited, all religions and cultures, paths and ways. And I see also that the sanyasin's happiness, like everyone else's, flows from a sense of being "inside." It is their womb, their protection, source of motivation and channel for their energies. Everything is manifested in form, and yet, the forms themselves are shifting and illusory. There is no inside or outside of form, and it does not matter anymore whether I'm in a trailer park, or a tavern, or a holy city. Everywhere people find, alternatively, delight and discouragement; they believe, then disbelieve; they build, then cease building; they pray and grow tired of prayers; they come and they go; they are born and they die...and it makes me weary. Not happy, not sad, just weary.

Weary was the right word, only this was no momentary weariness of the flesh, nor a temporary fatigue of the mind, but the beginnings of a deep soul-weariness with existence itself. Just as Mao's China had put an end to my dream of a secular utopia, so Rajneeshpuram signaled the demise of its spiritual counterpart. In the very flamboyancy of their contradictions, Bhagwan's sanyasins had shown me that there was nothing holier than anything else, no unmixed motives, no pure activities, no sacred communities. It was the same old world—and always would be —wherever I went. Thus, what I was seeking externally was a mirage— an ever-receding rainbow that I would never catch.

But far more serious, this weariness also extended inwardly to Samantha, though I tried not to let it show in my letter, the rest of which was taken up with wishing her well in her "new life." Nor was I the least bit bitter. On the contrary, she had done me a final, painful service. She had held a mirror up to my own incorrigible absurdity, for now, through her eyes, I could see myself truly for the first time. Instead of a twentieth-century Knight of the Dharma, I was a ludicrous Don Quixote. I had imagined myself on some heroic mission of the heart, but in reality I had been playing the buffoon in an impossible farce. Eschewing any ordinary relationship, I had envisioned an Eternal Amor on whose altar I had sacrificed everything; but this was a temporal world, and Samantha was a temporal girl, and the very things I had consigned to the flames of my deluded passion—career, home, security—were the things temporal relationships were made of. I had lost her before and won her back, but now the energy and means were utterly exhausted. What did I have left to offer? Mendicant wanderings? A life of saintly poverty? A future as tenuous as any itinerant farmworker's? No wonder she had kept her distance, and who could blame her? But the farce was finally over. The curtain had rung down. The theater had gone dark, and all I wanted to do now was slip out of her life as quietly as possible.

I ended the letter on what I thought was a light but carefully dispassionate note, signed it simply "love," and headed north once again. This time, however, there was no smile on my lips and no hope in my heart.

As I drove up through the center of Oregon, I felt something enormous had come to an end but could see nothing to take its place. The Shadow that had been dogging my travels—indeed, my whole life—had now crept inside my very soul and was slowly spreading its darkness into every corner of my being. Like the acrid clouds of loggers' smoke that rolled across the treeless country, I could smell the smoking ruins of my own life choking out the sun, and even the desolation of this denuded landscape seemed to pale beside the desolation that was growing within.

Eventually, the scenery changed, but my mood didn't; if anything, it deepened. In the Mt. Hood National Forest I pulled off onto a deserted logging road to take a pee in the wilderness. Afterwards, I climbed up on a giant tree stump and had a strange vision.

I saw the whole history of human consciousness unreel with dizzying speed, like a telepathic movie, before my mind. In the beginning there had been only the primate germ of a seminal self-awareness, but out of that single seed had been born a myriad, proliferating forms, multiplied and manifested through countless migrations and myths, visions and voyages, religions and wars; out of consciousness the first stick had scratched the soil, the first flint produced a fire, the first stone crushed a skull—but then whole herds were slaughtered, forests felled, rivers rerouted, entire continents terraced and sculptured like so much clay; out of consciousness cultures had sprouted and withered, civilizations flourished and died, temples and cities had been raised, then burned to make room for more. Consciousness had been the incorporeal source of all this corporeal activity, this surge of sheer busyness that was spilling across the globe and, now, even beyond to the stars; and I saw all its millions of agents in vast parade—mothers and maidens, sinners and saints, students and teachers, soldiers and sages, merchants and kings, madmen and murderers, artists and whores—all coming and going out of the void like a swarm of fabulous fireflies with their fantastic dreams, from the most sublime samadhis to the cruelest lusts, from the tinkerings of genius to the fractured schemes of fools—a universal flood of ideas and images, poems and prophecies, theories and songs—all pouring forth into existence then flowing away again in the general, endless flux and drive towards what? What was the purpose? What was the point? Where was it all leading?

I didn't know and drove on.

On the outskirts of Portland I stopped by another community, but they didn't want to be videotaped. "We got our own media," a man in a checkered shirt explained apologetically, but it no longer mattered. I didn't care anymore who carried the true Dharma and who didn't. I crossed into Washington and camped in a rain forest on the banks of the Columbia Gorge.

That night I searched my thoughts for Samantha, but she was gone. There was only an awful emptiness, and I brooded over it. In losing her love, I realized, I had not only lost the motive for my quest but something even more critical—my last link to the whole weave and web of social relations that is the life of humanity, that anchors us to the past, cradles us in the present, and out of which we spin our dreams for the future. Everywhere I had gone, I had carried her in my heart as a reference point. She had been the final arbiter of my destiny and the sole measure of its meaning. In her name I had wielded Athena's sword, slashing everything else from my life. But now that sword—"double-edged and deadly"—had swung back to make its last, ironic cut, and without Samantha's love I found myself completely severed from the race of men. I had put all my spiritual eggs in one basket, and the bottom had fallen out.

August 11th:

In the morning I awoke to overcast skies and intermittent rain.

I meditated, then made a soggy breakfast of undercooked pancakes and lukewarm coffee. Afterwards, I washed up and got out the map. The next community on my list was located near Olympia. The shortest way there was up Highway 5, but I had been trying to stay off the Interstates. Besides, there was another community just outside of town called Goldendale that I had half-heartedly planned to check out as well. I settled on a route that would take me east on 14, then north on 97 through Goldendale, and finally west again on 12 toward Olympia.

I packed up my utensils and climbed behind the wheel of the Old Gray Mare, ready to leave just as I had left countless campsites before—only this time I couldn't. I was literally frozen in my seat. There was simply no reason to go on, no game left to play, no candle to burn, and no brass ring to snatch. The entire journey had suddenly been rendered futile, and I could feel my whole merry-go-round life crash into a deathly silence. Nothing like this had ever happened to me before. I was absolutely immobilized.

I thought of going back to L.A., but to what? Colette? My job? Topanga? They were all gone. There was nothing left of the past, and I couldn't envision anything in the future. My mind refused to produce any images at all. Time had stopped, and I was suspended over a great nothingness. I thought of the nursery rhyme,

> Humpty-Dumpty sat on a wall,
> Humpty-Dumpty had a great fall.
> All the King's horses
> And all the King's men
> Couldn't put Humpty-Dumpty
> Together again.

After a while I got out my tape recorder and started making a tape for Samantha. I had no intention of ever sending it to her—it was just that there didn't seem to be anything else to do. I felt like I was leaving a last will and testament, but there wasn't a trace of sorrow or self-pity. I was beyond all emotion. The only sensation I felt was a kind of absence of sensation, a complete hollowness inside.

The tape was full of long pauses while I waited for words to come. In these silences I could hear the rain drumming on the Old Gray Mare's roof. I described the rain and the previous day's drive up through central Oregon and Mt. Hood. I told her of my vision and said I had an intimation that the journey would soon come to an end, but it was a prophecy uttered without joy. I spoke of the necessity of dispensing with all teachers—"If you meet the Buddha on the road, kill him!" (as the Zen masters used to say), but these were only empty ramblings.

Finally, I mentioned that if there was anything, it was a voice calling me north. North, someone had once told me, was the direction of power. Was there really power in the north? Could you go to the north, scoop up some power like snow, put it in your pocket, and come home? Or maybe it was the other way around; if you moved with power, the power would carry you north—north on the psychic compass in the geography of the soul...symbols and signs, images and forms. Up until now they had seemed to be guiding me, but I could no longer decipher their codes. I remembered what Jesus had said: "The Light...is hidden in the Image of the Light of the Father," but the Father's image remained stubbornly sealed.

I talked for forty-five minutes, filling up one side of the tape. Then I shut off the machine. The sky was clearing, and I found it possible to go on, but I did so mechanically and without any conscious motive.

For the next two days I traveled like this through a void. Only the barest whisper of thoughts and feelings ruffled its surface. Otherwise, it was empty. There was no sadness or depression in it, just a kind of strange absurdity. I often felt death was close at hand, but I was not the least suicidal. I neither welcomed my demise nor was frightened of it. Instead, I watched like a disinterested scientist observing an insect whose brain had been removed. Occasionally, I made notes on my tape recorder with some vague notion that all this might be of interest to someone in the future after I was gone.

I drove through the community at Goldendale as planned but had no desire to stop or talk to anyone and so pushed on. Ten miles outside of town, my fuel line broke. I pulled into a little roadside restaurant with gasoline leaking all over the Mare's hot engine. I knew it could ignite at any moment and cause a serious explosion, but I was strangely unconcerned. I phoned a mechanic in town who came out to fix it. He brought the wrong fuel line and had to make another trip back to Goldendale. The whole affair took two hours, yet the delay had no effect on me one way or another. I just sat in the Old Gray Mare and waited. I had nowhere else to be.

In the evening I pulled into a campground just east of Mt. Rainier. I went through the motions of cooking dinner, washing the dishes, brushing my teeth. Everything as usual. Later I even noticed that my feet were getting cold and took the trouble to pull on an extra pair of socks. I keep saying, "I", but it was more like someone else was doing it all for me. "I" was on automatic pilot.

During the night I awoke from a restless sleep, opened Meister Eckhart at random, and read the following:

> We can think what we like, that a man ought to shun one thing or pursue another—places and people and ways of life and environments and undertakings—that is not the trouble, such ways of life or such matters are not what impedes you. It is what you are in these things that causes the trouble, because in them you do not govern yourself as you should.
>
> Therefore, make a start with yourself, and abandon yourself. Truly, if you do not begin by getting away from yourself, wherever you run to, you will find obstacles and trouble wherever it may be ....People who seek in that way are doing it all wrong; the further they wander, the less will they find what they are seeking. They go around like someone who has lost his way; the further he goes, the more lost he is. Then what ought he to do? He ought to begin by forsaking himself, because then he has forsaken everything.[100]

It was a perfect description of my own predicament. I was lost, and the further I went, the more lost I became. What's more, I certainly felt this "self" of mine to have become very much a burden—would that I could forsake it! The trouble was, I mused ruefully, drifting back to sleep, no one ever tells you how.

August 12th:

The next morning I awoke feeling heavy and not at all rested. I found a spot where the light slashed through the pines and tried to meditate, but nothing happened. Afterwards, I ate some yogurt and watched the first leaves fall. This far north, autumn was already in the air. Then it would be winter. I was tired, but I could recognize in this tiredness a crazy kind of peace. I presumed it was the repose of the dead.

Eventually, I felt I should be pushing on toward the community in Olympia, following the program even though the programmer himself had long since disappeared.

I spent the whole day behind the wheel not thinking about anything in particular, hardly aware of where I was going. At the town of Randle I had an impulse to detour south and see Mt. St. Helens, the famous volcano. It was a grueling, dusty drive up and down one-lane mountain roads with turnouts for oncoming traffic. When I finally did get a look at Mt. St. Helens, it was just another mountain with a few wisps of vapor blowing off the top. I sighed and drove back to the main highway.

It was early evening when I arrived in Olympia. The streets were jammed with people going home from work, dashing through yellow lights and honking at each other impatiently . I just followed the flow not really caring where it took me. As I crossed the main bridge that spans the Deschutes River (dividing the Olympic Peninsula from the mainland), I saw a sign saying Percival Harbor and for a moment I thought of Samantha and my own lunatic quest for some modern-day Grail. What nonsense it all seemed like now.

After driving around on the west side of town for a while, I finally located the community I was looking for. The address turned out to be a house in a campus suburb, but apparently no one was home. I knocked several times and peered through the screen door. Inside, the living room was strewn with New Age pamphlets and posters protesting the killing of whales and nuclear power. A bumper sticker plastered to the window read Ecotopia Now. Somehow it looked very familiar — like places I had lived during the sixties, only then we had posters of Mao on the walls and bumper stickers that said Get Out of Vietnam. Yes, I knew that house well and what its occupants would be like — bright-eyed, zealous kids bent on reforming the world — and suddenly, I had no stomach for their company. I had heard it all before and had grown too old and too tired to listen anymore. Instead of waiting around for them to return, I decided to take their absence as the sign of a merciful fate that I was not meant to videotape here.

It was getting late now, and I felt utterly exhausted, as though the whole dark burden of this journey was catching up with me all at once. Also, I hadn't bathed in nearly a week, and every pore of my flesh felt clogged with grime. To hell with discipline, I thought, and decided to splurge on a really good meal and a motel room with a shower for the night. My first priority, however, was to get out of the city with its jarring traffic and smoggy streets. I looked at the map. The closest town was Shelton, located on the southeastern shore of the Olympic Peninsula. This was a bit off my route, but I was no longer concerned about that.

In Shelton I discovered a surprisingly elegant Italian restaurant. Their menu featured a variety of sophisticated pasta dishes and salads. I chose the seafood fettuccine, drank a glass of nicely chilled white wine, and suddenly found myself flirting with the waitress. It gave me a wonderfully giddy sensation. Here I was indulging myself shamelessly, and far from feeling guilty, I was actually reveling in it—even if it was the revelry of the damned.

Nevertheless, a man without a future has certain prerogatives. He passes beyond the pale of all purpose and desire. True, I had gambled with an "eternal mistake" and lost, but slowly it was beginning to dawn on me that I also had—as Bob Dylan used to sing—"nothing anymore to live up to," no more preparations to make, no more discipline to follow, no more dreams to fulfill, spiritual or otherwise.

In the midst of these thoughts a poem appeared. It went like this:

> What did I do
> when I lost my best girl?
> What everyone does—
> Got drunk and had satori!
> My heart was really broken,
> but still I had to laugh:
> There is only one sin
> and it's called Necessity.

This poem just popped into my head, and I really didn't know what it meant. I certainly had had no satori, and why should necessity be a sin? But for some reason it pleased me. I jotted it down on a napkin, ordered another glass of wine, and drank a light-hearted toast to Samantha. By the end of the meal, however, my exhaustion had returned.

On the way into town I had driven by a place called the Mill Creek Motel. In passing, it had looked like one of those charming but inordinately expensive country inns, so I hadn't bothered to stop. Now, however, with two glasses of wine under my belt plus an after-dinner Irish coffee, I threw fiscal prudence to the winds and doubled back to find it.

As I pulled up to the entrance, I realized that the Mill Creek Motel was going to offer something less than luxury accommodations. On closer inspection its peaked, shingled roof—which I had thought "charming"— was actually in a sad state of disrepair, and its coat of paint was chipped and peeling like scales off a dead fish. Screen doors banged, dogs barked, and somewhere inside I could hear a television blaring. In my new mood of extravagance I was mildly disappointed but too weary to look further.

There was no one in the front office when I entered, and I had to call loudly for the manager several times before she appeared—an overweight, middle-aged woman with her hair in curlers. As I scrawled my name on the registration pad, she picked through the clutter behind her desk until she found what she was looking for. It was the key to Room No. 4, for which I paid twenty dollars plus tax.

The room itself had shabby cinderblock walls and was furnished only with the barest essentials. The bed sagged, and the bathroom was hardly larger than a closet, but I didn't care. It had a shower, of sorts, and I plunged in, grateful for anything that was hot, wet, and soapy.

I had brought a couple of books in from the Old Gray Mare, but after the shower I was too tired to read. I stretched out on the shapeless mattress and fell immediately asleep.

Sometime in the middle of the night I woke up feeling agitated and restless. For a while I tossed and turned, trying to go back to sleep, but found it impossible. Finally, I gave up, switched on the light, and opened *Zen Flesh, Zen Bones* by Paul Reps. Skipping over the first chapters, which contained Chinese and Japanese Zen stories, I turned to the last section titled *Centering*. According to the preface this was a translation of an ancient Sanskrit manuscript detailing, in 112 short verses, Shiva's instructions to his consort, Devi, on various ways to attain enlightenment. I read through them quickly and found a lot of the material familiar from other sources. Most of the verses dealt with points of concentration, like the gap between the in and the out breaths. In the past I had at least been able to grasp intellectually the purpose of such exercises, but what was peculiar about this reading of them was that I no longer seemed to be able to make sense of them at all. It was like reading pure gibberish. Apparently, my cognitive powers had ceased functioning altogether.

Disgusted, I put down the book, turned out the light, and tried to go back to sleep. As I lay in the darkness, however, verse number 50 crept back to mind. It read,

> At the point of sleep when sleep has not yet come and external wakefulness vanishes, at this point *being* is revealed.[101]

These words were the last things I thought about as I approached that very point between waking and sleeping described by the verse. I had not planned it that way, it just happened—and suddenly, lo and behold, BEING WAS REVEALED!

Several days later I wrote a hurried account of what occurred next. It is perhaps worth quoting here:

> I jump up, turn on the light, and look around. Sure enough, I no longer see through a glass darkly. The veil has been lifted, and the glass has cleared—no, more than cleared—it has vanished! I see the Kingdom, and now I am laughing wildly, because the great joke of it all is that this exalted Kingdom I have been searching for in such anguish and despair is none other than the very room I have been sleeping in, with its dirty, cinderblock walls, frayed curtains, and horribly grungy, blue-green rug! Oh, I could have kissed that rug and those walls! I could have shouted! I could have danced! I could have done anything, for that matter, because it really didn't matter. It didn't even exist and never had. I was free.
>
> What was it like? What was it not like? How can I tell you? I can't, but I'll be brave and try, anyway... It was not a thought. It was not a feeling. It was not an experience. I was everything. I was nothing. I was everywhere and I was nowhere—nowhere to be found, hence, nowhere to be lost. Amazing Grace! Sacred Grace! Silly Grace!—like those nonsensical little phrases that children make up and then laugh and laugh over while poor perplexed adults just shake their heads. And no wonder! You have to be a child to get it. And I was a child, a child sitting on a bed, bathed in rapture...
>
> But there were thoughts, too: Zen stories popped to mind and made me laugh uproariously. I remembered the koan about killing the Buddha on

the road, and now the Buddha was dead! He, too, had never existed, yet I was celebrating his demise. Eckhart's words floated by, and my own woeful remark that no one ever tells you how to forsake yourself. But of course not! It's impossible as long as you are still there; first you have to forsake yourself! Even my poem now made sense. Truly, a broken heart —if you really let it break—is the Gate to Paradise; and Necessity, sad necessity—whoever slays this Gorgon gets instant Enlightenment!... these were my thoughts, and many more, only they were no longer "mine." They came and went like a parade of rainbows. Where do rainbows come from? If you know, you don't need to read this; you can write your own description!

And there was feeling. Oh, such feeling. Relief. Joy. Gratitude—gratitude most of all, not because something had happened but because something had ceased—like waking up from a nightmare, you want to laugh, you want to cry. There's nothing special about waking up. It's simply that the ordeal you thought so real is ended, the Furies have gone. Well, I was awake and I was free—free of this journey, free of my Dream and all the other dreary destinies I had conjured for my life. I was FREE, and that was the supreme bliss in a measureless sea of bliss.

And yes, there was also an experience, like the ones I had so enviously read about—and yet, I had never expected this! What had I expected? Something exceptional, luminous, visionary—the Platonic Forms behind all forms, or a Transcendental Light wiping out the universe, or maybe the Cosmic Voice of God calling me from eternity—I don't know, but it wasn't this. This was much, much too obvious. It wasn't even right under my nose, it was my nose. And it was a finger uncurling miraculously in front of my eyes. It was a car horn, sharp and crisp in the night. It was the sound of my sheets rustling as I shifted position on the bed. It was the doorknob effortlessly staring me in the face—they were all so effortless, and therein lies the true Oneness and Beauty of the world; we are all effortlessly together, brothers and sisters to the stars— nor do I mean this metaphorically (though metaphor it is), for this was no gauzy vision full of images and archetypes. The Image had burst, and the Light was out, and the Light was everything. The Metaphorical World had come to an end, and I was AWAKE in the REAL WORLD, the world without end.

I had begun this whole quest with the question, Who am I? but now, in the discovery of Gnosis, the question itself was seen to be predicated on a basic misconception. All along I had assumed that "I" must be a conscious being—that is, an entity in whom consciousness had somehow mysteriously arisen. But, in Reality, it was the other way around.

Consciousness had never arisen in my being; rather, my "being" had arisen in Consciousness as the perceived image of a particular body-mind with particular thoughts, feelings, desires, and experiences. Thus, in Gnosis 'I' is understood to be simply a trick of the imagination. It is only as if this body-mind—thoughts, feelings, etc.—constitutes a self-existent entity called "I". Actually, I am no more a particular body-mind than I am a particular flower, rock, or tree. All these are merely metaphorically differentiated "events" appearing somewhere, and I am the *where* they appear. With this realization the entire metaphorical world of individual entities is at once obliterated, and in its place the Real World emerges— the perfect, seamless Kingdom in which all "entities," "objects," and "things" are but imaginary distinctions superimposed on the One and Only Body of God from which nothing can ever be truly singled out or separated. This is Reality, and this is who I really am.

With the obliteration of all separateness also comes the obliteration of the whole problematic relationship between 'I' and 'Other,' or my 'self' and a 'world' (which I had dubbed the Shadow and experienced in its extremity as the Wasteland). But in the Grace of Gnosis the illusion of 'I' and 'Other' is pierced right through the middle and re-membered as the Very Consciousness that perceives them—a Consciousness that itself is neither an 'I' nor an 'Other' but the immutable Emptiness in which all 'I's and 'Others', 'selves' and 'worlds' ascend and subside only as metaphorical contrasts. Thus, just as a visible shadow, seen by the physical eyes, is not anything with a substantial reality of its own but simply the metaphorical absence of light, so, too, the Shadow of the World is seen by the Eye of Gnosis to be simply the metaphorical absence of my own true Identity. Once this Identity is revealed, the Shadow dissolves and the Wasteland vanishes, for there is no longer any separately existing "one" to experience them.

Likewise, there is no longer any "one" to experience that Ultimate Shadow of every "I"—Death—for birth and death, too, are only the comings and goings of metaphorical images. But once identification with every possible image is surrendered in Gnosis, then the passing of one particular image (this body-mind) has no more final significance than the passing of any other image; because, although all images are bound in time and space (hence, ephemeral and finite), the Consciousness in which they appear and disappear has no such limitations. In fact, Time and Space are themselves only the conceptual framework by which the whole of metaphorical existence is perceived in Consciousness; and being this Very Consciousness, I can neither come into existence nor leave it, for I am that which cognizes existence itself.

Death, then, is not something to be conquered, as I had supposed, but merely re-cognized as the disappearance only of a finite image (not an individual entity) in an infinite Consciousness. Yet paradoxically, this recognition cannot take place until the experience of "I" (as an individual entity) itself disappeared, or "died." This was the "task left undone" in Nam (where, indeed, in the face of actual physical death the potential for such a spiritual death had been unusually high). But once accomplished, I discovered the death of all Death, which is to say Eternal Life—not as the indefinite extension of the life of a particular body-mind, or spirit, or soul, or any other "thing" in time, but as the True Life of Consciousness that precedes Time and every other temporal restriction.

Finally, there was the problem of Destiny. Even death, I had felt, might be accepted with some measure of equanimity if I could but find and fulfill a destiny that would lend it meaning. Yet, in Gnosis this whole notion is understood to be based on the absurd attribution of choice and will to a mere metaphorical image. It is like watching a movie and thinking that the characters on the screen actually will their own actions and choose their own fates. But this is just what I had done. I had invented my "self" as an image in Consciousness and then been seduced into believing that this piece of fiction was real. Thus arose my sense of being a victim or protagonist in some private, tragi-comic drama of love, war, revolution, marriage, career, and even this final quest itself. But instead of being the protagonist in such a play, I had been, in Truth, its Author. In fact, this entire Cosmic Pageant was nothing more nor less than my own spontaneous and unwilled creation. And this is exactly what my Vision of Consciousness in the Mt. Hood forest had been trying to communicate. In spite of all its multifarious, metaphorical appearances, there is only ONE, and this ONE is absolutely free and undetermined.

Thus, from the beginning there had never been anywhere to go, anything to acquire, any experiences to have, any states to achieve, any destiny to fulfill. Nor is Gnosis a question of solving any problems, perceiving hidden relationship, or discovering new realms, as I had been trying so hard to do. Indeed, all these activities had merely perpetuated the old illusion of 'I' and' Other' in a new "spiritual" metaphor of a seeker and a sought, Parzival and his Grail. But in Reality the seeker and the sought are also only One, and I am already the Grail.

In this sense, then, nothing had happened, nothing had changed. Everything was the same — mind, body, thoughts, feelings, images, and energies. It was only their context that had been suddenly revealed, or Consciousness itself — that perennial FACT of facts, that RELATIONSHIP of all relationships, the infinite PRESENCE of every object and state. And just because Consciousness itself never happens, never changes, never manifests; is neither large nor small, light nor dark, in motion nor at rest — in short, is totally without attributes and, hence, unimaginable, I had simply never noticed that I was That.

And now that I did notice it, there was nothing more to do. All effort ceased. I spent the next several hours just sitting on that sagging mattress amid the crumpled sheets, flooded with ecstasy and gratitude, not desiring anything more than this, because this was ALL, and it was all so obvious.

After a while I passed into sleep again, deep and rich, yet it was also a conscious sleep — I don't know how else to put it. The revelation of Gnosis remained untouched and unbroken by anything that happened organically. My body just floated in a kind of radiance. Oh, that Light!

August 13th:

In the morning I woke up completely refreshed and, I think, a little surprised to find a physical body and its surroundings still present. Since "I" had vanished from existence, perhaps I had assumed that the world would, too. Amazingly, however, it continued to happen all on its own, and without a trace of me in it!

I performed all my usual morning rituals: washing, brushing my teeth, packing, etc. — nothing had changed, yet everything had changed. For the last few days I had been doing things mechanically, going through the motions of life without any reasons or motives. Now I still had no reasons or motives for doing anything, but it didn't matter. Life was the doing, and all motives had become superfluous, even a hindrance. Every action was sufficient unto itself — a crazy expression of pure joy, and this joy needed no further justification. It was simply the way things were, the only way they could be.

I drove back into Shelton for a delicious breakfast of apple pie and coffee. Originally, I had planned to return to the mainland to follow my route to the next community, but now, quite spontaneously, I decided to tour the Olympic Peninsula instead. I have become an ordinary tourist, I mused happily, and headed the Old Gray Mare west toward the Pacific.

During the trip my moods changed. I put on a cassette of Greek music and danced Zorba-like in my seat, pounding out the rhythm on the Mare's steering wheel. Later, I grew quiet, turned off the stereo, and just watched the scenery whistle by. I don't know what to say. Nothing unusual happened. Everything was perfectly ordinary — but that was just it: It was so perfectly ordinary. I shook my head and laughed at myself. How had I missed it all the years of my life?

In the evening I made camp on a beach near the town of La Push. I took a stroll through the surrounding forest and cooked up a meal on a small fire. Afterwards, I got out my tape recorder and began making notes of what had happened. In the middle of it, I was suddenly taken by how the sunlight filtered through the exquisitely delicate needles on the branch of an overhanging fir tree and stopped to describe it. I concluded by saying,

> I feel like something is over but nothing has begun — I've simply dropped into the middle of everything...It is truly indescribable.

August 14th:

The next morning I got up early, looked at the map, and decided to drive out to Neah Bay, the most westerly tip of the Olympic Peninsula. Again, there was no special reason to go there, no communities or anyone I knew. It just struck my fancy. When I reached the town of Sappho, however, and turned west on Highway 112, which runs along the northern coast, the scenery began to seem curiously familiar, though I had never been in this part of the country before. All around me, a piney wilderness ran right down to the shore, and as I looked out to my right over the water, I saw a huge hunk of land — Vancouver Island, Canada — rising from the mists. This was, indeed, familiar, and my heart began to sing.

Rounding a bend I spotted a sign that read *The Far West*, and then another, *Makah Indian Reservation*, and sure enough, the lush wilderness that surrounded me on all sides, save for the sea, looked as pristine and virgin as it really must have been before the white man came. Now I knew where I was going, and every cell in my body seemed to know it, too. I was heading as far west as one could travel by land (and being borne there by a horse, of sorts, as well!), back to where it had all started.

As the Old Gray Mare galloped through the turns (as though she, too, knew the way), I was filled with an overwhelming *deja vu*. In my mind's eye I could see what was coming next, and it made my flesh tremble.

Finally, we rounded the last bend coming into Neah Bay, and there it was —exactly as it had been in my Dream—*a fishing-boat harbor, complete with a long, rock jetty stretching out into the sea!*

I parked the Old Gray Mare at the foot of the jetty and scrambled out across the rocks. When I reached the end, I sat down and lit a cigarette. I suppose I was half-expecting something to happen, perhaps a new Dream or Vision to take the place of the one that was here completed. But there was only the cry of the gulls overhead and the sighing, putt-putt of the fishermen's boats bobbing after their nets. In front of me I could still see Vancouver Island shrouded in the mists, and then I realized something was different. Everything was the same as it had been in the Dream except that I was now on the *other shore* looking back the way I had come. I had crossed the sea.

And so it was over. There were no new rules, no more destinies—just this unutterable peace. Then I heard Athena's gentle, distant laughter for the last time, and finally, I understood. It was the laughter of my Guru. No wonder I had been allowed no others. All along, she had been leading me, first to the Mill Creek Motel, and now here, to this very spot, in this very moment. Nor did any of this surprise me in the least. It was merely a tangible symbol, the seal of fulfillment on a promise that had been made to me a long, long time ago.

I was home.

Epilogue: World Without End...

At first, I had no thought of communicating what had happened to anyone else. In Truth, there *was* no one else. There was only This One Consciousness newly dazzled by its own infinite manifestations. All distinctions of 'I' and 'other' within this flux were purely conventional and imaginary. To whom, then, should I communicate?

And even if there were someone with whom to communicate, what would I say? The path I had followed so intently seemed now to have no relation to its Fruit. All my searchings, all my inquiries, all my practices and disciplines apparently had proven futile. Indeed, I had abandoned them all in despair before the advent of Gnosis. Consequently, when that Supernal Sun finally did break, it appeared to be an act of sheer, unsolicited Grace. Thus, there were no lessons to be learned, no conclusions to be drawn, no teachings to impart. Far from being a teacher, I was, if anything, the primordial student: a Cosmic Child re-discovering the most mundane activities — from tying shoelaces to building a campfire — as the Radiant Play of Formless Divinity.

There is, however, a Sufi saying that the journey *to* God has an end, but the journey *in* God has no end. How true this would prove I had no idea, having had no formal training in such matters beyond the Spartan instructions of Athena who never deigned to elaborate her commands. For a Gnostic, then, I was abysmally ignorant about the laws of form, which is what the journey *in* God is all about. In Truth, my education was just beginning. From now on, Consciousness Itself — in the Form of form — would be my Teacher; for this kind of knowledge comes not from thought but from insight — thought being only the last and coarsest stage of its in-forming.

The first person I actually talked to was a fierce-looking logger hitching home to Port Angeles with a broken arm and a six pack of beer. "Don't you have a car?" I asked.

"Naw," he said, shaking his shaggy head with a beatific smile. "When I took up drinking, I figured I better get off the road."

Sure enough, during the next two hours he polished off the whole six-pack while giving me a running monologue on the forests we were passing through, how you could tell Doug fir from cedar and old growth from new. He also told me about a time he had shot a deer out of season because it absolutely refused to move from his path even when he sat down right in front of it to load his rifle. Listening to his stories, I laughed and laughed, because he was completely perfect just as he was.

Later, in Port Townsend, while waiting for the ferry, I mingled with other tourists chatting about hotels and restaurants, checking maps and watches, calling to their children, and I felt not the slightest difference between us. *Literally*. We were all eddies in a Single Sea, and it was only the power of metaphor that carved imaginary figures out of that Unity, then mistook such phantoms for realities. Nor did even this bit of foolery seem a problem. It was just part of a Holy Game of Hide-and-Seek, which I certainly had no inclination to interrupt.

It was only after we had finally gotten underway, and the old ferry was chugging out across the calm afternoon waters, that an idea arose about transmitting what I had discovered to somebody else. I was standing on the bow, watching my shadow race effortlessly across the waves, when suddenly it struck me that if anyone could see this, *really see it*, they would understand. It was that simple and that obvious.

At the time, however, it seemed just another passing metaphor, and I didn't give it a second thought. But several days later, traveling through the majestic Cascades, the urge to communicate arose again—this time as an impulse to set down something of what had happened in written form.

The prompting persisted and grew stronger, so just before sundown I pulled into Glacier Creek, a tiny town lying in the shadow of Mt. Baker, rented a cozy, one-room cabin, and went to work. At the end of four days I had produced a nineteen-page journal documenting my Gnosis "for the record." Still I had no notion of elaborating it further. I was simply obeying a spontaneous impulse.

With the writing completed, I now faced the first real decision of my new life: whether or not to finish the video newsletter. My own search had ended, so there was nothing in it for me anymore. Nevertheless, I had undertaken an obligation to the people who had already participated, and there was no good reason not to follow through. Thus, a decision was made, but not by 'me'. It just coalesced naturally out of the circumstances arising in Consciousness. So that's how it's done! I marveled. Truly, I had to re-learn everything anew.

For the next two months I continued on my original course, swinging down through Washington, then over to Idaho and Montana, then south through Colorado and New Mexico, staying one step ahead of winter, which was already breathing down from the chilly north. I visited half-a-dozen more communities but still told no one about the Kingdom I now saw everywhere "spread upon the earth." For myself, there was no need to give it verbal expression, and even my extemporaneous writings at Glacier Creek were temporarily forgotten. All thoughts paled compared to this Truth, all words seemed superfluous in the face of this Reality.

And yet, slowly, I began to realize that what was true of me was not true of everyone else. Paradoxically, the belief in metaphors created metaphorical beings trapped in their own creations — even as 'I' had been. Sometimes, in the midst of an ordinary conversation, it would strike me as hilariously funny that someone was taking such fancies so seriously, and I would burst into peals of laughter. At other times, however, I would be overwhelmed by the gulf of sorrows those delusions caused. And just because, in Truth, there really were no 'others', I realized these sorrows too were not other than my own. Thus, for the first time since Gnosis, I experienced ripples of real pain in an otherwise stainless sky of bliss.

In between visiting communities, however, I camped out in undisturbed solitude for days at a time, enjoying whatever arose — sun, rain, forests, streams — and I knew exactly how Adam felt wandering through Paradise. What wonders were everywhere at hand! A single leaf trembling in the light, or an industrious squirrel darting from rock to mossy rock, or the raucous gossip of birds in the dappled canopy overhead — all were manifestations of Holy Ecstasy.

Later, too, driving endless hours over the great highways of the Southwest, I would watch the land unfurl like an incandescent tapestry without a single stitch out of place. Even supposedly "ugly" things, like billboards and gas stations, were saturated with a kind of Absolute Beauty that was nothing less than the Light of Naked Being. What need had I of miracles? — the world itself was one. But it was also the very *same* world that it had always been. It was just that I had never really seen it before. And now it was so easy, so incredibly easy. Oh Light! Oh Love! Oh Laughter! How could I have missed you!

I also continued to sit for half an hour in the mornings, but it hardly qualified as meditation. What was the difference between this activity and any other? — except perhaps that it was a special mode of stillness in the Great Stillness that was the Root of the Universe. Indeed, stillness and action, sound and silence — all the opposites — were overthrown, exactly as the mystics had written, and I smiled, remembering how their words had once set my mind a-tumbling through a maze of imaginary hoops. How silly and sad such shenanigans all seemed now!

As for current reading, I did very little during those months — there seemed little point. When I did glance through one of the scriptures or pick up a sutra, I found them all instantly transparent. How sweet! How profound! How humorous! The Zen stories, in particular, struck me as wildly comical and actually made me roll on the grass. But at the same time I could also see the enormous chasm of ignorance such tales were meant to bridge and feel the frustration of dead masters trying to shout into deaf ears. Why had they bothered? Then, as now, there had been nothing to gain. It was all right here, like the amalaka fruit held in the palm of the hand, even as those ancient sages themselves had said.

One day I opened the *Lankavatara Scripture* and read again the Bodhisattva vow, which is never to accept the bliss of Nirvana for oneself alone, but always and everywhere to devote one's life to the emancipation of all beings. What could this possibly mean? In Truth, there were no beings to save and nothing to save them from! As for Nirvana — or, at least, the Reality I had fallen into — it was not something one could accept or reject. It just *was*. And it *was* blissful. How could I not go on enjoying it forever?

But the more I mixed with people, the more I realized it was not in my power to accept or reject suffering, either. I felt their pains and anxieties, guilts and fears, surging like waves through this bliss, breaching its walls and at times all but driving it from the field. Yet in spite of these storms,

Gnosis remained, untouched and indestructible, neither coming nor going. How, then, could bliss come and go?

Slowly, I began to discern that there are two kinds of bliss, or rather that Bliss has two modes. The first is Unmanifested — intrinsic to Consciousness Itself and, therefore, Eternal. The second is generated by Gnosis as the experience of a particular body-mind which, having been overwhelmed by the revelation of its own Nothingness, suddenly becomes capable of bliss in manifest form. But this secondary, manifested bliss is only a by-product of Gnosis and, like all manifest experience, is completely dependent on the relative conditions of the metaphorical world. In other words, it is neither Intrinsic to Gnosis nor Eternal. Eventually, it too must come and go...unless, of course, an effort were made to avoid the kinds of conditions that would tend to undermine it.

At first, such an effort seemed quite feasible. I had read about certain yogis who had developed techniques for maintaining the organism in a state of almost complete suspension, free from all physical and mental pain. Indeed, one need not go even this far. It would suffice simply to let the body-mind live out its biological life in relative solitude, enjoying the passing play of forms without in any way entering into it, much as a member of the audience in a movie theater views a film. In fact, precisely such thoughts began to arise. After the newsletter was finished, I imagined myself settling down in some anonymous town, taking whatever job would pay enough to satisfy the body's minimal wants, and so spend the rest of my days basking in these unutterable delights.

Yet here was the ultimate trap, for no matter how sublime, the motivation for such a strategy implied an identification with some form of manifestation — even as supremely subtle a one as bliss. But to want bliss, to pursue bliss, to cling to bliss in any form was impossible in Gnosis, for Gnosis precludes all identification with form and any motivations based upon it.

In the past, however, the body-mind had always relied on *some* motive, whether worldly or spiritual, for its existence. What reason could there now be for its manifestation? In Reality, there was none, and I would have been just as happy to see it cease. But it didn't. Moment by moment, the body-mind continued to arise in Consciousness, and I continued to watch it arise, almost as amazed by its appearance as I had been that very first morning at Mill Creek. What in this world was it doing?

Gradually, I came to understand that it wasn't doing anything. It was simply the expression of this very understanding, founded in Gnosis. In fact, the whole metaphorical world was nothing more than a great, on-going, over-flowing, out-pouring of the Divine Imagination that had no purpose whatsoever. It was an absolutely Free activity born of sheer Love. Purpose only arose under the veil of ignorance. It was only because of ignorance that activity took on meaning; and it was only in relation to ignorance that its ultimate purpose could be ascertained—namely, to put an end to ignorance through the discovery of the Real.

To reject Nirvana for oneself, then, was once again to submit to purpose, and this was the same purpose as before, only now seen from the other side, as it were—from the point of view of Gnosis. But since Gnosis was no longer something that I could attain—because there was no 'I' and no 'thing' to attain—this purpose must be a compassionate devotion to helping others discover the same. In effect, bliss, freedom, happiness—the three crown jewels of all human questing—had themselves to be sacrificed as soon as they were won to the merciless Law of Love. For this body-mind in particular, I realized, it would mean the surrender of bliss and the embrace of suffering in the service of That Law.

Was there ever really a choice? In one sense, no, because, as I have already described, there was no one to make any decisions. In another sense, yes, because Consciousness Itself is always absolutely Free. In Truth, however, it made no difference. What did I care about this body-mind, what it did or what it suffered? This whole life was nothing more than a blink in Eternity. To cling to the least shadow of its existence was to assume an intolerable burden. Thus, I gleefully consigned my life to the fire of service and, in so doing, became a slave of Love. Yet, by this very sacrifice (which was no sacrifice at all!), I actually escaped the last and most insidious link in the chain of delusion—the very link that masquerades as liberation; for both bondage *and* liberation are products of ignorance.

This, then, was the meaning and the mystery of the Bodhisattva vow: those who aspire to bliss alone, or selfishly succumb to the lure of personal freedom, are in the end the most deceived. For truly, there is no Gnosis without Love, no Freedom without Slavery. In Gnosis they are absolutely identical.

But in those early days I still had no idea what all this would actually mean or of the tasks ahead. As already mentioned, I could see no connection between Gnosis and the path that had preceded it. How then could anyone follow the way I had come?

> Rain on the mountains,
> thunder in the north;
> the sun rises in the east,
> what is there to teach?

—I wrote, and it was true. If nothing else, however, I could bear witness to this Truth and the Gnosis that had revealed it. Consequently, as my travels drew to a close, the idea for this book began to take shape. I envisioned it as a simple testimony to the fact that Gnosis *is* possible, even for an ordinary person like myself. Therefore, I resolved to write it as honestly as I could, with all the warts showing—the kind of book, in fact, that I had always wanted to read during my own journey but had never found. Even though I had no path to offer, then, I hoped others might at least take courage from my struggles.

When the newsletter was finished, I headed back to Los Angeles to make copies, stopping on the way for another visit to the Wolff's ranch in Lone Pine. Fortuitously, I learned there was a cabin for rent on the property and immediately took it. In L.A. I made copies of the newsletter and sent them off to the various communities. Then, with Captain Blood once again in tow, I returned to the cabin, set up my typewriter on a trunk in front of the fireplace, and started to work.

But the year in Lone Pine spent writing this book has proved fortuitous in more ways than one. The hush of the desert, the silence of the mountains, the luxury of simple living with not even a phone to interrupt concentration has provided, of course, an ideal setting for the accomplishment of this work. Far more importantly, however, I have been graced by the presence of the great Wolff himself. Too advanced in age to impart extensive formal teachings, he nevertheless has exercised a profound influence on my whole subsequent development.

To begin with, there are his own writings, *Pathways Through To Space*, *The Philosophy of Consciousness Without An Object*, and *Introceptualism*, in which he calls philosophy back to its ancient and original task of being "a *Way* of Realization, and not solely a monitor of *doing*." That is, like Plato and Kant, he shows how logic itself, if exercised to the limit, leads to the brink of Transcendence and, if thoroughly exhausted, can actually become a jumping-off point into that Ocean of Truth. Thus, reason need not be discarded, as I had supposed, but could be pressed into the service of Realization.

Secondly, he has guided me back to that most precious of human inheritances, the world's great mystical classics, where, in the records of Shankara and Mira Bai, of Rumi and Arabi, Teresa and Dionysius, Nargajuna and Lady Tsogyel (to name just a few), I found maps and journals describing the very same terrain I had traversed. Indeed, almost every incident of my own journey had antecedents in the journeys of others. Many before me have left family and friends to seek the Grail of Enlightenment. Many before me were graced with disincarnate guides, prophetic dreams, and archetypal visions to point the way. Many before me had to pass through the portals of doubt and darkness, and all had finally to die to themselves before Awakening to that Ultimate Reality that is the alpha and omega of every path and journey. Clearly, the Light of Gnosis reveals a universal landscape to all those who have eyes to see it. In this respect it appears every bit as "objective" to the Gnostic as do the pale phenomena of the physical world to the ordinary person blinded by ignorance. Thus, the Sufi sage Ibn Arabi proclaims, "He who has seen what I have seen will say what I say, whether openly or in secret."

More importantly, I realized from these deeper studies, which the Wolff inspired, that although Gnosis is never the outcome of causal factors (and thus, is always ultimately a matter of Grace), this fact does not in any way negate the value of spiritual practices and disciplines. Indeed, practices and disciplines are indispensable, for they render the seeker capable of that Grace that is always present as the redemptive Power of Consciousness Itself. Consequently, even that handful of Gnostics who have been spontaneously Enlightened by Grace alone had later to submit to these disciplines and learn these practices in order to fulfill their roles as Guides to others in obedience to the Law of Love.

Although there is no room here to elaborate, I mention this in case anyone mistakes the highly personal character of my story or the fact that I did not formally follow an established tradition as a signal that the Wisdom of the Traditions is overthrown. On the contrary, my path confirms the Traditional Wisdom in every essential respect. In particular, Athena's four commandments — Attention, Commitment, Detachment, and Surrender — summarize the four fundamental principles upon which all paths and traditions are based. No seeker can afford to ignore these principles or escape their demands.

At the same time, it is true that the purely formal aspects of any tradition evolve as appropriate responses to historical conditions and can out-live their appropriateness as those conditions change. When this happens, even the most revered metaphors from the past lose their ability to persuade us of the Transcendent Truths to which they point. Such is the case in our own time.

The old insular civilizations of Christian Europe, Islam, India, and the Far East, once the cradles and the glory of the Great Traditions, are crumbling under the onslaught of a technological revolution that is compelling the complete re-organization of all human affairs on a global scale. In short, a new, global civilization is in the making, and this new civilization will require new forms and new metaphors. The only question is, will this civilization be sacred or profane? Will it serve to further our common destiny by unifying humanity and aiming it towards Transcendence? Or must it reduce us to a desperate struggle for material goods and resources that will cut short our collective quest in an orgy of self-destruction?

So far, the greatest obstacle to the formation of a new Sacred Civilization has been the doctrine of materialism which, basing itself on the same science that produced our technology, aggressively denies any Transcendent meaning or dimension to human existence. Instead, it insists that life is finite, reducible to purely physical needs, and so counsels us to seize the things of this world while we can. With such a worldview to guide us, there seems little cause for hope, and the future looks bleak indeed.

Yet science itself is undergoing a momentous revolution—a revolution that at once points back to the Transcendent roots of its own truths in the mysticism of Pythagoras and Plato and to a new worldview in which Consciousness must be seen as fundamental to the manifestation of all physical phenomena. I am speaking, of course, of the most powerful of all theories so far formulated in the history of science—quantum mechanics —whose profound philosophical implications are still so little understood even by the average scientist. Listen, however, to one of the founders of quantum theory, the great Werner Heisenberg, speaking about those who oppose this revolution:

> It would, in their view, be desirable to return to the reality concept of classical physics or, to use a more general philosophic term, to the ontology of materialism. They would prefer to come back to the idea of an objective real world whose smallest parts exist objectively in the same sense as stones or trees exist, independently of whether or not we observe them.
>
> This, however, is impossible or at least not entirely possible because of the nature of the atomic phenomena.[102]

Wherever the quantum revolution finally takes us, the defenders of materialism can no longer look to science for support. Materialism is dead, but its demise also leaves science without a sound philosophical base. That science works no one can deny, but the question must still be asked, *why?* What sort of Reality does its very success imply? Since the philosophy of materialism can no longer answer this question, we must look elsewhere.

In the past many well-meaning people—both east and west—have tried to salvage mysticism by finding a "scientific" justification for its insights and methods. But mysticism does not need science to justify it—for mysticism is justified not by conceptual knowledge, which only *mediates* reality, but by Gnosis, which is the *immediate apprehension* of that Reality. This, however, does not mean mysticism and science have nothing to say to each other. In fact, today it may well be that science needs mysticism to render its own operations intelligible—and this by way of a new worldview, founded on an intuition of the Transcendent that can be ultimately verified through Gnosis. Such a worldview, while recognizing the inherent limits of conceptual knowledge, will certainly not reject science. On the contrary, between intuition and Gnosis there is ample room for the play of metaphor, whether logical or poetic, philosophical or scientific. In fact, this play is essential to us as human beings, for metaphor is both the source of our delusion and the means by which we may end it, as those sages who labored so hard to construct the ancient cosmologies well knew. Indeed, we have much need of such sages now.

Although this is not the place to argue for a worldview based on a recognition of the Transcendent, considerations along these lines permit us to hope once more. In addition, for spiritual seekers, they point the way to establishing a new vehicle, or *nava yana*, grounded in those universal principles discovered by our ancestors but expressed in modern terms, free from cultural accretions and parochial prejudices. Truly, for those who follow such a way a thousand springs will become a mighty stream, for in these wayfarers will merge all the rivers of that Superessential Wisdom flowing down to us from the dawn of time, forming and informing Consciousness to this Great Adventure which, if we could look into the mirror of Eternity, we would realize has only just begun.

But now I run ahead of myself into the future, revealing things which are not yet ready to be revealed. Let me, therefore, bring this testimony to a close. I have passed by the angels with their flaming sword and returned to the Garden. It is there where subject and object are destroyed. I have found the Tree of Eternal Life and eaten its fruit. It is the Fruit of Gnosis. Thus qualified to bear witness, what I bear witness to is this world, made of images and metaphors, and to other worlds as well: to the inner world, the subtle world, the archetypal world, and infinite worlds beyond, up to, and including That which Transcends all worlds, is the Truth of all worlds, is the Reality of all worlds, World without End—Incomparable, Inconceivable, Ineffable, yet closer to you than your very heart. May my testimony serve you on your own journey through this vast poem of creation back to our Original Home—the Uncreated Consciousness from which all things spring and to which all things return, including even yourself.

Verily, *Tat tvam asi*—That thou art.

World Without End

About the Author

Joel Morwood is also the author of *The Way of Selflessness: A Practical Guide to Enlightenment Based on the Teachings of the World's Great Mystics* and *Through Death's Gate: A Guide to Selfless Dying*. Since 1987, Joel has served as spiritual director of the Center for Sacred Sciences, a non-profit organization based in Eugene, Oregon. The Center for Sacred Sciences is dedicated to helping individual seekers on their spiritual paths, as well as fostering the creation of a new worldview, founded on the mystical teachings of The Great Tradition, but presented in terms appropriate to our present scientific age. Toward these ends, the Center offers a variety of educational programs.

>Center for Sacred Sciences
>1430 Willamette #164
>Eugene, Oregon 97401
>
>www.centerforsacredsciences.org

Naked Through the Gate

References

Blakney, R. B., trans. *The Way of Life: Lao Tzu*. New York: New American Library, 1955.

Campbell, Joseph. *The Masks of God: Creative Mythology*. New York: Viking Press, 1970.

Capra, Fritjof. *The Tao of Physics*. New York: Bantam Books, 1977.

Castaneda, Carlos. *The Teachings of Don Juan: A Yaqui Way of Knowledge*. New York: Ballantine Books, 1968.

Colledge, Edmund, and McGinn, Bemard, trans. *Meister Eckhart*. New York: Paulist Press, 1981.

Evans-Wentz, W. Y., ed. (rendered into English by Lama Kazi Dawa Samdup). *The Tibetan Book of the Dead*. London: Oxford University Press, reprint, 1976.

Goddard, Dwight, ed. *A Buddhist Bible*. Boston: Beacon Press, by arrangement with E. P. Dutton & Co., Inc., 1970.

Goswami, Amit. *The Bhagavadgita*. Unpublished. All citations refer to chapter and verse numbers.

Guillaumont, A., et. al., trans. *The Gospel According to Thomas*. San Francisco: Harper & Row, 1959.

Halifax, Joan. *Shamanic Voices*. New York: E. P. Dutton, 1979.

Heisenberg, Werner. *Physics and Philosophy*. New York: Harper Torchbooks, 1962.

Hoeller, Stephan A. *The Royal Road*, 2nd edition. Wheaton, Ill: A Quest Book, The Theosophical Publishing House, 1975.

Jung, Carl G. *The Portable Jung*. Joseph Campbell, ed.; R. F. C. Hull, trans., New York: Viking Press, 1971.

References

Krishnamurti. *Explorations into Insight*. New York: Harper & Row, 1980.

Marx, Karl, and Engels, Frederick. *Karl Marx and Frederick Engels: Selected Works*. New York: International Publishers, 1968.

Mishra, Rammurti S. *Fundamentals of Yoga*. New York: Julian Press, 1959.

Reps, Paul, ed. *Zen Flesh, Zen Bones*. Rutland, Vt.: Charles E. Tuttle Co., 1957.

Robinson, James M., ed. *The Nag Hammadi Library*. trans. by members of the Coptic Gnostic Library Project, San Francisco: Harper & Row, 1981.

Snyder, Gary, trans. "Twenty-four poems by Han-shan." *Evergreen Review*, vol. 2, no. 6, 1958.

Wilhelm, Richard, trans. (rendered into English by Cary F. Baynes, Bollingen Series XIX). *The I Ching or Book of Changes*. Princeton: Princeton University Press, 1967.

Endnotes

[1] The Long March was one of the great feats of military history. In 1934, surrounded by superior Kuomintang forces, the Communist Eighth Route Army, under Mao's leadership, broke out of its stronghold in central China and marched thousands of miles to the north and west to establish a new base with headquarters in Yenan.

[2] Marx & Engels, p.97

[3] Guillaumont, p.31

[4] Castaneda, p.79

[5] Hoeller, p.81

[6] Castaneda, p.79

[7] Castaneda, p.79

[8] Hoeller, p.89

[9] Wicca is the name that modern witches give to the pre-Christian religion of Europe from which witchcraft is supposed to have descended.

[10] John 18:37-38. All biblical quotes are taken from the King James version unless otherwise stated.

[11] Jung, p.518

[12] Capra, p.56-57

[13] Capra, p.126

[14] Capra, p.126

[15] i.e., Wolfram Von Eschenbach.

[16] Campbell, p.567

[17] Campbell, p. 38 (citing James Joyce, *A Portrait of the Artist as a Young Man*, London: Jonathan Cape, Ltd., 1916, p. 272).

[18] Campbell, p. 344 (citing Schopenhauer, *Transcendente Spekulation...Werke*, vol. 8, p. 220-225).

[19] Guillaumont, p. 3

[20] The third eye, located between the eyebrows, is one of the major chakras, or subtle energy centers, in Indian esotericism.

[21] Guillaumont, p. 3

[22] Luke 10: 20

[23] Luke 10: 24

[24] Krishnamurti, p.90

[25] All definitions cited are from *Webster's New Third International Dictionary*.

[26] Guillaumont, pp. 17-18

[27] Goddard, p. 189

[28] Colledge & McGinn, p. 181

[29] Goddard, p. 293

Endnotes

30 Goswami, 2:46
31 Blakney, p. 109
32 Goswami, 7:27-28
33 Colledge & McGinn, p. 227
34 Goddard, p. 292
35 Goswami, 7:14
36 Goswami, 9:4
37 Colledge & McGinn, p. 198
38 Blakney, p. 56
39 Goddard, p. 85-86
40 Goddard, p. 514
41 Evans-Wentz, pp. 95-96
42 Colledge & McGinn, p. 220
43 Goddard, p. 287
44 Robinson, p. 295
45 Colledge & McGinn, p. 190
46 Goswami, 4:23
47 Goddard, p. 341
48 John 8:32
49 John 8:51
50 Blakney, p. 68
51 Goswami, 2:12
52 Goddard, p.59
53 Colledge & McGinn, p. 179
54 Halifax, pp. 108-109
55 Castaneda, p. 196
56 Goddard, p. 341
57 John 3:3
58 Goddard, p. 339
59 Colledge & McGinn, p.203
60 Colledge & McGinn, p.183
61 Goddard, p. 370
62 Blakney, p. 101
63 Goddard, p. 622
64 Goswami, 18:65
65 Matthew 7:7-8
66 Goddard, p. 356

Endnotes

[67] Goddard, p. 514
[68] Colledge & McGinn, p. 182
[69] Blakney, p. 86
[70] Robinson, p. 189
[71] Goswami, 13:17
[72] Luke 17:21
[73] Mishra, p. 103
[74] John 10:20
[75] Snyder, p. 79
[76] Guillaumont, p.45
[77] Goddard, pp. 130-131
[78] Krishnamurti, p. 33
[79] Goddard, p. 323
[80] Goddard, pp. 29-30
[81] Goddard, p. 31
[82] Goswami, 3:39
[83] Goswami, 2:62-63
[84] Goswami, 3:19
[85] Colledge & McGinn, p. 292
[86] Matthew 19:21
[87] Matthew 6:25
[88] Blakney, p. 120
[89] Goswami, 15:5
[90] Luke 14:11
[91] Goswami, 12:13-14
[92] Goddard, p. 524
[93] Matthew 5:38-48
[94] Guillaumont, pp. 55-57
[95] Blakney, p. 72
[96] Goswami, 12: 19
[97] Goddard, p. 625
[98] Matthew 19:29
[99] Luke 9:61-62
[100] Colledge & McGinn, p. 249
[101] Reps, p.201
[102] Heisenberg, p. 129

www.ingramcontent.com/pod-product-compliance
Lightning Source LLC
Chambersburg PA
CBHW022057160426

43198CB00008B/267